The History of Books

*A Guide to Selected Resources
in the Library of Congress*

"L' Imprimerie," a pencil sketch by Gravelot for an illustration in volume 2 of J. R. de Petity's Bibliothèque des artistes *(Paris, 1766). Lessing J. Rosenwald Collection, Rare Book and Special Collections Division.*

The
History
of Books □

*A Guide to Selected Resources
in the Library of Congress*

Alice D. Schreyer   *The Center for the Book*
Library of Congress   Washington   1987

Library of Congress Cataloging-in-Publication Data

Schreyer, Alice D.
  The history of books : a guide to selected
resources in the Library of Congress.

  Includes bibliographies and index.
  1. Library of Congress. 2. Bibliography—
Library resources—Washington (D.C.) 3. Books
and reading—History—Library resources—
Washington (D.C.) 4. Printing—History—Library
resources—Washington (D.C.) 5. Learning and
scholarship—History—Library resources—
Washington (D.C.) 6. Transmission of texts—
History—Library resources—Washington (D.C.)
I. Center for the Book. II. Title.
Z1002.S35 1986   027.573   86-10493
[Z663.118.H56 1986]
ISBN 0-8444-0536-1 (alk. paper)

  For sale by the
Superintendent of Documents, U.S. Government Printing Office, Washington, D.C. 20402

To the memory of my mother,
who taught me to love books and reading,
and to Les, who shares my enthusiasm for them

❏ Contents

2   RARE BOOK AND SPECIAL COLLECTIONS DIVISION   57

❏ Foreword

The Library of Congress has acquired books for use by the Congress of the United States since 1800, when the American government moved from Philadelphia to the new capital of Washington City. The scope and size of the collection accumulated since then verifies an observation made in 1815 by Thomas Jefferson, one of the Library's founders: "there is, in fact, no subject to which a Member of Congress may not have occasion to refer." Today most subjects and more than 450 of the world's languages are represented in the Library's collection of about 20 million volumes and pamphlets—in all likelihood the largest gathering of books ever assembled. An unsurpassed reflection of American culture and national aspirations, this remarkable collection is available to all. The Library of Congress, in the words of Librarian of Congress Daniel J. Boorstin, is an "open national library" that takes "all knowledge for its province and a whole nation as its audience."

The Center for the Book in the Library of Congress was proposed by Librarian Boorstin and established by Congress in 1977 to "stimulate public interest and research in the role of the book in the diffusion of knowledge." In his testimony on behalf of the legislation, Dr. Boorstin explained that a Center for the Book was needed "to organize, focus, and dramatize our nation's interest and attention on the book." As the national library of a great free republic that was built on books and reading, the Library of Congress has "a special duty and a special interest" to promote books and reading and

encourage the study of books. For the book, the Librarian noted, "is the reservoir of all ideas we have forgotten and will be the reservoir for ideas still unborn."

The Center for the Book encourages the historical and interdisciplinary study of books by commissioning publications such as this guide, by sponsoring symposia, lectures, exhibitions, and projects, and by hosting events that mark significant anniversaries or occasions in the book world. Its history-of-books program, like its reading-promotion projects, is funded primarily by contributions from individuals, corporations, and foundations. This publication was supported by such contributions and by advice and help from many Library of Congress staff members. The Center for the Book is grateful to all who have offered it their financial support, to the Library of Congress staff, and above all, to Alice D. Schreyer, for the imagination and skill she devoted to turning an idea into a book.

John Y. Cole
Director
The Center for the Book

❏ Acknowledgments

In compiling this guide, I sought and received advice and assistance from individuals throughout the Library of Congress. I wish to acknowledge with thanks their help in identifying and locating relevant material. The responsibility for all decisions regarding inclusion and coverage is my own.

Special thanks are due to William Matheson, chief of the Rare Book and Special Collections Division, whose insights and encouragement contributed significantly to the project from its start and who read the manuscript as it evolved. Several other members of this division were particularly instrumental in the guide's development. Leonard Beck and Peter VanWingen served as untiring readers as well as superb resources for information on many collections. James Gilreath focused my attention on a broad range of American materials and engaged in a steady, stimulating dialogue about copyright resources, the guide, and the field. Kathleen Mang provided kind assistance with the Lessing J. Rosenwald Collection.

John C. Broderick, Assistant Librarian for Research Services and former chief of the Manuscript Division, read and commented on the introduction and Chapter 1. Gary Kohn and Charles J. Kelly of the Manuscript Division Reading Room staff were especially helpful.

Lewis Flacks and Waldo Moore of the Copyright Office shared their historical and legal expertise with me. Roberta Shaffer, special assistant to the Law Librarian, substantially facilitated my work in the Law Library and carefully read what I wrote about it.

Assistance provided in the special format divisions enabled me to survey vast quantities of uncataloged materials. John Wolter and Richard Stephenson in the Geography and Map Division, and Jon Newsom, Gillian Anderson, and Wayne Shirley in the Music Division were especially helpful in this regard. Renata Shaw, Annette Melville, and Bernard Reilly provided advice and answered questions about many collections in the Prints and Photographs Division.

Lois Fern and Rosalinda Raher prepared the index for this volume with care and thoughtfulness, considerably enhancing the usefulness of the book with their work. Several colleagues outside the Library of Congress took an interest in the guide and offered suggestions for it. These include Roger E. Stoddard, curator of rare books, Houghton Library, Harvard University, G. Thomas Tanselle, vice president of the John Simon Guggenheim Memorial Foundation, and Michael Winship, editor of the *Bibliography of American Literature*. In the course of extensive discussions about archival sources for the history of books, William L. Joyce, associate university librarian for rare books and special collections, Princeton University, made many valuable contributions.

My deepest debt of gratitude is to the Center for the Book in the Library of Congress, which sponsored this project as part of its program to promote research in the history of books. Linda Cox provided a seemingly endless supply of good humor and expert technical assistance on the manuscript. John Y. Cole, executive director of the center, conceived the guide and supported it at every stage. His exhaustive knowledge of Library of Congress organization and history made the entire process possible, and working with him made its accomplishment a pleasure for which I offer warm thanks and appreciation.

Alice D. Schreyer

❏ The History of Books

A Guide to Selected Resources
in the Library of Congress

❑ Introduction

The purpose of this guide is to suggest research opportunities at the Library of Congress for those interested in the history of books. The guide also serves as an introduction to the range of inquiry the history of books encompasses and to the diverse types of resources that can support studies in this field.

In the broadest sense, the theme of the history of books is the influence of printed materials on the development and transmission of culture. This approach, part of intellectual and social history, focuses on the activities and relationships by which texts in the form of printed books are conveyed from authors to readers—authorship, printing, publishing, distribution, and reading. By examining the economic, technical, and cultural context of these spheres of activity in a particular time and place, historians of books achieve an understanding of the role of books in society.[1]

The scope of this developing discipline is defined by the common element of printed artifacts. Thus the history of books includes the study of all products of the printing press, such as maps, music, photographs, and prints, whether or not they are in book form. Other forms of communication—recordings, film, and television—are usually excluded. The production and distribution of manuscript and printed books involves many similar and sometimes related activities, and comparison of these two forms of textual

---

1. See Robert Darnton, "What Is the History of Books?" in *Books and Society in History,* ed. Kenneth E. Carpenter (New York: R. R. Bowker, 1983), 3–26.

transmission is an important part of the study of early printed books. This book follows these distinctions in defining its scope so as to reflect current trends and to anticipate future needs of scholars as well.

The history of books as a unifying, interpretive point of view evolved from several studies of changes brought about in Europe by the shift from written to printed texts. In *L'Apparition du livre* (1958), Lucien Febvre and Henri-Jean Martin considered the book as a force for change by examining the impact that printing had on the production and consumption of books, on the transmission and standardization of classical, humanistic, and scientific texts, on the development of modern vernacular languages, and on the Reformation.[2] In *The Printing Press as an Agent of Change* (2 vols.; Cambridge: Cambridge University Press, 1979), Elizabeth Eisenstein concentrated on literate groups that had previously relied on scribal transmission to analyze how printing may have affected the Renaissance, the Reformation, and the scientific revolution. Robert Darnton, using the archives of the Société typographique du Neuchâtel, a Swiss firm that produced books for readers all over Europe during the last two decades of the eighteenth century, investigated the organization of work and the lore of the printing trades, censorship in the ancien régime, and connections between the publishing history of a single book—the *Encyclopédie*—and the Enlightenment.[3]

These examples and recent research on the book in America, much of it under the auspices of the American Antiquarian Society's Program in the History of the Book in American Culture, indicate the broad range of themes that book historians are addressing. Papers presented at a conference held in 1980, published as *Printing and Society in Early America* (Worcester, Mass.: American Antiquarian Society, 1983; ed. William L. Joyce et al.), and at a conference to discuss "needs and opportunities" in 1984, covered topics that included readers and reading, technology and labor, the book and popular culture, the religious press, and the newspaper press. In his lecture, published as *On Native Ground: From the History of Printing to the History of the Book* (Wor-

2. *The Coming of the Book: The Impact of Printing 1450–1800,* trans. David Gerard; ed. Geoffrey Nowell-Smith and David Wootton (London: NLB, 1976; reprinted London: Verso, 1984).

3. See *The Business of Enlightenment: A Publishing History of the "Encyclopédie," 1775–1800* (Cambridge, Mass.: The Belknap Press of Harvard University, 1979); *The Great Cat Massacre* (New York: Basic Books, 1984); *The Literary Underground of the Old Regime* (Cambridge, Mass.: Harvard University Press, 1982).

cester, Mass.: American Antiquarian Society, 1984), David D. Hall enumerated various aspects of "the history of the book as the history of culture and society." Foremost among them was the need to apply the insights and information acquired by historians of printing, publishing, and the book trades to the study of the book as an economic, social, cultural, and intellectual force.

Our knowledge of printing and publishing history is derived from archival records and from analytical bibliography, the study of books as physical objects. This approach was first applied by textual editors to assess how the transmission of a text might have been affected by printing processes, but the examination of evidence preserved in books—such as compositorial spelling patterns, recurring type, and paper—also inevitably reveals many details of a book's production history. Thus physical books and archival documents together constitute the primary sources for the history of books. As G. Thomas Tanselle noted, "any facts uncovered by bibliographical analysis are historical facts, facts of interest in their own right as the data out of which the broader history of printing and publishing is built.[4]

As the history of books is developing, efforts are being made to characterize and locate sources, and the need for a variety of approaches is now recognized. Printers' and publishers' archives, for example, reveal facts about the economic and technical aspects of authorship and book production, but theories derived from these sources must be tested against the products: the books themselves. On the other hand, multiple copies of a printed text and, if possible, publishers' records must be examined to verify conclusions, for books may deceive, intentionally through false imprints or new title pages on old sheets or accidentally through variants produced in the printing process. Accordingly, the resources for the study of the history of books described in this guide include both archival documents and printed books, sources which illuminate and complement each other.

The resources of the Library of Congress, unique in size and scope, offer extraordinary opportunities to benefit from the interdependence of bibliographical and archival evidence. The collections comprise 80 million items, of which nearly 20 million are books, and span all countries, all centuries, and all print and nonprint formats. The predominant strength of these vast holdings is in American materials, primarily because responsibility for copyright

---

4. *The History of Books as a Field of Study,* The Second Hanes Lecture (Chapel Hill: Hanes Foundation and Rare Book Collection, Academic Affairs Library, University of North Carolina, 1981), 7.

registration and deposit has been centralized at the Library of Congress since 1870. Records created as part of the copyright registration process—complete for the post-1870 period and extensive for the years between 1790 and 1870— form a principal archival source for American printing and publishing history. Copyright deposits constitute the core of the general collections and the holdings of the special format divisions. The Library thus brings together documents relating to the writing, printing, and publishing of American books and the books themselves, which in the case of the deposits are often in multiple and always in historically significant copies. In addition, the Library of Congress has strong holdings in many other areas relevant to the study of American and European book history.

This guide focuses on groups of materials rather than on individual authors or texts. As the title states, it is a guide to selected resources, and the principles of selection were shaped by the desire both to indicate existing strengths and to suggest the diversity of potential research. The scope was limited to the Western printed book and thus the African and Middle Eastern Division and the Asian Division were omitted, but they have superb resources, especially for the study of the Hebraic and Oriental book. Separate guides are needed to illuminate research possibilities in these collections.

The arrangement of the guide follows the organization of the Library of Congress into custodial units. Although at first a thematic approach was considered, it soon became apparent that a structure reflecting the Library's own organization would provide the most useful introduction to a large and complex institution that has no comprehensive published guide. *Special Collections in the Library of Congress: A Selective Guide* (Washington: Library of Congress, 1980), compiled by Annette Melville, covers "thematically related groups of material maintained as separate units within the general holdings" and should be consulted as a companion to this more specialized compilation.

The guide is divided into two parts. In the first, pertinent collections in the Manuscript Division and the Rare Book and Special Collections Division are described in alphabetically arranged, separate entries preceded by an overview of each division. The collections included in this section represent the full range of bibliographical and archival sources: imprints; printers' and publishers' records; and papers of book collectors, book designers, and members of the book trades.

Part 2 comprises narrative essays on the copyright collections, the Law

Library, and three separate divisions—the Geography and Map Division, the Music Division, and the Prints and Photographs Division. Each of these chapters describes the Library's holdings from the perspective of the history of books and gives an overview of significant developments and themes. Chapter 3 surveys U.S. copyright laws and registration requirements over the past two hundred years as the background for evaluating the Library's unique resources for historians of American authorship, printing, publishing, and book manufacturing and outlines the role copyright deposits have had in the growth of the collections of the Library of Congress. The chapter on the Law Library suggests the influence printed books have had on the development of law and the legal profession in areas well represented in the collection. Parallel trends that emerge from the chapters on the special format divisions point to possible interrelated lines of research in the graphic arts, the relationship between these and the book trades, and the role of printed images in shaping society and culture.

The emphasis on the separately maintained custodial divisions means that the general collections remain a vast and largely uncharted territory. Sampling reveals extraordinary strength in bibliography and library history. Subject, author, and book-trade bibliographies have always been exhaustively collected for use in the Library's reference and acquisitions activities. These materials, developed as "a basic reference collection separate from the general collections,"[5] facilitate historiographical study of bibliographical scholarship. The holdings of library catalogs and reports, catalogs of private libraries, and auction and booksellers' catalogs in both the general collections and the Rare Book and Special Collections Division are remarkably strong. Newspaper and periodical holdings are especially comprehensive at the Library of Congress, and these strengths are not addressed in this guide.

Certain categories, such as trade catalogs and paper sample and type specimen books, were neither routinely registered for copyright nor actively acquired by the Library of Congress. The Division of Graphic Arts of the National Museum of American History, Smithsonian Institution, however, is exceptionally strong in these areas, and the proximity of the two institutions enables scholars to use their resources together. Records at the National Archives document the development and role of government printing from

---

5. *Classification: Class Z, Bibliography and Library Science,* 5th ed. (Washington: Library of Congress, 1980), iii.

its early days as a form of political patronage to the current position of the Government Printing Office as a major modern printer, publisher, and distributor.

The future development of the history of books, still a relatively new field, will depend on the nature and extent of available scholarly sources. This guide is intended to encourage use of material at the Library of Congress and examination of holdings in other libraries and archives from a similar perspective. By focusing attention on interdisciplinary approaches, intercultural comparisons, and previously neglected genres, formats, and activities, the history of books stimulates innovative uses of research resources, of which those included in this guide to selected resources in the Library of Congress are preeminent examples.

❏ Part One

Pen-and-ink drawing for the front cover of Mark Twain's Life on the Mississippi *(Boston: James R. Osgood, 1883). The cloth binding is stamped with the design in gold and the ornaments and border in black. Benjamin Holt Ticknor Papers, Manuscript Division.*

1□ Manuscript Division

INTRODUCTION

Throughout the nineteenth century, manuscript collections acquired by the U.S. government were maintained by the Bureau of Rolls and Library in the Department of State. During this period, the Library of Congress received historical documents with the libraries of Thomas Jefferson and Peter Force, with the Smithsonian Institution transfer, and from several other sources. By 1888 the need to bring original materials together was recognized, and a department of manuscripts was established for that purpose in 1897 in the newly opened Library of Congress building. The holdings of the Library's Manuscript Division now number nearly 40 million items in approximately 10,000 collections today housed in the James Madison Memorial Building. The original collecting focus was on American statesmen. Presidential papers, the papers of cabinet members and the judiciary, including approximately half of the men who have served as U.S. secretary of state or chief justice, and the papers of selected senators and representatives have been acquired. Papers of military leaders and prominent American families and the archival records of organizations that have significantly affected American life are very well represented.

In the twentieth century, the collecting scope has been broadened to encompass contributions to American literary, cultural, and scientific life. Com-

prehensive holdings exist for writers such as Harold Frederic, Oliver Wendell Holmes, Archibald MacLeish, Edna St. Vincent Millay, Vladimir Nabokov, Edwin Arlington Robinson, Muriel Rukeyser, Walt Whitman, and Owen Wister; for performing and visual artists like Charlotte Cushman, Daniel Chester French, Lillian Gish, Groucho Marx, and James McNeill Whistler; and for scientists, sociologists, and technologists Alexander Graham Bell, Margaret Mead, Samuel F. B. Morse, and J. Robert Oppenheimer. Although the focus is chiefly on American individuals and institutions, papers of prominent non-Americans have also been acquired, a notable example being Sigmund Freud.

Although documenting the role of the book trade, bookselling, and book collecting in shaping American life has never been a collecting priority in the Manuscript Division, its resources highlight the interaction between books and economic, cultural, and political life. Many of the papers of printers, publishers, and book collectors now in the division were sought for their creators' or compilers' political activities: the papers of Thomas Jefferson, Benjamin Franklin, and Peter Force are preeminent examples. Several records of the late eighteenth- and early nineteenth-century Washington printers described below—Blair & Rives, William Duane, Force, Gales & Seaton, Gideon & Company, Samuel Harrison Smith—document political and cultural life in the new capital and the importance of political patronage in early government printing as well as the economics and technology of printing in this period. The R. Hoe & Company Records are unique in the division as solely concerned with printing technology.

Vast collections of the personal and professional papers of newspaper editors and publishers—Roy W. Howard, Henry Robinson Luce, Eugene Meyer, Joseph Pulitzer, the Reid family (Whitelaw Reid, Elisabeth Mills Reid, Ogden Mills Reid, Helen Rogers Reid), William Allen White—reveal the close connections between journalism and politics in American life. They also document the editorial and business operations of newspapers and syndicates. For example, the papers of Whitelaw Reid, who was an early and powerful backer of Ottmar Mergenthaler and who has been credited with naming the Linotype, chronicle the adoption of the machine in the *Tribune* composing room. These voluminous collections, part of the larger history of communications, have not been separately described in this guide, which does not focus on newspaper or periodical publishing. Finding aids for these collections are available in the Manuscript Division Reading Room.

Walt Whitman's involvement in printing, publishing, and distributing his works extended to technical details. On a proof title page for Complete Poems & Prose of Walt Whitman, 1855–1888 (Philadelphia: Ferguson Bros. & Co., Printers, 1888) he noted, "I want the pressman to keep up as good a strong color as can be maintained . . . ." Feinberg-Whitman Collection, Manuscript Division.

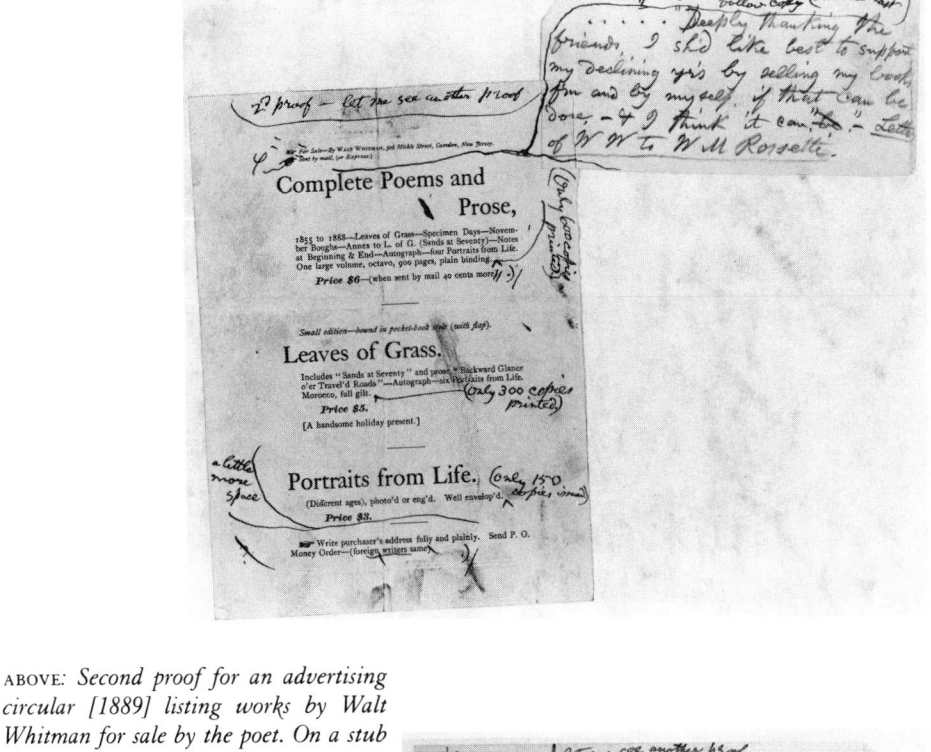

ABOVE: *Second proof for an advertising circular [1889] listing works by Walt Whitman for sale by the poet. On a stub pasted to the proof, Whitman added a quotation from a letter he had written to William Michael Rossetti, "I sh'd like best to support my declining yr's by selling my books f'm and by myself, if that can be done—and I think it can." Feinberg-Whitman Collection, Manuscript Division.*

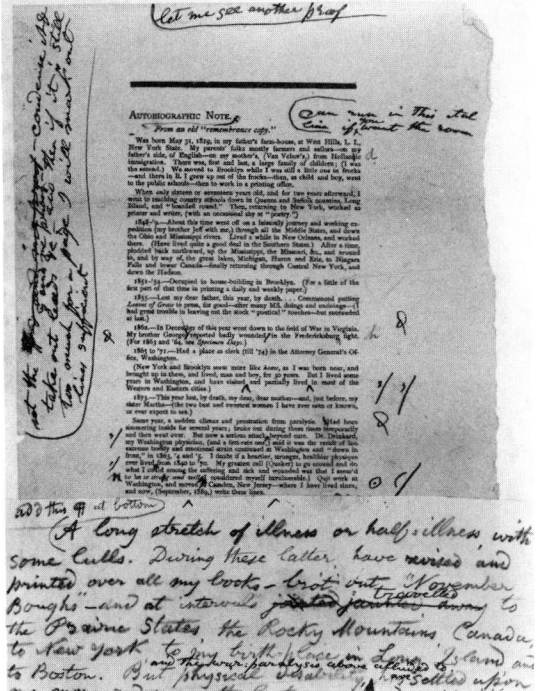

RIGHT: *Second proof for an "Autobiographic Note" by Walt Whitman [September 1889], to be printed on the verso of the circular advertising his works. Whitman brought an earlier "Personal Note" up-to-date by adding autobiographical information for the years 1873 to 1889. Feinberg-Whitman Collection, Manuscript Division.*

No comprehensive commercial publishers' archive is maintained in the Manuscript Division, although important resources exist for every period, beginning with a small group of Isaiah Thomas items in the Miscellaneous Manuscripts Collection. The papers of Benjamin Ticknor provide insights into author-publisher relations, an aspect of publishing history better illuminated by the author collections in the division.

The Thomas Biggs Harned Collection of the Papers of Walt Whitman and the Charles E. Feinberg Collection of the Papers of Walt Whitman reflect the poet's close involvement in every aspect of bringing his work to the public. Whitman's activities as editor, printer, compositor, publicist, and bookseller are revealed in such unique items in the Feinberg-Whitman Collection as the original brass dies used in the 1860–61 edition of *Leaves of Grass;* the title-page plate for the "Death-bed" edition, not used because of Whitman's illness; plate proofs of *Passage to India* (1871) and *Democratic Vistas* (1871); announcements; copyright notices; and instructions to printers, publishers, and binders and other correspondence with them. (See John C. Broderick, "The Greatest Whitman Collector and the Greatest Whitman Collection," *Quarterly Journal of the Library of Congress* 27: 109–28, and the exhibit checklist "Walt Whitman, the Man and the Poet," ibid., 170–76.) Correspondence in the Harned-Whitman Collection between Whitman and James R. Osgood concerns the suppressed edition of *Leaves of Grass* (Boston: J.R. Osgood, 1881–82), which was withdrawn after Whitman refused to make changes demanded by the district attorney. By a memorandum of agreement between Osgood and Whitman (May 17, 1882), plates and copies were transferred to the poet.

The Elbert Hubbard Family Papers consist of letters received by Hubbard, the author, editor, printer, and publisher who founded the Roycroft Press at East Aurora, New York, his wife, and other family members. A program for a Society of the Philistines dinner in honor of Stephen Crane (1895) is included. A small number of Hubbard letters are scattered among other collections. The papers of James D. Barbee, a Methodist minister who served as book agent for the Methodist Episcopal Church (South) in the post-Civil War years, concern Barbee's efforts to settle a claim by the Methodist Publishing House against the government, as well as other topics. Testimony in the collection covers a thirty-year period and touches on "enemy acts" conducted by Confederate printers and the subsequent confiscation of property and equipment by the Union army.

There are several collections for the study of twentieth-century popular and specialized magazine publishing. The editorial files for *Harper's Magazine* begin in 1869 but date almost entirely from the years between 1942 and 1965. The archives of the radical journal of literature and the arts *Earth,* founded and edited by Joseph Niver and published between April 1930 and July 1932, are supplemented by a run of the periodical in the Rare Book and Special Collections Division. The papers of Lawrence Spivak include a series relating to the *American Mercury* from 1933 through 1950. Correspondence, memorandums, and other items in the general editorial files of the *American Scholar* pertain to all aspects of publishing the magazine, including policy, organization, advertising, circulation, relations with the editorial board, printing, production, promotion, and publicity. Similarly, the records of the American Historical Association include material relating to the *American Historical Review,* published by the organization.

The records of the American Council on Learned Societies (ACLS) reflect the wide range of this organization's involvement in bibliographical scholarship. Files from the 1920s document the interest in an international survey of current humanistic bibliography and the distribution of American learned publications in Europe. Major projects which received early support or encouragement from ACLS include the *Census of Medieval and Renaissance Manuscripts in the United States and Canada,* compiled by Seymour de Ricci. The council's most direct and sustained contribution to American scholarship and scholarly publishing is the *Dictionary of American Biography.* A great deal of material in the archive relates to the publication of the first twenty volumes (1928–36) by Charles Scribner's Sons with a subvention of $500,000 from the *New York Times* and to arrangements for a revision, an index, an inexpensive edition, and a supplement. Additions to the collection covering the fifth supplement have continued through 1979.

The two most comprehensive publishers' archives in the Manuscript Division—the Benjamin Huebsch Papers and the Bollingen Foundation Records—reflect innovative and experimental developments in twentieth-century publishing rather than mainstream commercial ventures. The selection process of a major book club may be studied in the Book-of-the-Month Club Records. An unpublished manuscript (in the Miscellaneous Manuscripts Collection) by William Patten, best known at the Library of Congress for beginning the Cabinet of American Illustration in the Prints and Photographs Division, records the origin of the Harvard Classics, a series

Patten developed while manager of the Book Department at P.F. Collier's in 1909.

Collections relating to book design and illustration are not large in number, although—as the description of the Thomas Maitland Cleland Papers that follows demonstrates—there are some outstanding resources. A typescript by author and book illustrator Theodore Bolton for an unpublished, revised edition of his *American Book Illustrators* (New York: R.R. Bowker, 1938) records appearances in book form of work by late nineteenth- and early twentieth-century book illustrators. Letters written by English bookbinder Douglas B. Cockerell to his brother T. D. A. Cockerell in the United States between 1939 and 1945 in the Douglas Cockerell Papers chronicle wartime family and social conditions and political and military developments. Among the professional topics covered were the effect of the war on the book trade and Cockerell's efforts to restore some water-damaged manuscripts belonging to a Cambridge college.

The Pennell-Whistler Collection documents many aspects of Whistler's career, in particular his relationships with his publishers and art galleries; the Pennell portion of this collection includes correspondence from Elmer Adler, Walter Crane, A. Edward Newton, William E. Rudge, John Singer Sargent, and many others. This collection is enriched by Pennell and Whistler holdings in the Prints and Photographs Division and the Whistler manuscripts in the Lessing J. Rosenwald Collection in the Rare Book and Special Collections Division. The papers of author and cartoonist William Henry (Bill) Mauldin consist of manuscripts and correspondence; original drawings and cartoons by him are in the Prints and Photographs Division.

The history of the Library of Congress and its relationships with American bookselling, publishing, and librarianship are documented in the voluminous Library of Congress Archives and in the personal papers of Librarians of Congress George Watterston (1815–29), Ainsworth Rand Spofford (1864–97), John Russell Young (1897–99), Herbert Putnam (1899–1939), Archibald MacLeish (1939–44), Luther H. Evans (1945–53), L. Quincy Mumford (1954–74), and Daniel J. Boorstin (1975–). The Library of Congress Archives (about 1 million items) document activities that begin with the establishment of the Library in 1800, but they are comprehensive only for the period beginning with Herbert Putnam's librarianship in 1899. Major record groups contain acquisitions and accessions records, including want lists and correspondence with domestic and foreign booksellers and agents, letterpress copies of corre-

spondence from the Librarians of Congress (1843–), and records, correspondence, blueprints, drawings, and photographs relating to the construction of
the Thomas Jefferson Building (1873–97). Other categories include annual
reports, binding, cataloging, and fiscal records, legislative and congressional
matters, literary activities, personnel, and services of the Library. Some material relating to the disposition of copyright deposits is in the Library of
Congress Archives, but the Copyright Office, Exchange and Gift Division,
and several other Library divisions retain custody of their own records. (See
John Y. Cole, *For Congress and the Nation: A Chronological History of the
Library of Congress* [Washington: Library of Congress, 1978], especially
"Sources for Further Study," 177–79.)

The papers of Thorvald Solberg (1852–1949), the first Register of Copyrights in the United States, relate to his efforts to protect literary rights in
America and abroad. The broad base of support for international copyright
in the late nineteenth century is confirmed in the R. R. Bowker Papers. The
Ross Alexander Collins Collection and the Frederic Melcher Papers preserve
evidence of successful lobbying on behalf of the purchase of the Otto
Vollbehr Collection now in the Rare Book and Special Collections Division.

Censorship is the focus of two manuscript collections described below, the
papers of Huntington Cairns and Elmer Gertz. Library history and reading
programs are the subjects of the papers of Lyman Bryson and J. C. Thomas
and the records of the Washington Library Company. The development of
bibliographical scholarship is reflected in the Edmund Bailey O'Callaghan
Papers.

Scattered through the Miscellaneous Manuscripts Collections are several
booksellers' account books. The earliest of these, entered as "Book sales,"
records the names of William Byrd, Col. Benjamin Harrison, and John Randolph among its customers, and therefore may be assigned to Virginia in the
1750s. There are two items relating to James Rivington; three items from the
New York bookseller Robert Moore, 1813–17, including a receipt from
Mathew Carey; a letterbook and daybook from Georgetown stationer Robert
Cruikshank covering the period between 1827 and 1831; an account book
and letterbook from Peabody & Company, a New York City book and stationery store, for the period 1831 to 1833; and a small group of papers from
Fred E. Woodward (1898–1922), a Washington, D.C., merchant and bookseller who ran the book department of the Woodward and Lothrop department store. None of these is comprehensive enough to sustain extended re-

search, but each gives important information for the time and location it covers.

The acquisition of books and the formation of private libraries in the early years of the republic are revealed in superb detail in the papers of Thomas Jefferson and James Madison. The Pierre Eugène Du Simitière collection and the papers of Peter Force testify to the foresight and resourcefulness of some of our earliest book collectors.

The descriptions that follow suggest the strength and diversity of the division's resources for the study of the history of books. These collections illuminate the role of books and reading in the lives of men and women who have shaped American culture and thus reveal the influence of books on the society they shaped.

REFERENCES

United States. Library of Congress. American Revolution Bicentennial Office. *Manuscript Sources in the Library of Congress for Research on the American Revolution.* Comp. John R. Sellers et al. Washington: Library of Congress, 1975.

United States. Library of Congress. Manuscript Division. *Handbook of Manuscripts in the Library of Congress.* Washington: Library of Congress, 1918.

————. *Library of Congress Acquisitions: Manuscript Division.* Washington: Library of Congress 1981–.

————. *The National Union Catalog of Manuscript Collections.* Washington: Library of Congress, 1959/60–.

❏   BLAIR & RIVES RECORDS

For the first years of the country's existence, government printing was dispensed by contract to the lowest bidder, and printers in New York, Philadelphia, and finally Washington recognized in official printing the possibility of a steady source of income. The system resulted in delays, inaccuracies, and controversies over costs, and the population of the nation and the business of government soon expanded sufficiently to require a schedule of fixed prices and the selection of a printer by each congressional house. Until the Government Printing Office was established in 1861, printers changed with each election. For most of this period, two firms, Gales & Seaton and Blair & Rives, alternated as government printers. Both firms issued newspapers—the *Intel-*

ligencer was published by Gales & Seaton and the *Globe* by Blair & Rives—which provided them with a commercial outlet for the information they received in the course of their government work and guaranteed them employment while they awaited the next election when they had none.

Francis P. Blair (1791–1876), a Kentucky journalist and politician, came to Washington to form a newspaper that would serve as an organ for Andrew Jackson's administration. Blair founded the *Globe* in 1830 to replace Duff Green's *United States Telegraph.* It was an immediate success, with a range of influence far wider than its circulation. Two years later a fellow Kentuckian, John C. Rives (1795–1864), arrived with a recommendation to Jackson from Duff Green, in whose *Telegraph* office Rives had worked. Rives served as the financial manager of the *Globe* and in 1833 initiated the *Congressional Globe,* the first complete and impartial report of congressional debates. With a change in the political environment, Blair was discharged by President Polk in 1845 and forced to sell his share in the *Globe* to Thomas Ritchie. The firm was dissolved in 1855, because Blair's antislavery stand had lost them many contracts. The *Congressional Globe* was published by Rives until 1864 and by his son through 1873, when Congress began to issue the *Congressional Record.* Both Blair and Rives were affluent and influential members of the Washington political and social scene.

The records of Blair & Rives comprise about 800 items in seven volumes, including business papers, speeches, and printed matter. Letters received, primarily dating from the 1830s and 1840s, relate to national politics, the selection of congressional printers, and the publication of the *Congressional Globe.* The collection includes a document dated July 20, 1842, in which Matthew St. Clair Clarke relinquishes his share of the contract to publish *The Documentary History of the American Revolution* to John Rives and printer's copies of acts, proclamations, and petitions printed by the firm.

❑   BOLLINGEN FOUNDATION RECORDS

The Bollingen Foundation, founded in 1945 by Paul and Mary Conover Mellon, supported publications and research in a broad range of humanistic fields, including aesthetics, anthropology, literary criticism, mythology, poetry, philosophy, psychology, and religion. The program of publication, the Bollingen Series, established under the auspices of the Old Dominion

Foundation in 1943 to publish a new and uniform edition of the collected works of Carl Jung in English, was transferred to the Bollingen Foundation in 1945. Under the direction of John D. Barrett, president and editor of the Bollingen Series, who took over after Mary Conover Mellon's death in 1946, and Vaun Gillmor, vice president and assistant editor of the Bollingen Series, the founding ideal was understood to encompass scholarly and creative work of an interpretive, analytical, or critical nature. Volumes selected for the series would not have been published in the usual commercial channels because of their great length, difficult production requirements, or limited commercial appeal. The Bollingen Series published original works and translations of works previously unavailable in English, many in multiple volumes, such as the collected works of Jung, St. John Perse, and Paul Valéry, the selected works of Miguel de Unamuno and Hugo von Hofmannsthal, and the collected works and notebooks of S. T. Coleridge.

The records of the Bollingen Foundation include extensive files (95 linear feet, about 78,000 items) documenting the administration and operations of this unique philanthropic and publishing venture. Three black binders titled "Publishing History and Information" contain a set of forms, arranged alphabetically by book title, recording contract and rights information, financial arrangements, and publication information. Topics covered in general memoranda include copyright, reprint agreements with domestic and foreign publishing firms, publication costs, and royalty schedules.

Pantheon Books, founded by Kurt and Helen Wolff in 1942, assumed responsibility for production and distribution of the Bollingen Series in 1943. Correspondence and contracts in the collection cover all aspects of this close relationship, which lasted until 1967, when the foundation transferred the Bollingen Series to the Princeton University Press. In 1961, when Pantheon merged with Random House, alternative arrangements were considered in a memorandum on the "Status of Publication Problems." As a result, the foundation assumed responsibility for publication of the series and Pantheon continued as the distributor. Other recurring themes include book club and paperback reprint arrangements. Several paperback houses brought out Bollingen Series titles until 1961, when the foundation and Harper & Row agreed to select certain titles for publication as Harper Torchbooks. The philosophical and financial considerations leading up to this agreement are shown in correspondence and contracts in the collection.

Correspondence with designers, including E. McKnight Kauffer, who

designed the Bollingen Series logo, indicates the great care that went into each aspect of bookmaking. Over the years twenty-one Bollingen Series volumes received awards from the American Institute of Graphic Arts (AIGA). AIGA Certificates of Excellence were awarded in 1960 and 1964. Files for individual titles record international negotiations with translators, editors, compilers, and authors.

Besides sponsoring the Bollingen Series, the foundation donated copies of the publications to over two hundred libraries free of charge and awarded fellowships and grants-in-aid to individual scholars for research and writing. Through 1966, 322 projects were supported in all fields represented by Bollingen Series publications. Other foundation programs included direct grants to institutions and the subvention of scholarly publication by university presses and learned societies. The entire range of these activities is fully represented in the collection.

The Bollingen Collection in the Rare Book and Special Collections Division demonstrates the contributions made by the foundation to twentieth-century scholarship. An archival set of over 600 volumes in the Bollingen Series was given to the Library with the papers in 1973. Both books subventioned by the foundation and books written by fellows but not officially part of the foundation's publishing projects are included. The Princeton University Press continues to send copies of Bollingen titles upon publication, which are added to the collection on receipt.

REFERENCES

"Bollingen Series: A Numerical Listing" and "Bibliography of Publications Resulting from Research and Writing Done with the Aid of Bollingen Foundation Fellowships and Grants-in-Aid (1945–1965)." In *Bollingen Foundation Twentieth Anniversary Report of Its Activities from December 14, 1945, through December 31, 1965.* New York: Bollingen, 1967.

McGuire, William. *Bollingen: An Adventure in Collecting the Past.* Princeton: Princeton University Press, 1982.

McGuire, William. "The Bollingen Foundation: Mary Mellon's 'Shining Beacon.'" *Quarterly Journal of the Library of Congress* 39 (1982): 200–211.

Quarterly Journal of the Library of Congress 31 (1974):181.

Quarterly Journal of the Library of Congress 31 (1974): 261–63.

❑   BOOK-OF-THE-MONTH CLUB RECORDS

Approximately 9,500 preliminary readers' reports in this collection span the period from 1939 to 1958 and relate primarily to books not selected by the club. Readers, among them William Rose Benét, Basil Davenport, Amy Loveman, Allan Nevins, and Ralph Thompson, wrote candid evaluations of the literary merit, suitability, and cost of various books. The reports are arranged chronologically, then alphabetically by title within each year. Over 5,200 letters from editors and publishers in the correspondence files (1947–50) relate to books submitted by publishing firms for consideration by the club. They are arranged chronologically, then alphabetically by correspondent. Clifton Fadiman, Dorothy Canfield Fisher, John P. Marquand, and Christopher Morley are represented in this sequence.

REFERENCES

Library of Congress Information Bulletin 23 (May 25, 1964): 232–33.

Quarterly Journal of the Library of Congress 21 (1964): 199.

❑   RICHARD ROGERS BOWKER PAPERS

Editor, publisher, bibliographer, and author Richard Rogers Bowker (1848–1933) was actively involved in late nineteenth-century efforts to secure an international copyright agreement. In 1878 he issued a circular letter requesting information and opinion on the subject and circulated petitions for delivery to Congress. Responses from leading publishers and authors such as Theodore Low DeVinne, Oliver Wendell Holmes, Charles Eliot Norton, Edmund Clarence Stedman, and Harriet Beecher Stowe, originally printed in *Publishers Weekly,* form part of this collection of 2,200 items. Manuscripts and journals written by Bowker in London, where he served as Harper's agent from 1880 to 1882, are also included, as well as papers relating to his activity as an early organizer of the independent Republican movement in 1879, manuscripts by authors such as Thomas B. Aldrich and Austin Dobson, and a collection of miscellaneous autographs. The largest body of Bowker papers, however, is at the New York Public Library and provided the basis for the biography *R. R. Bowker, Militant Liberal* (Norman: University of Oklahoma Press, 1952), by E. McClung Fleming.

❏ LYMAN LLOYD BRYSON PAPERS

A radio and television broadcaster, an author, and an educator, Lyman Lloyd Bryson (1888–1959) directed the Readability Laboratory at Columbia University from 1936 to 1940. Among his ideas to promote communication of difficult subjects to average readers was the "People's Library." This series, published by Macmillan, was developed by a group of educators, librarians, and psychologists who studied theories of lucidity, communication, and comprehension. Their findings were reported by Bryson in a "Manual for People's Library," intended for authors, the manuscript of which is with his papers. Other activities represented in the collection (15 linear feet, about 10,000 items) include a project to provide librarians with a basic bibliography of nonfiction books graded according to difficulty and suitability.

REFERENCE

Library of Congress Information Bulletin 18 (March 2, 1959).

❏ HUNTINGTON CAIRNS PAPERS

The papers of lawyer and author Huntington Cairns (1904–1985) include correspondence, corrected galley proofs, entries contributed to the *Dictionary of American Biography,* and professional and administrative papers (35 linear feet, about 28,000 items). Between 1934 and 1937 Cairns worked for the U.S. Treasury Department as federal censor of imported books and movies. He had long staunchly supported freedom of expression. As early as 1931, in reply to a letter from Morris Ernst about a case brought by the New York Society for the Suppression of Vice, Cairns observed, "You state that a bill has been introduced in Albany to repeal its charter; I can only say that I hope the day of reckoning is at hand."

The case and subject files for this period include correspondence relating to particular cases and chronological "Lists of Decisions on Books, Booklets, & Pamphlets under the Provisions of Section 305 of the Tariff Act of 1930 (and Related Statutes)." These cover censorship cases primarily relating to contraceptive literature and cases distinguishing the "free fine arts," which were not subject to import duties, from the "decorative or industrial arts,"

which were. The regulations were revised during this period to admit commercial quantities of mechanically produced reproductions formerly considered "industrial drawings."

Huntington Cairns served as an adviser for the Bollingen Series and wrote several works on aesthetics and legal philosophy. In 1943 he became secretary-treasurer and general counsel to the National Gallery of Art, a position he retained until his retirement in 1965. His interests and activities brought him into contact with the worlds of literature, publishing, film, and the law. Correspondents in the collection include Jerome Frank, Lillian Gish, Joseph Hergesheimer, Edith Hamilton, St. John Perse, Henry Lewis Mencken, Ezra Pound, Max Lincoln Schuster, and Allen Tate. An extensive series of letters from Henry Miller, which began when Cairns was writing a report on "Freedom of Expression in Art," includes several lengthy discussions of the effect of censorship on Miller's life and art.

REFERENCE

Quarterly Journal of the Library of Congress 23 (1966): 280–81.

❏ THOMAS MAITLAND CLELAND PAPERS

Thomas Maitland Cleland (1880-1964) worked as a typographer, book designer, artist, and illustrator. Correspondence (1920-63) with printers, publishers, clients, and fellow artists in the collection reveals his day-to-day working habits, business arrangements, and design philosophy. There are 700 items of correspondence to and from Daniel Berkeley Updike, founder of the Merrymount Press. Other correspondents include Elmer Adler, Paul Bennett, Harry Carter, Warren Chappell, Fritz Eichenberg, Mitchell Kennerley, Rockwell Kent, Fritz Kredel, Francis Meynell, Will Ransom, Bruce Rogers, Carl Purington Rollins, Hans Schmoller, Oliver Simon, and Beatrice and Frederic Warde. There are approximately 1,200 pieces of family correspondence among the 6,700 items (11 linear feet).

Original drawings, designs, typographical arrangements, specifications, and corrected proofs document Cleland's versatile and productive career. As art director of *Fortune* and in his work for *Newsweek* and *PM* magazines, Cleland created distinctive typographical styles and layouts, the philosophy

and development of which may be studied through correspondence and drawings in the collection.

The Cleland Papers contain designs for insignia, emblems, printers' marks, trademarks, and bookplates that he did for individuals and institutions. Among his clients were the Century Club, the Grolier Club, and the Metropolitan Museum of Art.

Cleland's work as a book designer and illustrator is represented by original drawings, sketches, and proof copies. These include very early private press publications and *The Book of the Locomobile* (1916-17). Josephine Preston Peabody's *In the Silence* was privately printed by Cleland in 1900, and two copies of it are present. The annotated typescript of *The Veil of Happiness* was privately printed in 1920 by Cleland, who also translated the work and acted in the play. In his work for the Limited Editions Club, Cleland experimented with printing techniques to achieve perfect register and with silkscreen, or pochoir, printing. These efforts are apparent in the marked copies of Modern Library editions of *Tom Jones* and other works and in correspondence from Cleland's publishers, impatient for the overdue results of his labors.

The manuscript of Cleland's lecture "Progress in the Graphic Arts," delivered at the Newberry Library in 1948, is in the collection. A list of "Books Designed or Illustrated by TMC, Including Some That Have Parts Designed by Him" was prepared from Library of Congress catalog cards by Herbert Sanborn. This list, annotated and amended by Cleland, is also in the collection.

REFERENCES

Quarterly Journal of the Library of Congress 20, no. 3 (June 1963) : 186.

Sanborn, Herbert J. "The Cleland Papers," *Quarterly Journal of the Library of Congress* 20, no. 3 (June 1963): 163-73.

☐   ROSS ALEXANDER COLLINS COLLECTION

As representative to Congress from Mississippi, Ross Alexander Collins (1880-1968) introduced legislation in support of the purchase of the Otto H. Vollbehr Collection of incunabula now in the Library of Congress. A scrap-

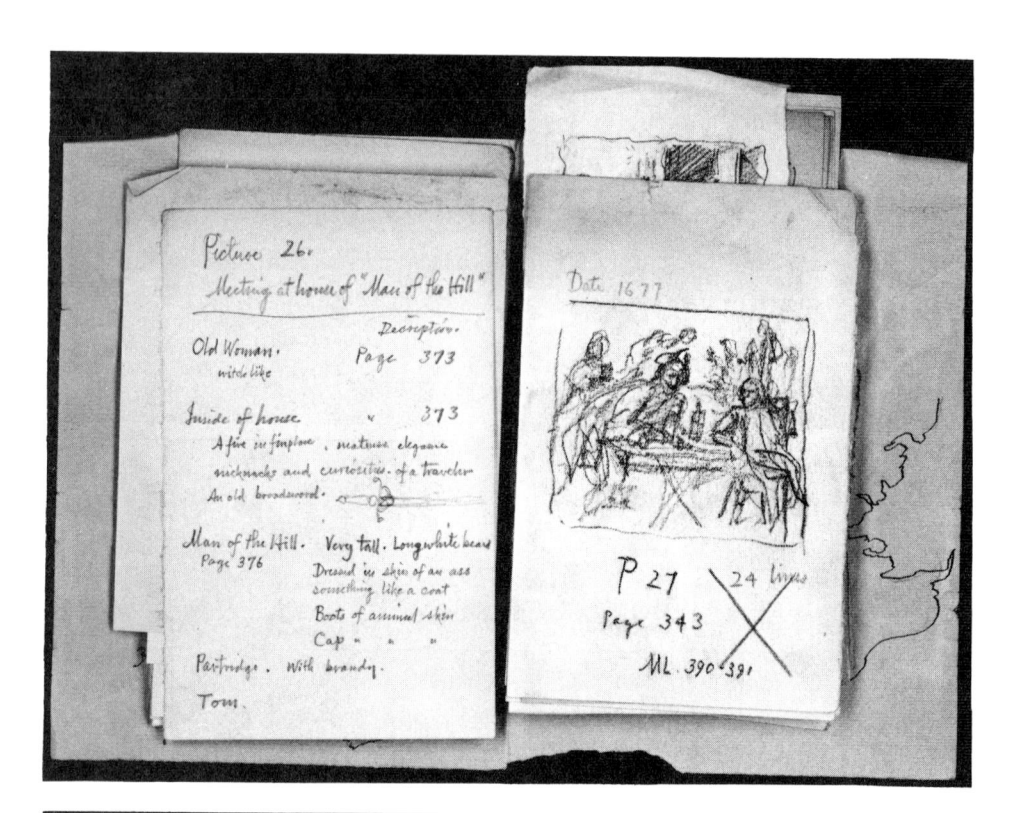

'"I am sorry for it with all my heart," quoth he, "and I wish thee better success another time. Though, if you will take my advice, you shall have no occasion to run any such risk. Here," said he, taking some dice out of his pocket, "here's the stuff. Here are the implements; here are the little doctors which cure the distempers of the purse. Follow but my counsel, and I will show you a way to empty the pocket of a queer cull without any danger of the nubbing cheat."'

'Nubbing cheat!' cries Partridge: 'pray, sir, what is that?'

'Why that, sir,' says the stranger, 'is a cant phrase for the gallows; for as gamesters differ little from highwayman in their morals, so do they very much resemble them in their language.

'We had now each drank our bottle, when Mr. Watson said the board was sitting, and that he must attend, earnestly pressing me at the same time to go with him and try my fortune. I answered he knew that was at present out of my power, as I had informed him of the emptiness of my pocket. To say the truth, I doubted not from his many strong expressions of friendship, but that he would offer to lend me a small sum for that purpose, but he answered, "Never mind that, man; e'en boldly run a levant" [Partridge was going to inquire the meaning of that word, but Jones stopped his mouth]: "but be circumspect as to the man. I will tip you the proper person, which may be necessary, as you do not know the town, nor can distinguish a rum cull from a queer one."

'The bill was now brought, when Watson paid his share, and was departing. I reminded him, not without blushing, of my having no money. He answered, "That signifies nothing; score it behind the door, or make a bold brush and take no notice. Or—stay," says he; "I will go down-stairs first, and then do you take up my money, and score the whole reckoning at the bar, and I will wait for you at the corner." I expressed some dislike at this, and hinted my expectations that he would have deposited the whole; but he swore he had not another sixpence in his pocket.

'He then went down, and I was prevailed on to take up the money and follow him, which I did close enough to hear

391

An illustrator's sketches and working notes reveal how he sets about interpreting and depicting scenes and characters from a text. Thomas Maitland Cleland made extensive notes from the Modern Library edition of Tom Jones *in his work for the 1952 Limited Editions Club edition of Henry Fielding's novel. His preparations for integrating image and text included an exact and careful character count from the Modern Library edition. Thomas Maitland Cleland Papers, Manuscript Division.*

book of clippings and five of letters received between March and July 1930 from librarians, teachers, and others indicate widespread and enthusiastic support for the acquisition.

REFERENCE

Quarterly Journal of the Library of Congress 20, no. 3 (June 1963): 180.

❑   ## ROBERT CRUIKSHANK RECORDS
HUGH T. TAGGART COLLECTION

The letterbook and daybook of Robert Cruikshank, a Georgetown stationer, cover the period between 1827 and 1831. In the letterbook, press copies of outgoing correspondence to suppliers of books and paper in Baltimore, Philadelphia, and Hartford provide a full picture of the firm's business. There are orders for books that cannot be found "in the district," among them textbooks. The discount structure and other transactions may be studied in the exchanges concerning payments and the complaints of nondelivery.

In the daybook, sales were entered for each day along with the customer's name and the price of each item. The high proportion of nonbook sales is immediately apparent: copy books, binder's board, writing equipment, household products, and engravings constitute the most frequent items entered, although in monetary value total book sales were substantial. These volumes constitute a partial but detailed record of an early nineteenth-century bookseller operating outside a publishing center.

REFERENCE

Annual Report of the Librarian of Congress, 1916, 46.

❑   ## WILLIAM DUANE COLLECTION

Journalist and politician William Duane (1760-1835) edited the Philadelphia *Aurora,* an influential Jeffersonian newspaper. He followed Jefferson's government to Washington and opened a store in anticipation of a contract for government printing and stationery that never materialized.

This group of fourteen letters dating from 1800 through 1832 covers political and printing activities. Citing his government connections, Duane requested assistance from Joseph Nancrede (1761-1841), who imported and published books in Boston, in establishing a London correspondent.

◻ PIERRE EUGÈNE DU SIMITIÈRE COLLECTION

The Swiss-born naturalist, artist, and antiquary Pierre Eugène Du Simitière (1737-1784) collected pamphlets, broadsides, newspapers, and clippings for a projected history of North America and specimens and curiosities for a museum that opened in Philadelphia in 1782. As early as 1774 Du Simitière perceived the importance of preserving primary documentary material relating to contemporary events. He lacked the resources to build a collection of the size and rarity of those of his contemporaries like James Logan, but he showed remarkable insight in recognizing the need to preserve fugitive publications. Du Simitière classified his reading and constructed elaborate bibliographical indexes of material he had or sought to acquire.

The collection formed by Du Simitière was sold at auction in Philadelphia the year following his death. Most of the manuscripts and much of the printed material was acquired by the Library Company, which published the *Descriptive Catalogue of the Du Simitière Papers in the Library Company of Philadelphia* in 1940. The five volumes acquired by the Library of Congress with the Peter Force Papers consist of a letterbook (1779-84), a commonplace book, a memoranda volume (1774-83), and two volumes of notes on publications. A commonplace book of 1770 was added by a later purchase. These materials provide fascinating details about books in prerevolutionary and revolutionary society and about the contacts and collections of this remarkable figure.

In the memoranda book, Du Simitière recorded a list of books purchased in October and November 1781 and added "NB all the above books were once part of that large and valuable Library of the late Col. [William] Byrd of Westover in Virginia, which is now selling piece meal in this city." The list of "Things lent" in this volume records the names of Benjamin Rush, John Jay, who borrowed *Thoughts on govt &c* in 1776, Thomas Paine, Maj. John André, and Pierre L'Enfant, the planner of Washington, D.C., who borrowed a manuscript "plan of a map of Charles town." After the start

of hostilities, Du Simitière's library remained open to Revolutionary and Loyalist alike.

Du Simitière's efforts to preserve documentary evidence relating to colonial and revolutionary events make him the spiritual ancestor of Peter Force. The lists and indexes of articles, books, and pamphlets afford valuable insight into the process by which a contemporary attempted to organize and classify events before and during the American Revolution. Du Simitière's work constitutes an early recognition of the relationship between bibliography, collecting, and historical scholarship.

The volumes also include lists of "Drawings and paintings done by me" and notes of natural curiosities, Indian relics, medals, and coins sent to Du Simitière, along with records of the donors. Correspondents in the letterbook include François Barbé-Marbois, George Clinton, Robert Morris, Benjamin Rush, Nathaniel Scudder, and Baron von Steuben.

❑ PETER FORCE PAPERS

The career of Peter Force (1790-1868) illuminates nineteenth-century printing, historical bibliography, and book collecting. As a young boy, Force was apprenticed to William A. Davis of New York, from whom he learned the printing trade. In 1812 Force was elected president of the New York Typographical Society. Three years later he moved to Washington with a contract for some government printing from Davis, who remained in New York. The Washington firm, known as Davis & Force, compiled and published the *National Calendar.* Force also edited the *National Journal,* and in 1833 he was authorized by Congress to compile and publish, with Matthew St. Clair Clarke, a documentary history of the American Revolution, which was published as *American Archives* between 1836 and 1853. This monumental project, which consumed all of Force's energies and finances, was terminated in 1855 after nine volumes had appeared. The project provided the stimulus to his collecting books, manuscripts, and transcripts that are of invaluable historical importance today.

The Peter Force Papers, purchased by Act of Congress in 1867, measure over 300 linear feet, with over 150,000 items. The collection consists chiefly of Force's personal papers, in addition to the transcripts and originals of manu-

Pierre Eugène Du Simitière operated an informal circulating library in revolutionary America, and he maintained this record of books, artifacts, and other materials that he lent or gave to his Philadelphia and foreign friends. For August 28, 1779, he noted, "lent Mr. Ch. Thomson narrative of Col. Allen's captivity," a reference to Ethan Allen's Narrative of Colonel Ethan Allen's Captivity, *first published that year by Robert Bell in Philadelphia.* Peter Force Papers, Manuscript Division.

Pierre Eugène Du Simitière listed books, journals, and pamphlets relating to the American Revolution and acquired as many of the works on his bibliography as he could. Among those recorded here are the Journals of Congress *and* A Narrative of Col. Ethan Allen's Captivity. Peter Force Papers, Manuscript Division.

scripts gathered for *American Archives.* The personal papers document Force's career as a Washington printer, newspaper editor, compiler, and collector; his military and public service (Force served as mayor of Washington from 1836 to 1840); his scientific and intellectual pursuits; and his contributions to the field of history, manifested in his role in organizing the first American Historical Society in 1836. The papers reveal Force's plan and method of compiling *American Archives* and his relationships with historians and antiquarians who sought his advice or the use of his library and with the dealers who shaped the collection.

The first series in the collection, the general correspondence, consists of letters received with drafts of letters sent. They relate to the proposal and congressional inquiries on the *American Archives,* the work of transcribers engaged by Force to copy manuscript material, and his book collecting. Force was the friend of both Henry Stevenses; there are 100 letters from Henry Stevens of Vermont (the younger) in this sequence. Also included are inventories of trunks of books sent by Stevens for Force's consideration in Washington, bills for books purchased, and extensive commentary on the availability and price of books relating to America.

Letters between Force and antiquarian and bibliographer John Russell Bartlett (1805-1886), from whose New York firm, Bartlett & Welford, Force purchased many books, include Bartlett's 1840 response to an order from Force: "Nos. 496 571 & 624 are sold, and No. 626 Las Casas has been missing for a week past from our shelves. We fear some lover of the Black letter has taken it without our knowledge." The interconnections between dealers and collectors are evident in Bartlett's comments in 1846: "Soon after my return from Washington, our Mr. Welford went to London—He writes that our friend Mr. Stevens is the great monopolist of American Books in London— He not only buys everything of value, but prevents all the respectable dealers from selling to others. The fact is, he has some rich customers in Boston & Providence, and I understand he makes them pay high prices." In later years Bartlett became closely connected with John Carter Brown, to whom these remarks directly refer, and cataloged his library.

Other correspondents in the book trade include Hilliard, Gray & Co., Samuel Drake of Boston, Joel Munsell, Joseph Sabin, and George Putnam. Among the collectors in this series are Henry C. Murphy, George Livermore, Lyman Draper, and E. B. O. Gallaghan. Correspondence from George Ban-

croft, James Buchanan, Mathew Carey, Matthew St. Clair Clarke, Joseph Gales, Robert Hoe, John C. Rives, Henry Rowe Schoolcraft, William Seaton, Daniel Webster, Roger C. Weightman, and others documents the full range of Force's activities and provides insights into political, military, social, and scientific aspects of early nineteenth-century America.

The second series consists of the papers of Force's son, William Quereau Force (1820-1880), who assisted in copying and indexing *American Archives* and also edited *The Army & Navy Chronicle and Scientific Repository* before joining the staff of the Smithsonian Institution. This group includes correspondence, diaries, and printer's copy for articles which were published in the *Chronicle* and in the *Bulletin of the Proceedings of the National Institute for the Promotion of Science.*

The Peter Force printer's file, which makes up the third series, includes correspondence and papers related to the *National Journal* (1823-32) and the *National Calendar,* and printer's copy and correspondence for books printed by Force or Davis & Force between 1818 and 1846. Included here are manuscripts of addresses by John Quincy Adams, some with proof copy; Henry Lee's *Memoirs of the War . . .* (Philadelphia: Bradford and Inskeep, 1812) with manuscript annotations, additions, and corrections interleaved for the second edition, together with a request for a cost estimate and proposed arrangements for payment; manuscript poems, pamphlets, and speeches, some with printed copy and many marked by the printer; and the manuscript of Robert Strange's *"Eoneguski, or the Cherokee Chief: A Tale of Past Wars,* by an American (Washington: F. T. Taylor, 1839). Strange, U.S. senator from North Carolina (1836-40), forwarded his work to Force with a request that he "commit it to the press, or the flames, according to your judgement of its merits."

The subject file includes records of a circulating library run by Force as early as 1820, when two catalogs of its contents were printed. A "Catalog of Books Belonging to Davis & Force 1822" records 3,500 volumes in all fields. The "Record of Books Lent 17 Sep 1835-25 Mar 1844," and the "Receipts for Books Borrowed" for 1846-61 reflect the expansion of available material over this period. This sequence is followed by the financial papers, which include bills, receipts, and account books spanning the years 1816 to 1867. There is an account of printing by William A. Davis for the Fourteenth Congress, 1816-17, when Davis was still Force's employer. A Davis & Force Bill Book cover-

ing the period between 1820 and 1824, in which the work and rate for each compositor is recorded week-by-week, records the job, book, and government work in the shop at one time and the rate (in time and cost) at which each job was completed. Cash books and miscellaneous financial documents date primarily from the 1820s. Force's voluminous historical working papers document—in lists, surveys, and index sheets—the process by which *American Archives* was planned and compiled.

Manuscript and printed sources collected for and used in *American Archives* include printer's copy and transcripts from the Papers of the Continental Congress, the Papers of George Washington, state records, and records from historical societies, private collections, and foreign archives. Individual manuscript collections acquired by Force as part of this effort, including those of George Chalmers, Ebenezer and Samuel Hazard, and a Hispanic Collection, are maintained in separate sequences. Several of these were acquired with pamphlet collections now in the Rare Book and Special Collections Division.

Numerous documents and letters relate directly to Force's printing activities. These include arrangements for paper and supplies from New York and type from Boston and statements on the printing costs of individual volumes of the *American Archives,* submitted to the secretary of state. Force supervised the printing in his own shop quite closely and reported on it in great detail. Also in the collection is a "Letters Patent," signed by Secretary of State John Quincy Adams on August 22, 1822, for an invention by Peter Force "of an improved manner of making the paper hangings and machines for printing on calicoes and letter-press printing."

With the purchase of the Peter Force Library in 1867, the Library of Congress acquired significant resources for the study of American history. Printed materials in the collection included 22,529 books; nearly 1,000 volumes of bound newspapers, about a quarter of them from the eighteenth century; nearly 40,000 pamphlets; and over 1,000 maps, about a third of them in manuscript. Force also collected early printed books and the Library received 161 of his incunables and 250 sixteenth-century books he had owned.

In a *Special Report of the Librarian of Congress to the Joint Committee on the Library Concerning the Historical Library of Peter Force, Esq.* (Washington, 1867), Ainsworth Rand Spofford noted that "in the field of early printed American books . . . this library possesses more than ten times the number to be found in the Library of Congress." Many early imprints were gathered in

five pamphlet collections, which had originally been assembled by Ebenezer Hazard, William Duane, Jacob Bailey Moore, Oliver Wolcott, and Israel Thorndike. Spofford noted, too, that "The [Force] collection is not only unmatched, but at this day unmatchable for completeness." The books from the Peter Force collection have been dispersed, although many were recorded without source designation in the *Catalogue of Books Added to the Library of Congress from December 1, 1866, to December 1, 1867* (Washington, 1868). Incunabula, early American imprints, the pamphlet collections, and other rare materials have been incorporated into the collections of the Rare Book and Special Collections Division. Maps in the collection are now in the Geography and Map Division.

REFERENCES

Goff, Frederick R. "Peter Force." *Papers of the Bibliographical Society of America* 44 (1950): 1-16.

McGirr, Newman F. "The Activities of Peter Force." *Records of the Columbia Historical Society* (1940): 35-82.

Stephenson, Richard W. "Maps from the Peter Force Collection." *Quarterly Journal of the Library of Congress* 30 (1973): 183-204.

Sung, Carolyn. "Peter Force: Washington Printer and Creator of the *American Archives*." Ph.D. diss., George Washington University, 1985.

United States. Library of Congress. *Special Collections in the Library of Congress: A Selective Guide.* Comp. by Annette Melville. Washington: Library of Congress, 1980. See no. 84.

❏   BENJAMIN FRANKLIN PAPERS

The collection of Benjamin Franklin material acquired by Henry Stevens, the American bookseller in London, from William Temple Franklin's widow through H. A. Pulsform, was purchased by the U.S. government in 1882. This forms the core of the Library of Congress collections of papers and books by and relating to Benjamin Franklin (1706-1790), statesman, diplomat, scientist, printer, and publisher.

The Benjamin Franklin Papers in the Manuscript Division (12 linear feet, about 8,000 items) date primarily from the 1770s and 1780s and pertain to Franklin's activities in France. There are copies of letters to Cadwallader

Colden about Colden's proposed new plan of printing; a letter to Pierre Simon Fournier, the Paris typefounder, on the shape of types; and letters to Ferdinand Grand about payment for types ordered from François Ambroise Didot for Franklin's grandson, Benjamin Franklin Bache, to whom Didot later taught typefounding. A volume of notes with the title, "Medical, Nature Printing and Addenda" contains twenty specimens of nature printing. Several of Franklin's letters to the English printer William Strahan comment on English political affairs in printing terminology and relate to the book trade, noting the advantages to "holders of copy Rights in England" of the increased demand for English books.

The Benjamin Franklin Collection in the Rare Book and Special Collections Division is composed of the 204 items from the Stevens purchase and additional volumes from the Peter Force Library, the Brinley auction, the Pennypacker sale, and the Library's general collections. Approximately 270 Franklin imprints represent printing establishments that bore his name as well as the products of presses for which he worked or in which he had a financial interest. Works by Franklin and works about him are also included among the 850 volumes.

REFERENCES

Ford, Worthington Chauncey, comp. *List of the Benjamin Franklin Papers in the Library of Congress.* Washington: Library of Congress, 1905.

U.S. Library of Congress. *Benjamin Franklin: A Register and Index of His Papers in the Library of Congress.* Washington: Library of Congress, 1973.

□   GALES & SEATON RECORDS

Joseph Gales (1786-1860) came to Washington in 1807 from North Carolina to work as a reporter for Samuel Harrison Smith's *National Intelligencer.* He became a partner in 1809 and the sole proprietor the next year. In 1812 William W. Seaton (1785-1866), Gales's brother-in-law, became his partner. In 1814 the *Intelligencer's* office, including the type, presses, and paper, was destroyed by the British, but the firm of Gales & Seaton soon firmly reestablished itself in the field of congressional reporting and printing. Both men served as mayor of Washington as well: Gales from 1827 to 1830 and Seaton from 1840 to 1850.

Gales and Seaton were the exclusive reporters of Congress between 1812 and 1829. Seaton reported the debates in the Senate while Gales, also the practical printer, reported from the House. They were elected again in 1833 and 1835. The firm also compiled and printed the proceedings and debates of Congress in the *Annals of Congress* (1834-56), the *Register of Debates in Congress* (1825-37), and the *American State Papers* (1832-61). The rates for government printing set by the law of 1819 were unchanged until 1846. Technological advances in these years made such work quite profitable, a fact noted in congressional testimony on March 26, 1840, when a 15 percent reduction was first proposed. In 1829 Gales & Seaton imported the first flatbed steam press, a Napier, from England.

The records comprise 148 items including advertisements, announcements, articles, letters to the editors, notices submitted for publication, subscription correspondence, and a notebook of House debates recorded by Gales in 1816. Topics covered include Washington politics, banks, bridges, and canal and steamboat traffic.

❏   ELMER GERTZ PAPERS

The papers of lawyer and author Elmer Gertz (b. 1906) include correspondence and case files relating to censorship and copyright infringement cases among some 243,000 items or 270 linear feet. Gertz, who successfully defended Henry Miller in the *Tropic of Cancer* obscenity trials, also represented Frank Harris, about whom he wrote, with A. I. Tobin, *Frank Harris: A Study in Black and White* (Chicago: Madelaine Mendelsohn, 1931). Other clients include Otto Eisenschmil, who sued Fawcett and Harper & Bros. for copyright infringement, and Nathan Leopold. Case files, subject files, and correspondence document these activities and Elmer Gertz's long fight for "Books and Their Right to Live," which he described in the speech he delivered at the University of Kansas in 1964.

❏   GIDEON & COMPANY RECORDS

The papers of the Washington, D.C., printing firm Gideon & Company consist of thirty items dating primarily from 1843 to 1863, comprising order

books, account books, and business records. The firm, originally Way & Gideon, came from Philadelphia with the federal government. George Saile Gideon, who took over from his father, Jacob Gideon, printed for the Twenty-ninth and Thirtieth Congresses and published a newspaper, the *Republic*. Transactions for printing government documents, speeches, and pamphlets for congressmen and statesmen Albert Gallatin, Abraham Lincoln, Daniel Webster, and others are recorded.

JAMES ORCHARD HALLIWELL-PHILLIPPS COLLECTION

This collection of fifty-three volumes (about 7,000 items) of bills, accounts, and inventories, primarily dating from 1660 to 1750, was compiled by antiquarian and Shakespearean biographer James Orchard Halliwell-Phillipps (1820-1889) for a projected work on the history of prices in England. He presented the volumes to the Smithsonian Institution after abandoning the project, hoping that the work would be continued by an American scholar. They were transferred to the Library of Congress with the Smithsonian deposit in 1866.

Volumes containing receipts and tradesmen's bills cover every possible aspect of economic life. Indeed, the collection is so miscellaneous that it will not support sustained inquiry into most areas represented. Stationers' bills, for example, are scattered and difficult to locate. Following these volumes is a series of inventories and household accounts, for example "An Inventory of those bookes which was left in my custody when my master went to Tinmouth, taken this 20th of October, 1669." Estate accounts in this sequence focus on household and agricultural concerns. One school bill, "Miss Windhams bill from 25 July 1742 to 25 July 1743," records expenditures for books along with those for purses and allowance money.

Halliwell-Phillipps's *Some Account of a Collection of Several Thousand Bills, Accounts, and Inventories, Illustrating the History of Prices between the Years 1650 and 1750 Presented to the Smithsonian Institution, Washington, by James Orchard Halliwell* (Brixton Hill: [Privately printed], 1850) serves as a finding aid.

❏   HERMANDAD DE SAN JUAN APOSTOL Y
EVANGELISTA DE LOS PROFESSORES DEL ARTE
DE LA IMPRENTA Y MERCADERES DE LIBROS
(SEVILLE, SPAIN)
MISCELLANEOUS MANUSCRIPTS COLLECTION

These forty petitions, decrees, printed items, and other documents relating to
the book trade in Spain and to the Seville guild of printers and booksellers
date primarily from the 1750s. Topics covered include the exemption of
printed books, pamphlets, and paper from taxes; a requirement that all books
and gazettes be printed on fine paper; and the quality of metal for
typefounding. A royal privilege stamped 8 April 1755 granted to the Brother-
hood of St. John the Apostle the right to print specified books.

❏   R. HOE & COMPANY RECORDS

Beginning early in the nineteenth century, advances in printing technology
transformed the craft into an industry and provided the cheap printed matter
required to meet the needs of an increasingly literate population in the
United States and Europe. One of the most important factors in this development was the widespread availability of power printing presses manufac-
tured by R. Hoe & Company. Richard March Hoe (1812-1886) built the first
true rotary press or "type-revolving machine," patented in 1845. This was in
use, especially for newspaper work, until it was superseded by the Hoe web-
perfecting press of 1871. The company continued to introduce improved
printing machines, such as the four- to six-color offset sheet press, in the
twentieth century.

Family correspondence and business records in the R. Hoe & Company
Records date from 1830, when Richard March Hoe, the son of the firm's
founder, Robert Hoe (1784-1833), took over the business with his cousin
Matthew Smith III, son of Robert Hoe's partner, Matthew Smith II (d. 1820).
Robert Hoe II (1815-1884) and Peter Smith Hoe (1821-1902), younger sons of
Robert Hoe, entered the firm later. The collection is strongest for the period
between 1855 and 1870, when Richard M., Robert II, and Peter S. Hoe were
engaged in extensive European travel while conducting the Hoe business
abroad. A long file of letters (1856-59) documents the shipping and import

activities that eventually led to the establishment of a manufacturing plant in London and the purchase of the Isaac Adams Press Works in Boston. Correspondence from the period between 1860 and 1870 refers to efforts to obtain extension of the U.S. patent rights to the Hoe cylinder press inventions.

The records (8.4 linear feet, about 5,100 items) include letters relating to day-to-day business transactions; letterpress books containing outgoing letters of both a family and business nature; an account book of profit and loss summaries from 1856 to 1910; samples of advertising cuts and displays; and a group of patent reports and transfers. There are additional Hoe records at Columbia University, the Grolier Club, and the University of Texas-Austin.

REFERENCE

Quarterly Journal of the Library of Congress 15, no. 3 (May 1958): 180-81.

❑   BENJAMIN W. HUEBSCH PAPERS

The papers of American publisher Benjamin W. Huebsch (1876–1964) span the two major phases of his career: from 1900 to 1924, when he published under his own name, and from 1925 to 1964, when he was vice president and editor at Viking Press, with which his firm merged in 1925. Huebsch had high standards of literary excellence and great courage in publishing unknown or controversial works under his own imprint. These included the first American edition of D. H. Lawrence's novel *The Rainbow* and the first printings of James Joyce's *Portrait of the Artist as a Young Man* and Sherwood Anderson's *Winesburg, Ohio*. At Viking, Huebsch arranged for the first American publication of works by Harold Laski, Thomas Mann, Erich Maria Remarque, Franz Werfel, and Stefan Zweig.

The papers number about 10,500 items (17 linear feet). Among the writers represented by substantial correspondence are Sherwood Anderson, Theodore Dreiser, D. H. Lawrence, Siegfried Sassoon, Patrick White, and Stefan Zweig. There are both manuscripts and correspondence relating to the *Freeman,* a liberal weekly published by Huebsch from 1920 to 1924. Huebsch was involved in efforts to stimulate and modernize the distribution and sale of books, and these activities are documented in correspondence about the National Association of Book Publishers, which he helped to establish. A group

of notebooks and scrapbooks cover the years from 1893 to 1940. Beginning in 1900, Huebsch pasted advertisements for books he published into these scrapbooks, and they constitute a valuable record of his publishing career.

REFERENCES

Gilreath, James. "The Benjamin Huebsch Imprint." *Papers of the Bibliographical Society of America* 73 (1979): 225–43.

Quarterly Journal of the Library of Congress 22 (1965): 326.

❏   THOMAS JEFFERSON PAPERS

The Thomas Jefferson Library (about 2,400 volumes) and the Thomas Jefferson Papers (about 25,000 items) comprise the private library and personal papers of Thomas Jefferson (1743–1826), third president of the United States. Jeffersonian scholars and historians of all aspects of eighteenth-century life and thought have long recognized the importance of the insights afforded by the books Jefferson selected or which were presented to him, the marginalia in his books, and related commentary in his correspondence. Historians of the book are equally fortunate in the survival of these magnificent collections, for they illuminate eighteenth-century bibliography, book collecting, and the book trade in ways that have been explored but by no means exhausted.

The details of the offer and purchase of Jefferson's library—the second of three formed by him during his life—are revealed in the correspondence between Jefferson and the agents who acted for him in Washington and the records of the congressional debates. They indicate that Congress probably had in mind a narrow professional library when it appropriated money for the purchase of "such books as may be necessary for the use of Congress" on its move to Washington in 1800. One month after the existing library of some 3,000 volumes was destroyed when British troops burned the Capitol in August 1814, the former president offered his personal library to Congress. Jefferson's library, formed over fifty years and covering every field of knowledge, was described by him as one of the finest in private hands in the United States. This estimation, confirmed by later scholars, was not sufficient for Congress, and the nature of the collection occasioned bitter partisan debate.

Jefferson responded that "I do not know that it contains any branch of science which Congress would wish to exclude from their collection; there is, in fact, no subject to which a Member of Congress may not have occasion to refer."

Federalists objected to paying for books "good, bad, and indifferent, old, new, and worthless, in languages which many can not read, and most ought not." Their opposition was also based on more legitimate arguments, however, such as the financial problems of the young country. The bill was nevertheless approved by a margin of ten votes on January 30, 1815, permanently establishing the future character of the Library of Congress as a comprehensive, universal collection.

The library numbered about 6,500 books on its arrival in Washington. The price, arrived at by a calculation based on format, amounted to $23,950. With his books, Jefferson sent a fair copy of his manuscript catalog (Jefferson's original is in the Massachussetts Historical Society, but the fair copy no longer survives), in which he had classified his collection according to an arrangement based on Francis Bacon's "table of knowledge." In a letter to Librarian of Congress George Watterston, Jefferson explained the advantages of this arrangement by subject over an alphabetical classification. Watterston adopted Jefferson's scheme with some modification, and this system was retained throughout the nineteenth century, earning Jefferson the title of the founder of American library science along with his other accolades.

Over one-half of the books from Jefferson's library were destroyed in a fire in the Capitol in 1851, and approximately 2,400 volumes survive in the Rare Book and Special Collections Division and the Law Library today. To these have been added a small number of books from Jefferson's third and last library, sold at auction in 1829. The contents of the 1815 library were reconstructed by E. Millicent Sowerby in the five-volume *Catalogue of the Library of Thomas Jefferson,* based on the 1783 catalog. In addition to full bibliographical descriptions for each surviving volume or identified title, Sowerby provided lengthy excerpts from marginalia and relevant correspondence, making it possible to study the formation of the library and the influence of individual works on Jefferson.

Jefferson wrote about the price of books, the availability of books, and the nature of publishing at every stage of his career and from every location in which he pursued his book-collecting activities. In his letter offering his library to Congress, Jefferson described the manner in which he acquired it:

While residing in Paris I devoted every afternoon I was disengaged, for a summer or two, in examining all the principal bookstores, turning over every book with my own hands, and putting by everything which related to America, and indeed whatever was rare & valuable in every science. Besides this, I had standing orders during the whole time I was in Europe, in its principal bookmarts, particularly Amsterdam, Frankfort, Madrid and London, for such works relating to America as could not be found in Paris. . . .

Correspondence with booksellers and book agents confirms the role played by these figures in the formation of Jefferson's collection and points to their importance in the eighteenth-century book trade. There are bills and receipts for every period covering books and binding costs as well. Jefferson was willing to accept pirated editions when they were cheaper and to mutilate a volume for the sake of convenience, as for example when he bound together pamphlets on the same subject or destroyed many Bibles to create a polyglot volume, *The Morals of Jesus.* Because of these biblioclastic tendencies, Millicent Sowerby judged Jefferson to be a bibliomaniac but not a bibliophile.

Sowerby's work illustrates many other areas of inquiry suggested by the Jefferson collections, especially with respect to provenance and association. Whenever possible Jefferson purchased entire collections or parts of them, as he did with those of William Byrd of Westover, Samuel Henley, George Wythe, and Benjamin Franklin. He frequently lent books from his library to his colleagues; some books in the 1783 catalog which never reached the Library of Congress are presumed to have been out on loan at the time Congress purchased his collection. Correspondence and marginalia relating to the almost 500 presentation copies in the collection provide information on authorship and the printing and publishing history of several of the most significant works of the late eighteenth century. Two pamphlets were identified as the work of Citizen Genêt. *Colony Commerce,* which purports to have been written "By Alexander Campbell Brown," was actually the work of an American, Mark Leavenworth. Authorship of individual essays in Jefferson's copy of *The Federalist Papers,* once owned by Mrs. Alexander Hamilton, is attributed in Jefferson's hand to Jay, Madison, and Hamilton.

Information on matters of great historical and bibliographical concern is provided in the Jefferson collections. Jefferson was involved in the planning of John Carey's edition of George Washington's *Official Letters to the Honorable American Congress,* and correspondence in the collection firmly establishes the London, 1795, appearance as the first issue. Jefferson received from James

Madison the first copy of the first part of Thomas Paine's *Rights of Man* (1791) to arrive in the United States. Jefferson sent it to Jonathan Bayard Smith, a Philadelphia printer, who printed his edition with Jefferson's accompanying note without Jefferson's permission. This "indiscretion of a printer" caused Jefferson great embarrassment with John Adams, then vice president, described in letters to Washington, Madison, Adams, and others in the Jefferson Papers. (See the description of the Jonathan Bayard Smith Family Papers below, pp. 49-51.) No copy of the first part was sold by Jefferson to Congress, and Sowerby appends this documentation to her description of the *Rights of Man, Part the Second,* sent by Paine to Jefferson in 1792. The material relating to the printing, publication, and distribution of Jefferson's *Notes on the State of Virginia* covers the origin of the work, initial efforts to have it printed in the United States, the printing and distribution of the first (Paris, 1785) edition, and subsequent editions and revisions. Each of these entries and many others like them illustrate the rich resources of the library and papers of Thomas Jefferson.

Because Sowerby was only concerned with books represented in the 1815 library, many areas of inquiry remain to be explored. The Jefferson Papers include, for example, lists prepared by Jefferson in response to a request for advice on building a book collection. One such list, sent in 1771 to Robert Skipworth, displays a thorough familiarity with current publications and concern for bibliographical detail not evident in the 1783 catalog. While in Paris, Jefferson was introduced to François Hoffmann's "polytype" printing, an early effort at printing from stereotype plates. Jefferson's fascination is reflected in his comment to James Madison that "Types for printing a whole page are all in one solid piece. An author therefore only prints a few copies of his work from time to time as they are called for. This saves the loss of printing more copies than may possibly be sold, and prevents an edition from ever being exhausted." Jefferson requested a price estimate for printing his *Notes* by this method, which he described in letters to Benjamin Franklin, David Rittenhouse, Ezra Stiles, and others. His interest in new printing techniques extended to an improvement on a process of copperplate engraving originally developed by Franklin, described in the manuscript "For engraving in the Abbé Rochon's method."

Jefferson wrote to Madison from Monticello in 1821 in support of an effort to remove the duty on the importation of books: "Books constitute capital. A library book lasts as long as a house, for hundreds of years. It is not

then an article of mere consumption but fairly of capital, and often in the case of professional men setting out in life it is their only capital." For the historian of the book, the Library of Thomas Jefferson and the Thomas Jefferson Papers constitute capital with which studies of eighteenth-century books, the book trade, and political, cultural, scientific, and intellectual life may be built.

REFERENCES

Adams, Randolph G. "Thomas Jefferson, Librarian." In *Three Americanists,* 69–96. Philadelphia: University of Pennsylvania Press, 1939.

Gilreath, James. "Sowerby Revirescent and Revised." *Papers of the Bibliographical Society of America* 78 (1984): 219–32.

Goff, Frederick R. "Jefferson, the Book Collector." *Quarterly Journal of the Library of Congress* 29 (1972): 32–47.

Johnston, William Dawson. *History of the Library of Congress,* vol. 1, *1800–1864,* 65–104. Washington: Government Printing Office, 1904.

Malone, Dumas. *Thomas Jefferson and the Library of Congress.* Washington: Library of Congress, 1977.

Sowerby, E. Millicent. "Thomas Jefferson and His Library." *Papers of the Bibliographical Society of America* 50 (1956): 213–28.

Thomas Jefferson and the World of Books. Washington: Library of Congress, 1977.

U.S. Library of Congress. *Catalogue of the Library of Thomas Jefferson.* Comp. with annotations by E. Millicent Sowerby. 5 vols. Washington: Library of Congress, 1952–59. Reprint ed. Charlottesville: University Press of Virginia, 1983.

U.S. Library of Congress. *Index to the Thomas Jefferson Papers.* Presidents' Papers Index Series. Washington: Library of Congress, 1976.

———. *The Thomas Jefferson Bicentennial, 1743–1943 . . . .* Washington: Government Printing Office, 1943.

❏ FREDERIC MADDEN PAPERS
MISCELLANEOUS MANUSCRIPTS COLLECTION

Sir Frederic Madden (1801–1873), antiquary, paleographer, and keeper of manuscripts at the British Museum, took "Notes on Illuminated Manuscripts in the Public and Private Libraries of Great Britain, and in Foreign Libraries, and on Most Ancient Greek Manuscripts," between 1847 and 1850. He recorded observations and information on the provenance, sales, binding,

illumination, and textual history of manuscripts he examined during this period in these three unpublished notebooks.

☐   JAMES MADISON PAPERS

James Madison (1751–1836) is remembered as one of the most intellectual of the founding fathers. He read intensively under private tutors at his plantation home in Montpelier, Virginia, and at Princeton. When he returned to Montpelier to take up life as a planter, Madison spent considerable time and money ordering books from Williamsburg, Fredericksburg, and London. In 1781 he purchased books at the sale of the large library of William Byrd of Westover. At his death the library at Montpelier numbered several thousand volumes. Although Madison had intended them for the University of Virginia, they were sold at auction on May 30, 1854, following the death of his wife in 1849. No catalog of the library was made, and the majority of the books in his collection have never been located. The James Madison Papers (about 12,000 items) offer evidence of the importance of books and reading to Madison.

Sent as a delegate to Williamsburg in 1776, Madison met Thomas Jefferson. The voluminous correspondence between them in the James Madison Papers and the Thomas Jefferson Papers covers every issue of importance to the new nation. In this fifty-year friendship and collaboration, the exchange of books and ideas about books played a significant role. While Jefferson was in Philadelphia and in Paris, he served as Madison's book buyer. Madison trusted his friend's selections and gave him carte blanche, writing: "I must leave to your discretion the occasional purchase of rare and valuable books, disregarding the risk of duplicates. You know tolerably well the objects of my curiosity." Jefferson was eager for more specific instructions and pressed for a catalog. Occasionally he urged a particular purchase. When subscriptions for the new edition of the *Encyclopédie* were announced, for example, Jefferson advised Madison that he could still get the original folio edition for him, as he had for himself, for the new edition was better, he said, "in far the greater number of articles: but not in all." Madison occasionally acted on Jefferson's behalf in book purchases, as in 1785 when he arranged for Jefferson to buy the library of Samuel Henley.

The only book list Madison is known to have prepared was in response to

a motion adopted by Congress to compile "a list of books to be imported for the use of the United States in Congress assembled." The "Report on Books for Congress," dated January 23, 1783, is in Madison's hand and reflects the breadth of his reading. Jefferson, who was rooming in Madison's Philadelphia boardinghouse during January 1783, may have been consulted on it. The list, in the Madison Papers, consists of many form or subject entries, such as "Laws of each of the United States," "Collections of best Charts," and "Best Latin Dictionary with best grammar." Unlike Jefferson, Madison seems to have paid little attention to bibliographical detail or bindings. The motion to purchase the books was defeated, however, and in "Notes on Debates" Madison attributed the success of the opposition to the pressing need for funds and to "the difference of expense between procuring the books during the war & after a peace." He also remarked that "It was further observed that no time ought to be lost in collecting every book & tract which related to American Antiquities & the affairs of the U.S. since many of the most valuable of these were every day becoming lost."

Had the motion passed, it is possible that James Madison would be remembered today as the founder of the Library of Congress. From his retirement at Montpelier in 1815, he must have taken great pleasure in the purchase of his friend's library, in which so many of the works Madison had recommended were to be found. The James Madison Papers, together with the Thomas Jefferson Papers, document the role of books in the life of the fourth president of the United States and thus in the founding of the nation.

REFERENCES

Rutland, Robert A. *James Madison and the Search for Nationhood.* Washington: Library of Congress, 1981.

Rutland, Robert A. "Madison's Bookish Habits." *Quarterly Journal of the Library of Congress* 37 (1980): 176–91.

U.S. Library of Congress. *Index to the James Madison Papers.* Presidents' Papers Index Series. Washington: Library of Congress, 1965.

❏   FREDERIC GERSHOM MELCHER PAPERS

The papers of publisher and editor Frederic Melcher (1879–1963) comprise 52 items relating to the acquisition of the Otto H. Vollbehr Collection by the Library of Congress for $1.5 million in 1930. Melcher actively lobbied for the purchase. Correspondence with congressmen, including Ross Alexander Collins and Nicholas Longworth, indicates his concern over the importance and price of the collection. Congressional testimony on whether the forty-two-line Bible of Johann Gutenberg was included in the purchase price and the relationship between appropriations for the Vollbehr collection and for the Library annex (the John Adams Building) was given by George Parker Winship, John C. Oswald, and others. Telegrams to Melcher, dated June 9, 1930, from Otto Vollbehr and others attribute unanimous passage of the bill to Melcher's efforts.

Press releases, pamphlets, and editorials in the collection dating from 1940 relate to the virulent attack on the purchase by Burton Rascoe in "Uncle Sam Has a Book," an article in the *Saturday Review of Literature.* In a *Publishers Weekly* editorial, Melcher responded that "national satisfaction" with the acquisition was not disturbed by the fact that Vollbehr spent the proceeds of the sale on pro-Nazi and anti-Semitic propaganda.

❏   EDMUND BAILEY O'CALLAGHAN PAPERS

The papers of physician, historian, book collector, and bibliographer Edmund Bailey O'Callaghan (1797–1880) include approximately 2,000 items of correspondence relating to early American books, historical material on America in European archives, editions of the Bible, and book collecting. Among the correspondents are James Lenox, John Carter Brown, George Bancroft, John Dawson Gilmary Shea, and J. Larson Brevoort.

O'Callaghan emigrated from Ireland to Canada, from which he fled in 1837 after participating in an insurrection. He wrote a *History of New Netherland* (1846–48) and edited *The Documentary History of the State of New-York* (1850–51) and the colonial archives of the state of New York (1852–70). There are drafts and correspondence relating to these and other bibliographical projects.

❏ JONATHAN BAYARD SMITH FAMILY PAPERS

The Jonathan Bayard Smith Family Papers include 530 items of correspondence, memorabilia, printed material, and genealogical papers relating to members of the Smith family, including Samuel Harrison Smith (1772–1845), printer and publisher. Smith, the son of Jonathan Bayard Smith (1742–1812), a Philadelphia merchant and member of the Continental Congress, was a newspaper publisher and printer in Philadelphia between 1791 and 1800. He followed Jefferson and the federal government to Washington, where he continued these activities and was involved in political and social life. The Smith family papers and the three account books acquired by the Library of Congress with the papers of Peter Force reflect both periods of his career.

In 1791 John Beckley, later the first Librarian of Congress, obtained the first part of Thomas Paine's *Rights of Man* from London. He lent it to James Madison, from whom it went to Thomas Jefferson. Jefferson sent it, at Beckley's request, to Jonathan Bayard Smith. In a letter of April 26, 1791, accompanying the pamphlet and now in the collection, Jefferson observed that he was "extremely pleased to find it will be re-printed here" and requested "to engage three or four copies of the republication." The work was reprinted by Samuel Harrison Smith with Jefferson's note to Jonathan Bayard Smith prefixed to it, causing Jefferson great political embarrassment. In letters to Washington and Madison written in May 1791, Jefferson explained that he had sent it at the request of Jonathan Bayard Smith, "who had asked for it for his brother to reprint it." Jefferson did not know either Jonathan Bayard or Samuel Harrison Smith. He wrote to Madison that "I never saw J. B. Smith or the printer either before or since," and he mistook the father and son for brothers.

Correspondence in the Jonathan Bayard Smith Family Papers reveals that the relationship between Samuel Harrison Smith and Thomas Jefferson, which began on this inauspicious note, flourished over the next nine years. In 1797 Smith purchased the *Independent Gazetteer* from the elder Joseph Gales, and in the next three years published the *Universal Gazette.* After his move to Washington, Smith established the *National Intelligencer and Washington Advertiser,* a Jeffersonian organ in which abbreviated reports of congressional proceedings were published after they were submitted to members for comment, a system that resulted in great delays.

The Jefferson and Smith correspondence between 1800 and 1810 reflects the political strength of the newspaper and its editor during that period. Smith's other printing activities, which included government and private work, are also documented. Jefferson sent Smith a circular letter to potential office seekers, a detailed letter relating the progress of the Lewis and Clark expedition, and other notices to be published in the *Intelligencer*. In 1813 Smith was appointed commissioner of revenue by James Madison and correspondence relating to the appointment and the parchment commission are in the collection. That year Smith delivered a July Fourth oration that was printed by Roger Weightman. Two printed copies of it are in the collection, along with letters thanking the author for presentation copies.

When Jefferson decided to offer his library to Congress in 1814, he chose Smith to act as his agent, a reflection of Smith's connections, perhaps, as well

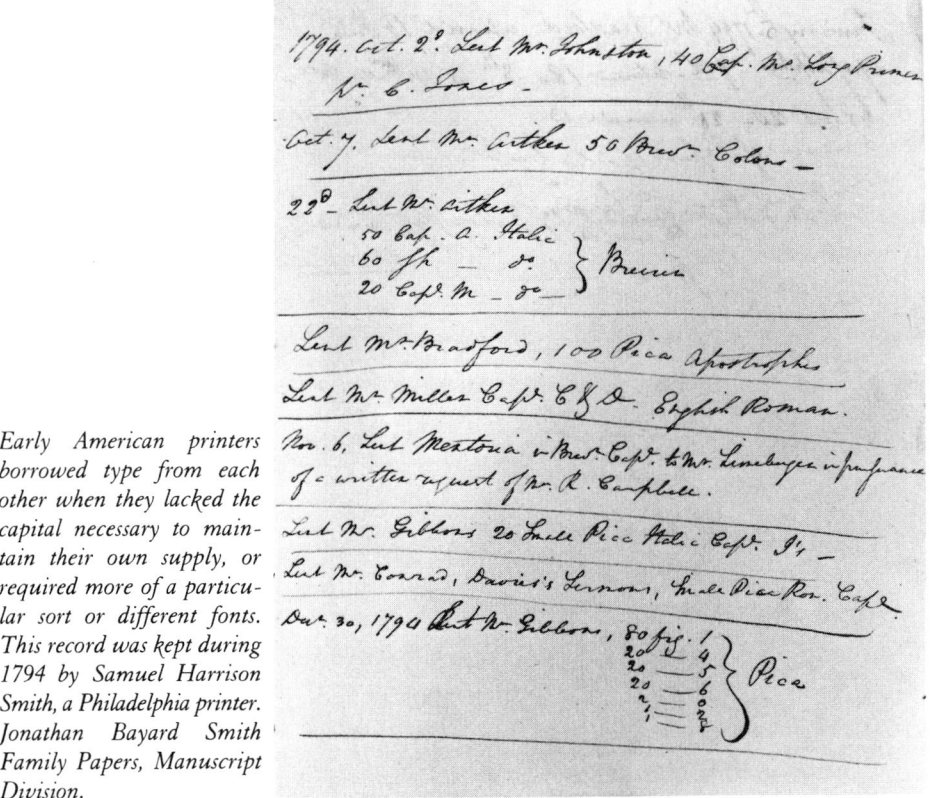

Early American printers borrowed type from each other when they lacked the capital necessary to maintain their own supply, or required more of a particular sort or different fonts. This record was kept during 1794 by Samuel Harrison Smith, a Philadelphia printer. Jonathan Bayard Smith Family Papers, Manuscript Division.

as of their close friendship. In the initial request, dated September 21, Jefferson assured Smith that he did not anticipate any difficulty. Subsequent correspondence from Jefferson and copies of Smith's responses document the transaction in great detail, including deliberations over where, when, and by whom the books were to be valued and how and by whom the library was to be transported from Monticello to Washington. Finally, on May 8, 1815, Jefferson reported "Our 10th and last waggon load of books goes off today. This closes the transaction here, and I cannot permit it to close without returning my thanks to you who began it."

Samuel Harrison Smith and his wife, Margaret Bayard, were central figures in Washington life. Letters, invitations, and tickets in the collection reflect the blend of practical printing, political influence, and social connections that was part of the career of Samuel Harrison Smith.

Insight into Smith's Philadelphia business is provided by the account books received with the Peter Force Papers. They cover the period between 1794 and 1796, when Smith was engaged in book and job printing as well as newspaper publishing, and consist of a receipt book in which Smith's employees signed for their wages; a week-by-week record of labor costs, recording how many pages and ems were composed, and how many tokens were printed, by each employee for each title in press; and a general account book, recording the costs of materials and the income derived from each job. During this period Smith's book-printing business expanded, requiring him to purchase new equipment. Close relations with other printers are reflected in recorded purchases of ink and paper and borrowed type. The account books were analyzed in detail by C. R. Kropf in "The Accounts of Samuel Harrison Smith, Philadelphia Printer," *Papers of the Bibliographical Society of America* 74 (1980): 13–25.

REFERENCE

Annual Report of the Librarian of Congress 1905: 32.

❏ JOSEPH CONABLE THOMAS PAPERS

Joseph C. Thomas (1833–1906) served as a chaplain with the Eighty-Eighth Illinois Volunteers during the Civil War and established regimental libraries

in the Army of the Cumberland while in Tennessee (1863–66). Correspondence, receipts, accounts, orders, and other papers among the 400 items in the collection relate to these activities, in which Thomas was assisted by the U.S. Christian Commission and the U.S. Sanitary Commission.

Thomas successfully solicited newspaper editors and book publishers to provide material at half-price for his program. In "A Reading System for the Army and Navy," he discussed how companies could raise the necessary funds by subscription and how the library could be transported on marches: "The regimental library is contained in eleven small boxes—each holding a cubic feet or less—one for each company, and one for the Field and Staff."

Following the war, Thomas became the general librarian of the U.S. Christian Commission. Testimonials in the collection note that "The library lessens profanity and intoxications" and that "The library has kept many from bad company, from strolling around nights, from drinking."

❑ BENJAMIN HOLT TICKNOR PAPERS

Benjamin Holt Ticknor (1842–1919), second son of William D. Ticknor, the founder of Ticknor and Fields, became a partner in its successor firm, Fields, Osgood & Co., in 1870. The following year James T. Fields resigned and the firm became James R. Osgood & Co. In financial difficulties in 1878, Osgood entered a brief partnership with Henry O. Houghton. In 1885 Benjamin Ticknor formed Ticknor and Co. and purchased the assets and assumed the debts of James R. Osgood & Co. Five years later Ticknor's business was transferred to Houghton, Mifflin and Company.

The papers of Benjamin Holt Ticknor date primarily from the period between 1870 and 1910 and consist of approximately 3,000 items of correspondence from American and European authors addressed to James R. Osgood, Benjamin Holt Ticknor, and Caroline Ticknor. A five-page manuscript by James R. Osgood dated 1871 recounts the history of the firm to that date. There are Ticknor family papers relating to William D. Ticknor and to Benjamin Holt Ticknor's children, Caroline and Thomas B. Ticknor.

Over 100 letters dating from 1882 from Julian Hawthorne to Osgood and Ticknor provide details of the negotiations for editing, printing, and publishing Nathaniel Hawthorne's unfinished story "Dr. Grimshaw's Secret." A Henry James letter of April 8, 1883, contains "Proposals" for two novels.

James described one as follows: "The scene is laid in Boston & its neighborhood; it relates an episode connected with the so-called 'woman's movement.'" The second involves "another 'international episode.'" In subsequent correspondence, terms and arrangements for the novels *The Bostonians* and *The American* are discussed.

A series of letters from Edward Bellamy span the years between 1885 and 1889. The English author first wrote to Ticknor and Co. to inquire what they were going to do about payments due at the time of Osgood's failure. By the following year his letters to Benjamin Holt Ticknor had become warm and detailed discussions relating to the printing, publication, and translations of *Looking Backward*. A letter dated 1889 expresses sincere regret at the news of "the transfer of your business to Houghton & Mifflin."

A manuscript of Mark Twain's introduction to "The New Guide of the Conversation in Portuguese and English" by Pedro Carolino (Boston: James R. Osgood Co., 1883) is in the collection, together with two pen-and-ink title-page designs for *Life on the Mississippi* (Boston: James R. Osgood Co., 1883) and a letter from Twain to his publisher concerning an illustration: "I care nothing about what the subject of the cut is so long as it bears no hint of the text, and is not funny. A landscape is a good thing, and can be called scene in the Adirondacks or Palestine or somewhere."

Other authors and illustrators represented include P. T. Barnum, W. H. Beard, Abby Morton Diaz, Henry Wadsworth Longfellow, James D. Smillie, and Walt Whitman. A letter from Benjamin Tauchnitz refers to the German publisher's practice of making agreements with American authors, despite the fact that in the absence of an American international copyright law he was not required to do so. Topics covered in the correspondence include the return of proofs, corrections to be made, the payment of royalties, and the style and placement of illustrations. Over 60 letters from James R. Osgood to Benjamin Holt Ticknor, written from New York, London, and Paris between 1870 and 1889, reflect the close personal and working relationship between the two publishers during and after their partnership.

❏   HORACE L. AND ANNE MONTGOMERIE TRAUBEL PAPERS

The papers of Horace Traubel (1858–1919) and his wife Anne Traubel (1864–1954) reflect Traubel's activities as a printer and journalist, friend and literary executor of Walt Whitman, and spokesman for American socialism. They show, too, the extent to which he shared these interests with his wife. In 1896 Elbert Hubbard reported the success of the Walt Whitman volume in his series Little Journeys to the Homes of American Authors, and three years later he suggested that the Roycrofters publish "a book containing some of Walt's best things." A long file of correspondence from Thomas B. Mosher concerns the publication of a Whitman anthology for which Traubel wrote the preface. Mosher remarked that "Personally, I don't quite like to see Whitman in Elbert Hubbard's typography." Mosher revealed that to him Whitman served as "a source of constant heartening up" and that he took great pains with the design and contents of *The Book of Heavenly Death,* published in 1905. Other publishers represented by correspondence in the collection include Thomas Fisher Unwin, who decided against publication of Traubel's book on Whitman in England because "it contained a large amount of copyright material and therefore it is illegal to publish and sell this book in the United Kingdom and the colonies," and Benjamin Huebsch, who wrote about the success of Traubel's *Optimos,* published by Huebsch in 1910.

Most of the material in the collection (about 7,000 items in processed sequences and 90,000 in backlog) is composed of manuscripts, proofs, and correspondence relating to Traubel's own writings, which include *With Walt Whitman in Camden* (1905–14). There is extensive editorial correspondence for Traubel's magazine, the *Conservator* (1890–1919). Subject files document his involvement with the Amateur Press Association. Traubel's social philosophy, formed under Whitman's influence, is revealed in correspondence with Eugene V. Debs, Joaquin Miller, Charles W. Stoddard, and Brand Whitlock.

REFERENCES

Quarterly Journal of the Library of Congress 13, no. 3 (May 1956): 166.

Quarterly Journal of the Library of Congress 14, no. 3 (May 1957): 120.

Quarterly Journal of the Library of Congress 33 (1976): 351–56.

❑   LEWIS McKENZIE TURNER COLLECTION

Lewis McKenzie Turner (1898–1960), proprietor of the Salt House Press, selected these 700 examples of early American watermarks found on letters and documents and arranged them according to correspondent. The folders are marked with the watermarks contained in them. The firms include J. Whatman Turkey Mill and Hagar & Co., with slogans such as "Work & Be Rich," "Pro Patria," and "Don't Tread on Me."

❑   WASHINGTON LIBRARY COMPANY RECORDS

Three volumes of journals, minutes, shareholder lists, accounts, clippings, and miscellaneous bills and receipts of the Washington Library Company span the period from 1811 to 1877. Topics covered include dues, book purchases, and facilities. Among the first shareholders of this circulating library were early Washington politicians and printers: John Q. Adams, James Madison, Samuel Harrison Smith, W. W. Seaton, and Roger C. Weightman. Members were permitted to contribute books in lieu of dues, and booksellers such as Joseph Milligan took advantage of this arrangement. There are valuation lists of books offered.

After the Capitol was burned in 1814, the shareholders voted to extend library privileges to members of Congress during session "on their complying with the rules respecting the return, injury, and loss of the books." In 1825 the Washington Library Company bought the circulating library run by Davis & Force; the 3,000 volumes were purchased for thirty-five cents on each dollar of the original cost.

According to a report by John Meigs, secretary of the Washington Library Company, the collection grew to 15,000 volumes before it began to suffer financial difficulties in the 1870s. The books were transferred to the YMCA and then to the Central High School Library.

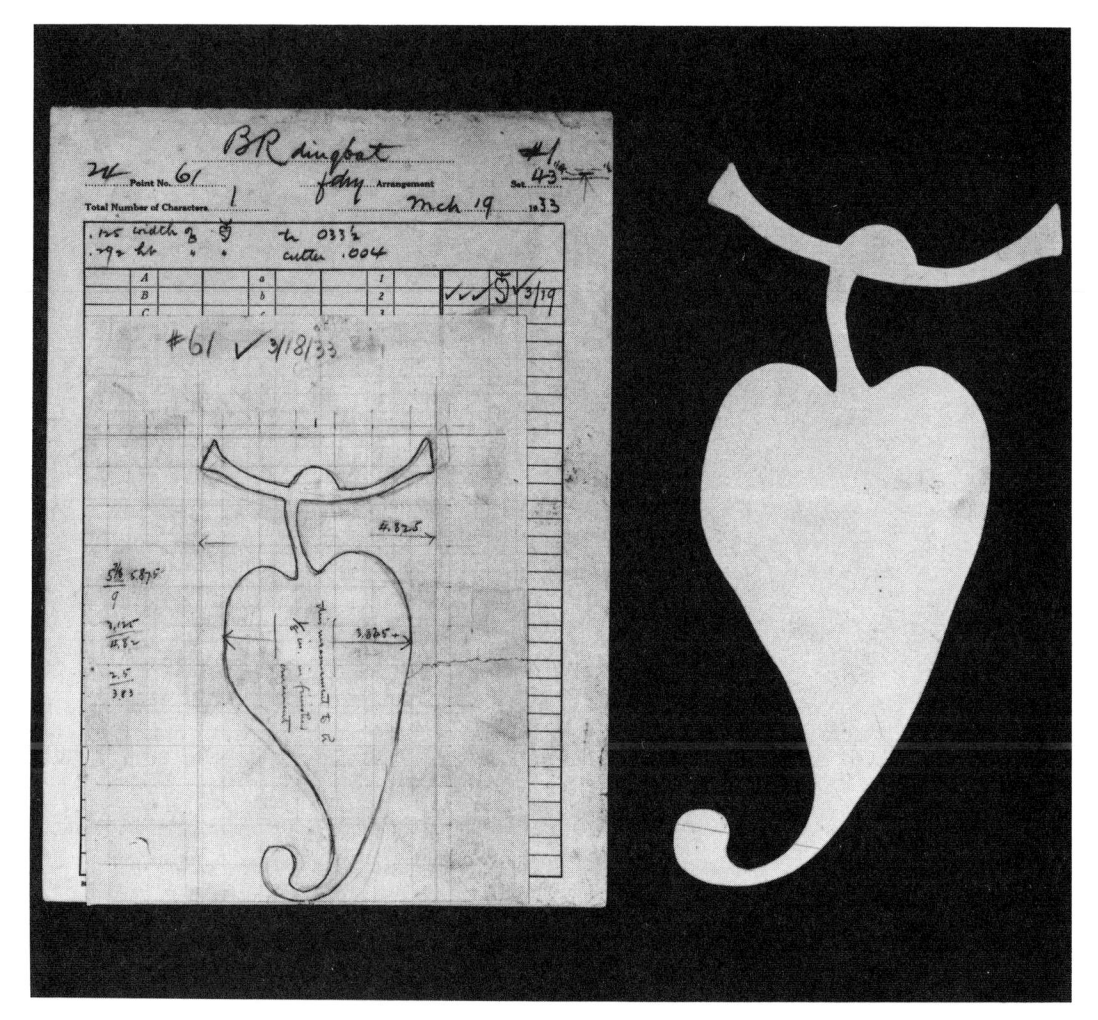

Sketch and cut-out for a dingbat designed by Bruce Rogers. His ornament was used throughout Stanley Morison's Fra Luca da Pacioli *(New York: The Grolier Club, 1933). Frederic and Bertha Goudy Collection, Rare Book and Special Collections Division.*

2 □ Rare Book and Special Collections Division

INTRODUCTION

The origins of the Rare Book and Special Collections Division date to the tenure of Librarian of Congress Ainsworth Rand Spofford (1864–97). Spofford separated materials of rarity or value from the general collections and designated them an "office collection," a term that still appears on some catalog cards. During the next half-century, the Library's collections grew at an enormous rate through purchase (the Peter Force Library was purchased in 1867 and the Yudin Collection in 1906) and transfer from other government agencies (from the Smithsonian in 1866 and the War Department in the 1920s). The Joseph Meredith Toner Collection of Americana and medical history, presented in 1882, was the first major gift from an individual. Copyright deposits dominated the growth of the general collections after 1870, but because contemporary publications were not perceived to merit or require special treatment, they were not added to the "office" collection.

When a separate rare book facility was established in 1927, the collection was already very strong in Americana, although it included rarities from every time and place. V. Valta Parma, the first curator, continued the process of transfer of materials to the division. By 1928 seventeen groups, including Bibles, miniature books, Confederate States imprints, and the Benjamin Franklin, Henry James, and Martin Luther collections, had been organized

to provide an "efficient aid to investigators." Under Arthur Houghton, the second curator, Lawrence C. Wroth, who served as a consultant for acquisitions, and Frederick R. Goff, who joined the staff in 1940 and became chief of the division in 1945, gifts and purchases assumed a more significant role.

In 1943 the division received the first of several major gifts from Lessing J. Rosenwald. These acquisitions contributed more than any other single factor to the development of the Rare Book and Special Collections Division over almost forty years. Individual rarities and the overall strength of the Rosenwald Collection in the history of printing and the western illustrated book established a commitment to developing resources and supporting scholarship in these fields.

The present collections number more than 500,000 books, pamphlets, broadsides, title pages, manuscripts, posters, prints, photographs, and memorabilia. The Rare Book and Special Collections Division holdings are divided between approximately one hundred "special collections" unified by format, subject, or provenance and the general collections of the division, shelved according to Library of Congress classification. The Alfred Whital Stern Collection of Lincolniana, for example, combines major rarities with supporting books, broadsides, sheet music, prints, cartoons, contemporary newspapers, autograph letters, and memorabilia.

Among the special collections are several of outstanding strength: 27,000 American broadsides, 15,000 children's books, early American magazines, eighteenth-century American pamphlets, and almanacs. Efforts to build a comprehensive American collection and an early recognition of the importance of ephemeral formats are reflected in these extraordinary holdings. They are enriched by European imprints of books influential in America or reprinted here. The American political pamphlets from the revolutionary period are complemented by extremely strong holdings of British imprints.

Several author and subject collections offer rich literary, historical, and bibliographical resources. These include collections relating to Hans Christian Andersen, Sinclair Lewis, and Hugh Walpole (gift of Jean Hersholt); Cervantes (gift of Leonard Kebler); Henry James (bequest of Mrs. Clarence W. Jones); Walt Whitman (gift of Caroline Wells Houghton; purchase from Charles E. Feinberg); cookery (gifts of Katherine Golden Bitting and Elizabeth Robins Pennell); cryptography (gift of George Fabyan); Sir Francis Drake (gift of Hanni and Hans Kraus); and magic (the Houdini and McManus-Young gifts).

The collections of the Rare Book and Special Collections Division are as wide-ranging as those of the Library as a whole. The most comprehensive and consistent holdings are the American imprints, which include approximately 43 percent of the titles recorded in Charles Evans's *American Bibliography*. Over 30,000 pre-1801 imprints have already been transferred to the Rare Book and Special Collections Division as part of an inventory of the Library's general collections begun in 1979. Although some areas, such as pre-1640 English printing, are not strong, there are other groups of materials, described in this introduction and in the individual collection descriptions that follow, important for the study of the history of books.

There are approximately 150 medieval and Renaissance western manuscripts in the Library of Congress, over three-quarters of which are in the Rare Book and Special Collections Division (others are in the Music Division and the Law Library). All but a small number date from the fifteenth century, and the texts are primarily biblical or liturgical. Among the most notable are the Nekcsei-Lipócz Bible, a fourteenth-century Hungarian illuminated manuscript; the Giant Bible of Mainz, 1452–53, and two contemporary manuscripts of Valturius's "De re militaria," which are three of eighteen manuscripts in the Lessing J. Rosenwald Collection; and a Flemish Book of Hours with fifty-six miniatures executed at Bruges during the last decade of the fifteenth century, the gift of Mrs. Felix Warburg in memory of her husband. A catalog of the medieval and Rennaissance manuscript collection is forthcoming.

The 5,600 incunabula in the Rare Book and Special Collections Division, primarily from the Peter Force Library, the John Boyd Thacher Collection, the Otto Vollbehr Collection, and the Lessing J. Rosenwald Collection (in order of acquisition), make up the largest collection of fifteenth-century books in the Western hemisphere. Thacher incunabula constitute one of four distinct collections formed by politician and historian John Boyd Thacher (1847-1909) and deposited in the Library between 1910 and 1921 (the others are early Americana, French Revolutionary material, and autographs). Thacher sought to gather notable specimens of as many fifteenth-century presses as possible. He ceased collecting in 1899, after acquiring examples of 500 presses from 128 cities. At the time of the Thacher deposit, the Library had 590 incunables. The 889 works in the Thacher Collection, arranged by country, town, and press in the order in which printing was introduced, included over 230 titles not in American collections at that time.

In 1928 Otto Vollbehr donated to the Library of Congress a collection of 11,000 printers' marks, devices or trademarks used by early printers. Vollbehr, who had left Germany with a collection of 3,000 incunables for sale, exhibited his books in several American libraries between 1926 and 1930. Extensive congressional testimony by Librarian of Congress Herbert Putnam, A. Edward Newton, Adolph Oko, John Clyde Oswald, George Parker Winship, and others focused on the appropriateness, significance, contents, and price of the collection. After considerable lobbying led by Mississippi congressman Ross Alexander Collins and publisher Frederic Melcher, documented in collections in the Manuscript Division, the purchase of Vollbehr's incunabula for $1.5 million was approved. The Vollbehr Collection included books from 635 presses; important editiones principes of Cicero, Livy, and others; books in vernacular languages; and one of the three surviving perfect copies on vellum of the Gutenberg Bible. The collection transformed the holdings of the Library of Congress from a representative sampling of early printing to an outstanding resource for the study of the products of the early presses. The Library's incunabula now more than fulfill the hope of Adolph Oko, who urged approval of the Vollbehr purchase to "help make American scholarship independent of European libraries." They are a resource of international renown and importance.

Imprints—the printed products of a particular time and place, the output of one printer, press, or publisher—constitute the foundation for historical and bibliographical investigations. Several collections in the Rare Book and Special Collections Division suggest the potential for imprint research at the Library of Congress. Hawaiian imprints and Spanish-American imprints illustrate the impact of missionaries and conquerors on an indigenous population. Approximately three-quarters of the narratives listed in Henry R. Wagner and Charles L. Camp's *The Plains and the Rockies* form a separate collection that is supplemented by strong holdings of western Americana in the general rare book collection. Imprint collections described below include the Bulgarian Renaissance Collection, Confederate States of America Collection, Documents of the First Fourteen Congresses, and the Yudin Russian Collection. The Benjamin Franklin Collection (see the description of the Benjamin Franklin Papers in the Manuscript Division, pp. 35-36) brings together approximately 270 imprints from all the printing establishments that bore his name, the products of presses for which he worked or in which he had a financial interest, and books by or about Franklin.

Several collections of publishers' imprints document significant late nineteenth- and early twentieth-century projects and trends. Over 40,000 dime novel titles from 280 different series and over 500 Big Little Books, received through copyright deposit, are maintained as special collections. Bollingen imprints in the division complement the archive in the Manuscript Division. A set of Dell paperbacks was presented to the Library in 1976 by Western Publishing Company. More than 6,000 volumes, often in multiple copies of popular titles, grouped by series and arranged in serial order, illustrate developments in cover design, merchandising strategy, and pricing.

Two archival collections point to possibilities for research in publishing programs of quasi-official status. The Armed Services Editions (ASE) and the Franklin Book Programs exemplify one aspect of the role of books now receiving increasing attention as a result of Curtis Benjamin's report *U.S. Books Abroad: Neglected Ambassadors* (Washington: Library of Congress, 1984). The Library's collection of 1,324 ASE titles, apparently the only complete set now in existence, was described in *Books in Action: The Armed Services Editions,* edited by John Y. Cole (Washington: Library of Congress, 1984), on the occasion of the fortieth anniversary of the series. The Franklin Book Programs, established in 1952 to encourage publishing of American books in developing countries, was administered by a U.S. nonprofit organization and operated on the principle of local selection of titles. The Library's collection includes all 3,000 titles published through 1978, when the programs were dissolved. The Franklin archives are at Princeton University, and the chronological correspondence files are at the University of Texas at Austin.

When in the 1960s Frederick R. Goff identified areas of strength within the division upon which to build, one area he pinpointed was fine printing. Resources for the study of late nineteenth- and twentieth-century American typography, fine printing, book design, and papermaking include the Harrison Elliott, Frederic and Bertha Goudy, National Endowment for the Arts Small Press, Bruce Rogers, and Stone & Kimball collections. Approximately 100 books by A. Edward Newton and a representative collection of Elbert Hubbard's Roycroft Press imprints are each maintained as special collections. The works of significant presses formerly dispersed throughout the division's classified collection are being brought together to form a Fine Printing Collection. Recent acquisitions include distinguished books from the Cranach Press and Victor Hammer's Stamperia del Santuccio, and these are supple-

mented by the superb holdings of modern fine printing and livres d'artiste in the Rosenwald Collection.

Private libraries form part of the history of the book trade, of reading, and of book collecting, and they reveal something about the role of books in the lives of individuals and groups. The books from the library of Thomas Jefferson that survived the fire in 1851 (see the description of the Thomas Jefferson Papers in the Manuscript Division, pp. 41-45) occupy a special place in the division. The collection is of immense importance as a reflection of Jefferson's encyclopedic interests, includes many important eighteenth-century editions, and has symbolic significance as the nucleus of the present Library of Congress.

Thirty volumes once owned by Abraham Lincoln and donated in 1928 by Mrs. Robert Todd Lincoln are held in the division, as are two other "presidential" libraries. The Hunting Library of Theodore Roosevelt, presented by his grandson Kermit Roosevelt in 1964, includes a number of early and important editions in the fields of hunting, natural history, exploration, ornithology, and sport (see Frederick R. Goff, "TR's Big-Game Library," *Quarterly Journal of the Library of Congress* 21: 167–71). Over 8,000 volumes acquired by Woodrow Wilson and donated by his widow in 1946 are housed in a separate Woodrow Wilson Room. The collection complements the Wilson Papers in the Manuscript Division. The books date from every period of Wilson's life and provide perspectives on his life as a scholar, educator, and statesman (see Vincent L. Eaton, "Books and Memorabilia of Woodrow Wilson," *Quarterly Journal of the Library of Congress* 4, no. 1, November 1946, 2–6).

The personal library of Susan B. Anthony was presented by her in 1905, along with her papers. Many of the 400 feminist and antislavery items were inscribed to the suffrage leader or annotated by her, and the library provides glimpses of both her influence on her contemporaries and her family and her feelings about them (see Leonard N. Beck, "The Library of Susan B. Anthony," *Quarterly Journal of the Library of Congress* 32: 324-35).

The Oliver Wendell Holmes Collection, formed by several generations of the Holmes family and received through bequest of Chief Justice Oliver Wendell Holmes in 1935, is rich in works on jurisprudence, constitutional law, philosophy, history, economics, and science. American literature collected by or presented to Justice Holmes's father, Dr. Oliver Wendell Holmes, includes volumes inscribed by James Russell Lowell, Henry Wadsworth Longfellow, and Ralph Waldo Emerson. There are several rare

nineteenth-century editions, such as one of six recorded copies of *Illustrations of the Athenaeum Gallery of Paintings* (1830), an anonymous collection of poems by several writers, one of whom is Oliver Wendell Holmes; the American edition of Lewis Carroll's *Alice's Adventures in Wonderland* (New York: Appleton, 1866), with the sheets of the suppressed 1865 English edition bound with a cancel title leaf; and one of fifty copies on Japan vellum of *Children of the Night* (1897), Edwin Arlington Robinson's second book of poems.

Two groups of books in the Rare Book and Special Collections Division are of interest because of their provenance. The Russian Imperial Collection, an accumulation of 2,600 volumes from one of the Romanov palaces, was purchased from a New York dealer in 1930. Many of these eighteenth- and nineteenth-century works of literature, military history, and social history were presented to the imperial family. The Third Reich Collection is a miscellany of books and albums collected by or presented to Nazi leaders and discovered by U.S. troops in a salt mine near Berchtesgaden. Many of the 1,000 volumes were presentation copies with dedications to Adolf Hitler. Almost none of the post-1933 imprints were bought by Hitler, and there are few editions of literary or historical importance.

Libraries formed by scholars compiling historical and bibliographical works frequently include rarities in the field. The collection formed by Peter Force has been dispersed throughout the Library of Congress (see pp. 30-35). Another such collection, the Henry Harrisse Collection described below, illustrates the relationships among book collecting, bibliography, and scholarship.

The general collections of the Rare Book and Special Collections Division include all forms of the book and are very strong in early nineteenth-century American materials. City directories, chapbooks, primers, books of instruction, annual reports, eulogies and orations, and auction, bookseller, and private library catalogs are only some of the many possible categories of genre research. The division is especially strong in nineteenth-century American natural history and ethnography. Frequently present in multiple copies or editions are the monuments of English and American color printing by Audubon, Catesby, Catlin, Charles Frederic Girard, John Edwards Holbrook, James Otto Lewis, and McKenney & Hall. Architecture and interior design books are an area of increasing strength, and American imports of classic works by Chippendale, Palladio, and Pain document influences and stages of popularization within this field.

REFERENCES

Beck, Leonard N. *Two Loaf-Givers: Or a Tour through the Gastronomic Libraries of Katherine Golden Bitting and Elizabeth Robins Pennell.* Washington: Library of Congress, 1984.

Goff, Frederick R. "The Oldest Library in Washington: The Rare Book Division of the Library of Congress." *Records of the Columbia Historical Society of Washington, D.C.* 69/70 (1968-70): 332-45.

Matheson, William. "Microcosm of the Library: The Rare Book and Special Collections Division." *Quarterly Journal of the Library of Congress* 34 (1977): 227-48.

———. "Recent Acquisitions of the Rare Book Division." *Quarterly Journal of the Library of Congress* 31 (1974): 166-82.

———. "Seeking the Rare, the Important, the Valuable: The Rare Book Division." *Quarterly Journal of the Library of Congress* 30 (1973): 211-27.

United States. Library of Congress. *A Catalog of the Alfred Whital Stern Collection of Lincolniana in the Library of Congress.* Washington: Library of Congress, 1960.

United States. Library of Congress. John Boyd Thacher Collection. *The Collection of John Boyd Thacher in the Library of Congress.* Washington: Government Printing Office, 1931.

United States. Library of Congress. Rare Book and Special Collections Division. *Library of Congress Acquisitions: Rare Book and Special Collections Division.* Washington: Library of Congress, 1982–.

United States. Library of Congress. Rare Book Division. *Catalog of Broadsides in the Rare Book Division.* 4 vols. Boston: G.K. Hall, 1972.

———. *Children's Books in the Rare Book Division of the Library of Congress.* 2 vols. Totowa, N.J.: Rowman and Littlefield, 1975.

———. *The Rare Book Division: A Guide to Its Collections and Services.* Rev. ed. Washington: Library of Congress, 1965.

———. *Some Guides to Special Collections in the Rare Book Division.* Washington: Library of Congress, 1974.

❏   BULGARIAN RENAISSANCE COLLECTION

The Bulgarian Renaissance Collection is an extraordinary example of the research potential of imprint collections. Books printed in the modern Bulgarian language between 1806, the year of the first such imprint, and 1877, the year before Bulgaria won independence from Turkish rule, document the nationalism and cultural revival of these years. Approximately 2,000 titles from this period were identified by Valerii Aleksandrovich Pogorelov in *Opis*

na starite pechatani Bulgarski knigi (Sofia, 1923), of which the Library has a representative collection of 40 percent, or 700 titles. A Bulgarian scholar is currently checking the collection against a newer, more complete bibliography by Man'o Stoıanov, *Bŭlgarska vŭzrozhdenska knizhnina* (Sofia, 1957). The collection was formed by Todor Plochev, a Bulgarian emigré who had been a well-known collector of rare Slavic books and manuscripts in Sofia and whose family had owned a printing press there. The Library's collection is unique outside Bulgaria.

Printing presses were prohibited in Bulgaria by the Turks, but little censorship was exercised at the borders. Books were printed for export primarily in Constantinople, but there are also imprints from Vienna, Belgrade, Bucharest, and Budapest. Some volumes in the collection have subscription lists, censor's marks, or acquisition notes. The material is not explicitly revolutionary in content, and the texts include liturgical books and religious tracts, grammars, readers, and textbooks, and histories, translations, and adaptations of foreign literary works, as well as didactic and patriotic works. The collection reflects the development of a national and historical consciousness, the codification of a Bulgarian literary language, the spread of education, and religious controversy. During a period of increasing resistance to foreign domination, the printed word played a crucial role in shaping and spreading national pride and revolutionary sentiment.

REFERENCES

Iovine, Micaela. "The Early Bulgarian Imprint Collections at the Library of Congress." Unpublished manuscript.

Jelavich, Charles. "Bulgarian 'Incunabula.' " *Quarterly Journal of the Library of Congress* 14, no. 3 (May 1957): 77-94.

United States. Library of Congress. *Special Collections in the Library of Congress: A Selective Guide.* Comp. by Annette Melville. Washington: Library of Congress, 1980. See no. 66.

❏   CONFEDERATE STATES OF AMERICA COLLECTION

One of the first acts passed by the Confederate government was to provide for public printing of all acts, journals of proceedings, and resolutions. Short-

ages of paper, type, and ink, all of which the South had obtained from the North before the war, made compliance difficult. Every effort was made to fill the gap with local materials and workers, and printers were exempt from military service in some states. To date, 7,000 bibliographic items have been identified as Confederate imprints, covering the full range of official and unofficial publications. Of these, the Library's collection contains 1,812 volumes. The diverse contents and the often imaginative materials of production testify to the importance of books in both political and everyday life to a government and a people at war.

In addition to the publications of every branch and department of the Confederate government—including the army, Bureau of Exchange, Bureau of Public Printing, Patent Office, Treasury Department, and War Department—and those of the individual states, the collection is rich in military, economic, and historical publications. The copy of *Uniform and Dress of the Army of the Confederate States* . . . (Richmond: Chas. H. Wynne, 1861), with lithographs by Ernest Crehen, is one of very few copies of the second edition of this Confederate plate book issued with color plates. Literary titles, sheet music, song sheets, educational material, and religious tracts indicate the central role that books played in the life of the Confederacy. There are books printed on bank-note paper and several novels bound in wallpaper published by the prolific S.H. Goetzel of Mobile. The Confederacy, anxious to maintain sound international relations, recognized international copyright, and fiction printed in the Confederacy includes editions of Hugo, Dickens, Bulwer Lytton, and Thackeray.

REFERENCES

Crandall, Marjorie Lyle. *Confederate Imprints: A Check List Based Principally on the Collection of the Boston Athenaeum.* Introduction by Walter Muir Whitehill. 2 vols. Boston: Boston Athenaeum, 1955.

Harwell, Richard B. *More Confederate Imprints.* 2 vols. Richmond: Virginia State Library, 1957.

Morrison, Hugh A. "A Bibliography of the Official Publications of the Confederate States of America." *Papers of the Bibliographical Society of America* 3 (1908): 92-132.

United States. Library of Congress. *Special Collections in the Library of Congress: A Selective Guide.* Comp. by Annette Melville. Washington: Library of Congress, 1980. See no. 50.

❑ DOCUMENTS OF THE FIRST FOURTEEN CONGRESSES COLLECTION

In an A. S. W. Rosenbach Lecture, published as *The Books of a New Nation: United States Government Publications, 1774-1814* (Philadelphia: University of Pennsylvania Press, 1957), J. H. Powell remarked that the study of "the printing history of the American government" is essential to "our humanistic understanding of ourselves as a free and democratic people." Despite their importance to historians, the nature and complexity of these early government documents have discouraged bibliographical study. Sabin, overwhelmed by the amount, omitted them; others, including Paul Leicester Ford and Worthington Chauncey Ford, did not distinquish between official publications and commercial reprints. The most successful effort to identify these documents was made by Gen. A. W. Greely, who recorded 5,000 congressional issues in *Public Documents of the First Fourteen Congresses, 1789-1817: Papers Relating to Early Congressional Documents* (Washington: Government Printing Office, 1900) and its supplement (1904).

The Documents of the First Fourteen Congresses Collection comprises legislative journals, committee reports, messages to Congress, petitions, and miscellaneous official printing between 1789 and 1817, the period of the presidential administrations of Washington, Adams, Jefferson, and Madison. Because early government publications were issued with separate or no pagination and no serial number, the total output is difficult to establish, and Greely knew that his list was not complete. Many of the 3,600 separate imprints in the Library's collection were not recorded by him. The government publications of the early years of the United States offer an excellent opportunity for bibliographical and historical research.

The Papers of the Continental Congress and the House and Senate papers, housed at the National Archives, record details of contracts, costs, and controversy relating to early government printing. They are a little known and very rich resource for the historian of American printing. Correspondence with the Clerk of the House and the Secretary of the Senate reveals increasing pressures on the printers who received the contracts for public printing and a growing necessity for expanded printing budgets and increased edition sizes. Topics covered include the quality of paper, the size of the type, and the size and pay of the work force. These papers reveal how the eight or nine printers who followed the government to Washington in 1800

established themselves in a village that had no printing trade, no paper mill within forty miles, no large population to support a bookstore, and no wholesalers to furnish supplies.

REFERENCES

Annual Report of the Librarian of Congress, 1904: 32.

Eaton, Vincent. "Documents of the First Fourteen Congresses." *Library of Congress Information Bulletin,* May 24, 1949, 14-15.

United States. Library of Congress. *Special Collections in the Library of Congress: A Selective Guide.* Comp. by Annette Melville. Washington: Library of Congress, 1980. See no. 63.

❏ LESTER DOUGLAS COLLECTION

Lester Douglas served as the director of art and printing for *Nation's Business* and the Chamber of Commerce in the 1930s and 1940s. This collection of 100 items includes original drawings, trial title pages, proofs, books, and ephemera illustrating Douglas's innovations in typography and book design. Several projects may be studied from the earliest stages of planning through the printed copy. The collection is arranged according to the numbers in *Books Designed and Directed by Lester Douglas Exhibited at the Library of Congress* (Washington: [Rufus H. Darby], 1949; Rare Book Z232.D7D6).

REFERENCE

Quarterly Journal of the Library of Congress 17, no. 3 (May 1960): 195.

❏ HARRISON ELLIOTT PAPER COLLECTION

Paper samples and historical and technical material were collected by Harrison G. Elliott (1879-1954). The collection comprises 5,000 secondary source items (articles, clippings, magazines, and pamphlets), 650 miscellaneous items (photographs, keepsakes, ream wrappers, commercial circulars), 4,500 specimens, and 10 paper molds. Elliott created handmade paper for use in limited

editions, and, as advertising and direct mail promotion manager for the Japan Paper Company, he designed, commissioned, and imported handmade paper. The collection is strongest in specimen sheets and sample books from the Japan Paper Company, its successor, the Stevens Nelson Paper Company, and Elliott's own work. Other paper companies and papers made before the twentieth century are represented as well. There is substantial personal and professional correspondence and memorabilia from Dard Hunter, Elliott's friend for over forty years. Folders containing trade journals, articles, and clippings represent Elliott's prolific writings on all aspects of the history and manufacture of paper (Rare Book TS1080.E4).

REFERENCES

Krill, John. "Harrison G. Elliott, Creator of Handmade Papers." *Quarterly Journal of the Library of Congress* 35 (1978): 4-26.

Quarterly Journal of the Library of Congress 31 (1974): 171-72.

United States. Library of Congress. *Special Collections in the Library of Congress: A Selective Guide.* Comp. by Annette Melville. Washington: Library of Congress, 1980. See no. 70.

❏ FREDERIC AND BERTHA GOUDY COLLECTION

All aspects of the career of American type designer Frederic W. Goudy (1865-1947) are documented in this collection of 1,791 volumes, 499 broadsides, 708 pamphlets, 3,321 printed ephemera, 654 prints, 189 nonprint items, and 3,169 manuscripts. There are works on typography and book design, examples of early and fine printing, and books, broadsides, and ephemera designed and printed by Goudy. Many proofs, dummies, extra copies, and unique items are included among the over 150 Village Press imprints, which are recorded in Melbert B. Cary's *Bibliography of the Village Press* (New York: Press of the Woolly Whale, 1938; Rare Book Z232.G68C3). American private presses of the early twentieth century are particularly well represented, many by inscribed copies. Goudy frequently annotated his purchases with revealing comments, such as the note in *An Endeavor Towards the Teaching of John Ruskin and William Morris . . .* (London: E. Arnold, 1901), by Charles Ashbee, the first Essex House imprint: "One of my earliest purchases for the especially vile type." Laid into Goudy's copy of Stanley Morison's *Fra Luca da*

Pacioli (1933), one of seven large paper copies, is a two-page autograph letter from Bruce Rogers, the book's designer, to Goudy, drawings by Rogers for several of the book's illustrations, and Rogers's design for the ornament used throughout.

Goudy's work as a commercial artist is exemplified in drawings, proofs, cover designs, and title pages for the Curtis Publishing Company, the Peerless Motor Car Company, and the Inland Printer. Many of the 124 typefaces Goudy designed may be studied in sketches and proofs that survived the 1939 fire at the Village Press and in the matrices for twenty-two-point Kennerley type. There are manuscripts and printed copies of Goudy's addresses, articles, diaries, and journals in the collection.

Most of Goudy's incoming correspondence was destroyed in the Village Press fire, but there are extant files of letters from Paul A. Bennett, Howard Coggeshall, Will Ransom, and others. Goudy's letters to Bertha from one of his first European trips also survive. The manuscripts include material for Goudy's *Half-Century of Type Design and Typography* and Paul Bennett's *Goudy: The Man and His Work*.

Photographs of Frederic and Bertha Goudy and the old mill that housed the Village Press are kept with the collection. Three films are held in the Motion Picture, Broadcasting, and Recorded Sound Division. Two are home movies and the third a 1935 Paramount short, "The Creation of a Printing Type from the Design to the Print," in which Goudy may be seen at work on the alphabet for Saks Goudy type.

REFERENCES

Beske, Kurt. "Craftsman in a Machine Age." *Quarterly Journal of the Library of Congress* 34 (1977): 97-115.

Haykin, Donald Hudson. "The Goudy Collection." *Quarterly Journal of the Library of Congress* 1, no. 3 (January, February, March 1944): 63-65.

Quarterly Journal of the Library of Congress 31 (1974): 170; 34 (1977): 240.

"Register of Manuscript Material in the Frederic and Bertha Goudy Collection." In the division files.

United States. Library of Congress. *The Collection of Frederic and Bertha Goudy, a Photostat Record of Cards Drawn to Form a Preliminary Checklist.* [Washington], 1945.

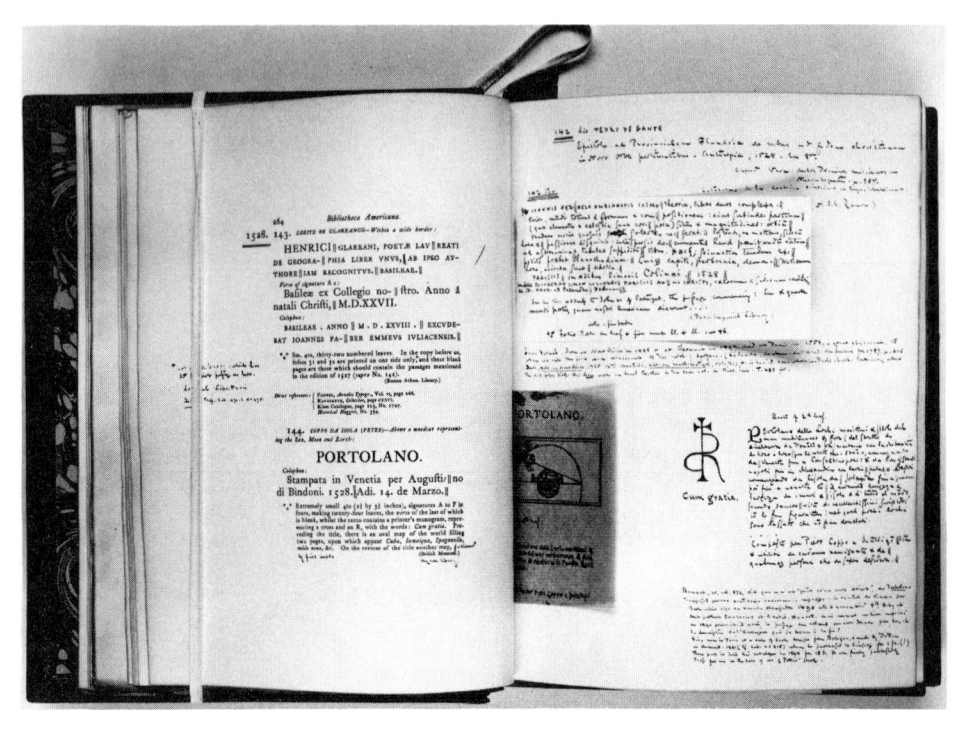

Henry Harrisse's copy of his Bibliotheca Americana vetustissima *(1866), a bibliography of works printed between 1493 and 1551 that relate to America. Harrisse expanded this copy with manuscript and tipped-in additions for a revision that was never published. Among the entries he interpolated here was Jean Fernel's astronomical and mathematical work,* Ambianatis cosmotheoria *(Parisiis: in aedibus Simonis Colinaei, 1527). Henry Harrisse Collection, Rare Book and Special Collections Division.*

❏   HENRY HARRISSE COLLECTION

The work of Henry Harrisse (1829-1910), bibliographer of Americana relating to the discovery period, demonstrates the importance of bibliographical scholarship to historical research. In *Bibliotheca Americana vetustissima (B.A.V.)*, published in 1866, Harrisse recorded over 300 books printed between 1493 and 1551 that refer to America, an increase of 250 over earlier compilations. Each entry is described, evaluated, and placed in its historical context, creating a narrative history of the period.

Throughout his career Harrisse was involved in disputes with publishers, book collectors, and librarians in the United States and in Europe. Henry

Stevens ridiculed *B.A.V.* because of one error he discovered in it. The publisher, G. Philes, claimed he had done much editorial work, and he undercut the subscription price by selling copies through Joseph Sabin. Private book collectors and public libraries restricted Harrisse's access to their collections. His mentor, Samuel Latham Mitchell Barlow, whose library of rare Americana Harrisse described in *Bibliotheca Barlowiana* (1864), was a notable exception to these embittered relationships. From 1870 until his death, Harrisse lived in Paris and investigated material in French, Italian, and Spanish archives relating to the discovery of the New World. During this period he published works on Columbus, John and Sebastian Cabot, the Corte-Reals, and Verrazzano, and he entered into debates concerning Christopher Columbus's birth, tomb, and letter reporting the discovery of America. Harrisse finally won the respect of the American scholarly community with *The Discovery of North America,* published in 1892, which was commended for "valuable contributions to science" at the Columbian Exhibition in Chicago in 1893.

Although Harrisse repeatedly attacked the custodial care and scholarly access afforded by public libraries, he divided his own collection among the Library of Congress, the Bibliothèque nationale, and a French bookseller. The Library of Congress received 213 volumes, 33 broadsides, 65 items of printed ephemera, 103 manuscripts, 15 seventeenth-century maps, and about 600 tracings, sketches, facsimiles, and photographs of early maps. These include Harrisse's own copies of all his works relating to America, which had been extensively annotated by him with corrections, additions, and comments. The collection includes one of four copies of *Bibliotheca Barlowiana,* and one of ten copies of *Letters of Christopher Columbus Describing His First Voyage to the Western Hemisphere.* Harrisse annotated two copies of *B.A.V.* and interleaved one with correspondence relating to the cost of production and the publishing history. A volume with the binder's title *Dossier de la Discovery* recounts Harrisse's unsuccessful efforts to find an American publisher for his most comprehensive work. Correspondence with Houghton Mifflin, Trübner, and others reveals the low esteem in which such ambitious projects were held by commercial houses. An attempt to arrange for the Grolier Club to undertake the work failed because of expenses related to their new house. These copies, along with the maps and manuscripts acquired by Harrisse in the course of his research, document the career of a significant and eccentric figure in nineteenth-century American bibliographical scholarship.

REFERENCES

Adams, Randolph. "Henry Harrisse." In *Three Americanists*, 1-33. Philadelphia: University of Pennsylvania Press, 1939.

Annual Report of the Librarian of Congress, 1915, 31-35.

Goff, Frederick R. "Henry Harrisse, Americanist." *Inter-American Review of Bibliography* 3 (January/April 1953): 3-10.

Stephenson, Richard W. "The Henry Harrisse Collection of Publications, Papers, and Maps Pertaining to the Early Exploration of America." *Terrae Incognitae*. Forthcoming.

United States. Library of Congress. *Special Collections in the Library of Congress: A Selective Guide*. Comp. by Annette Melville. Washington: Library of Congress, 1980. See no. 108.

❏   NATIONAL ENDOWMENT FOR THE ARTS SMALL PRESS COLLECTION

An archival set of the books published since 1975 with grant assistance from the National Endowment for the Arts Literature Program was established by the endowment in 1982. The initial deposit of approximately 1,500 volumes included works published with grant assistance between 1975 and 1980, and a recent addition covered the grant years 1979-82.

The Literature Program encourages and supports creative writing in America. Works of poetry, fiction, prose, and drama printed with grant support range from finely printed books to small paperback publications. The products of many of these presses are not deposited for copyright and are not automatically acquired by the Library. Among the presses represented are the Black Sparrow Press, BOA Editions, Capra Press, Ecco Press, Gallimaufry Press, Hanging Loose, Janus Press, Perishable Press, Red Dust, Inc., Salt-Works Press, Second Coming, Toothpaste Press, and Turkey Press. Authors represented by several titles include Tom Bridwell, Barbara Guest, David Hilton, Toby Olson, Charles Reznikoff, Dennis Schmitz, and Elka Schumann.

REFERENCE

Library of Congress Information Bulletin, May 7, 1982, 134-35.

❏   BRUCE ROGERS COLLECTION

The thistle mark of typographer and book designer Bruce Rogers (1870–1957) appears on the bronze door of the Rare Book and Special Collections Division Reading Room. His is the only twentieth-century printer's mark on the right-hand door, which is devoted to significant printers in the Americas. The year after the opening of the Rare Book Room in 1934, Rogers traveled to Washington from London to present a unique copy of the Oxford Lectern Bible, which had just been published by the Oxford University Press, to Herbert Putnam, then Librarian of Congress. This copy, printed on specially made Japan paper in England, is bound in pigskin tooled from a design made by Rogers and executed under his direction.

Extensive holdings of books designed by Rogers for commercial and private presses in the United States and Great Britain are to be found in the general rare book collections, the Goudy and Rosenwald collections, and the general collections of the Library, many in presentation and unique copies. This separate collection of 226 volumes, 114 miscellaneous items, and 790 manuscripts focuses on the period between 1897 and 1912, when Rogers served as the art director of Houghton Mifflin and the Riverside Press.

Among the original letters in the collection are one in which Rogers acknowledges his debt to William Morris and a file of correspondence with S. R. Shapiro, the donor of the collection. Transcripts record Rogers's working relationship with H. Watson Kent of the Metropolitan Museum of Art. An unpublished manuscript, "E-pistoleary Letter's to My Co-respondents Written on My Tipewriter by Gess Whoo?" displays Rogers's humor in a series of witty letters addressed to "elMOE Addle r," "Halfred & bl&che (wife) knopf," "Caril p. Rollings," and others, signed "bruise rogger printer ass, sum peeple coll mee."

REFERENCES

Quarterly Journal of the Library of Congress 17, no. 3 (May 1960): 195.

Quarterly Journal of the Library of Congress 31 (1974): 180.

United States. Library of Congress. *Special Collections in the Library of Congress: A Selective Guide.* Comp. by Annette Melville. Washington: Library of Congress, 1980. See no. 204.

❏   LESSING J. ROSENWALD COLLECTION

The collection of approximately 3,000 rare books formed by Lessing J. Rosenwald (1891-1979) and donated by him and his estate to the Library of Congress between 1943 and 1980 exemplifies an ideal relationship among the worlds of private book collecting, institutional rare book collections, and scholarship. Lessing Rosenwald sought complete and pristine examples of books within his special field—the western illustrated book from the fifteenth through the twentieth century—and at the same time maintained a flexible attitude toward significant books that fell outside this focus. His breadth of perspective and continued commitment to scholarly potential are reflected in a resource of preeminent importance for the historian of books and for scholars in many fields.

Lessing J. Rosenwald began to collect books in the late 1920s, several years after he had embarked on an equally dedicated, longstanding, and successful career as a collector of prints from the fifteenth through the twentieth century. His earliest purchases of fifteenth-century German illustrated books were compatible with his interest in the fifteenth-century woodcut print. For several years this buying pattern prevailed, with notable exceptions, such as the purchase of William Blake material from the William A. White estate, the start of a collecting interest that became the best-known and perhaps strongest part of the Rosenwald Collection. At the time of Lessing Rosenwald's first major gift to the nation in 1943, the shape of the collection as it would develop had been set. Over the next thirty-five years he donated prints to the National Gallery of Art and books to the Library of Congress. The collections were maintained at Alverthorpe Gallery, at his home in Jenkintown, Pennsylvania, during his lifetime.

Although the scope of the Rosenwald Collection soon expanded far beyond the fifteenth-century illustrated book, the holdings in this field are remarkable. Among the eighteen manuscripts is the Giant Bible of Mainz, considered by many to be the greatest single item in the collection. The manuscript, written in the same city and at the same time as the Gutenberg Bible was printed, was presented to the Library in 1952 on the 500th anniversary of the day the scribe began to work and is now on permanent display in the Library's Great Hall opposite the Vollbehr copy of the Gutenberg Bible.

Lessing J. Rosenwald acquired 4 superb block books in one of his major purchases from A. S. W. Rosenbach in 1929. The collection now has 10 of the

block books that appeared in the Netherlands and Germany about the same time as the first books printed from movable type and were common there to the end of the fifteenth century. Block or xylographic books, devotional or didactic works printed entirely from wood blocks, consist of image and text printed together on one side of a page. They were inexpensive and simple to produce because they did not require a supply of type or even a press, and the blocks could be reused when a new edition was required. A frequently re-printed block book, the *Biblia pauperum* or "poor man's Bible" is a series of subjects from the life of Christ accompanied by Old Testament parallels. It was primarily used by minor clergy in the preparation of sermons and not by laity. Block books have close ties to separately published fifteenth-century religious prints and are of great importance in the history of the graphic and typographic arts, although no direct influence on printing from movable type has been established.

There are over 500 incunabula in the Rosenwald Collection, including the Fust and Schoeffer *Durandus* of 1459; the 1460 *Catholicon;* the earliest printed law book, the *Constitutiones* of Clemens V (1460); the first dated book, the *Liber sextus decretalium* of Bonifacius VIII (1465); and the first printed book intended to be bound in two volumes, a Bible of 1462. There are superb copies and unique examples, many hand colored, of the most important illustrated books of this period, including Sebastian Brant's *Das Narrenschiff,* the *Dance of Death,* and Francesco Colonna's *Hypnerotomachia poliphili.* The existence of several illustrated editions of a single author, for example, Aesop or Virgil, permits the study of the migration of woodblocks. Technological developments are well represented. The mixture of type and woodblock in the 1473 *Speculum humanae salvationis* and the labor-saving factotum wood-cut, illustrations composed of several small blocks used in different combina-tions, found in the 1496 Strasbourg edition of Terence's *Comoediae* are exam-ples. Lessing Rosenwald resolved the sequence of two issues of the *Libro dei comandamenti di Dio,* printed in 1494, by using the number of titles in the "Libri necessarii alla salute humana corporale, temporale, spirituale, et eterna," the first printed list of recommended reading. His findings were published in *The 19th Book: Tesoro de Poveri* (Washington: Library of Con-gress, 1961). Even in areas of recognized strength, opportunities for new findings exist, as is seen in the recent discovery of an unknown indulgence from the press of William Caxton sewn in as quire guards for the binding

covering four complete Caxton texts. Paul Needham describes this discovery in *The Printer & the Pardoner: An Unrecorded Indulgence Printed by William Caxton for the Hospital of St. Mary Rounceval, Charing Cross.*

This combination of remarkable individual copies and comprehensive holdings characterizes the Rosenwald Collection for each century. Most of the books were purchased individually. A notable exception is the group of 167 fifteenth- and sixteenth-century Dutch and Belgian books from the Arenberg Collection acquired in 1956. Research opportunities presented by these volumes were recently explored in *The Early Illustrated Book: Essays in Honor of Lessing J. Rosenwald,* edited by Sandra Hindman. Many of the forty-one calligraphy books in the collection are from the sixteenth century and include works by Paccioli, Ludovico degli Arrighi, Dürer, and Tagliente. In addition to the 1529 *Champ fleury* by Geofroy Tory there are three manuscripts associated with this master. The Library's holdings of late sixteenth- and early seventeenth-century Latin and German editions and issues of the "Great Voyages" and "Small Voyages" of Theodor de Bry were immensely enriched by additions from the Rosenwald Collection, which also contains the second, 1590 edition of Thomas Hariot's *A Briefe and True Report of the New Found Land of Virginia,* the first volume of De Bry.

Many of the seventeenth-century books are milestones in the history of anatomy, architecture, astronomy, botany, cartography, dance notation, and mathematics. A great rarity is the only known complete copy of Braccelli's *Bizzarie di varie figure* of 1624, discovered and described by Henry Marguery and Kenneth Clark in the 1920s and hailed as a forerunner of cubism and surrealism. A two-volume facsimile of the Rosenwald copy has been published with an introduction by Tristan Tzara and an essay and notes by Alain Brieux.

The eighteenth-century French illustrated book is another area of particular strength. Among the special copies are the 1751 French edition of Erasmus's *L'Éloge de la folie* illustrated by Charles Eisen, with seventeen original drawings by the illustrator bound in; the drawings by Gravelot for Boccaccio's *Decamerone,* published in 1757; the edition of La Fontaine's *Contes* financed by the Fermiers généraux; and drawings by Prud'hon, Le Barbier, and other masters of rococo and neoclassical illustration.

In 1943, the year of his first major gift to the Library of Congress, Lessing Rosenwald acquired Tristan Bernard's *Tableau de la boxe,* illustrated by

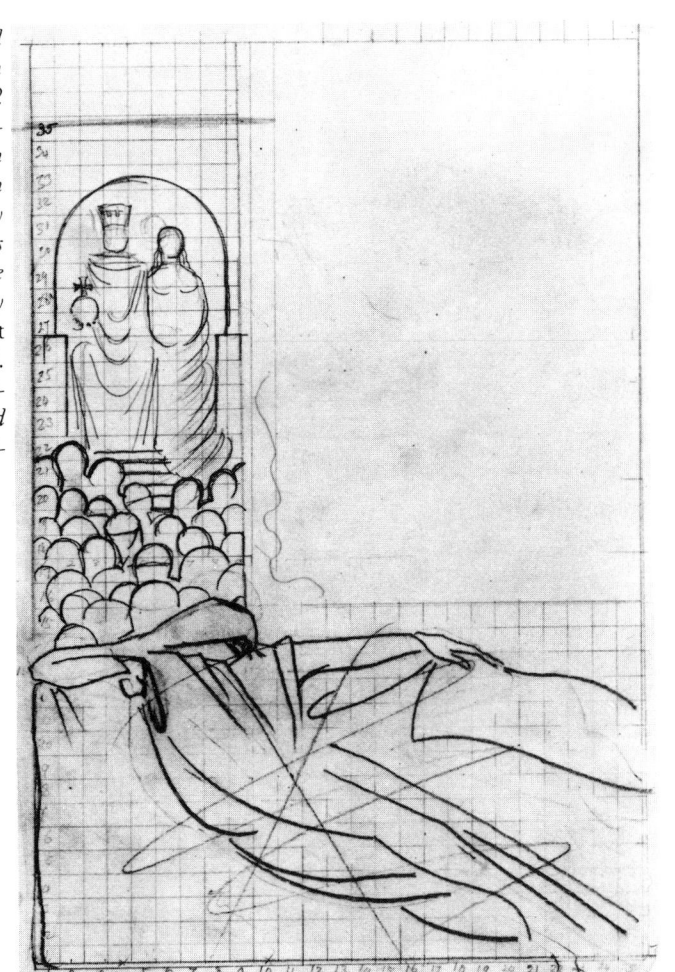

A pencil sketch by Edward Gordon Craig shows an unused design for page 12 of the Cranach Press Hamlet. Craig began work on the woodcut illustrations in 1913, the year Count Harry Kessler established the press in Weimar. Work on the edition was interrupted by World War I, but Hamlet finally appeared in 1929. Lessing J. Rosenwald Collection, Rare Book and Special Collections Division.

André Dunoyer de Segonzac, at the Crowninshield sale. The livre d'artiste, with its superb craftsmanship and close relationship between text and image, struck the collector as the modern equivalent of the early illustrated book. Lessing Rosenwald continued to acquire works with illustrations by major twentieth-century artists, including Verlaine's *Parallèlement,* with Bonnard lithographs; the Cranach Press edition of Virgil's *Les Églogues,* with proofs and sketches for the Maillol illustrations; Paul Éluard's *Liberté,* with pochoir illustrations by Léger; and Pierre Reverdy's *Sable mouvant,* with ten aquatints by Picasso. The work of modern fine presses, another focus of the

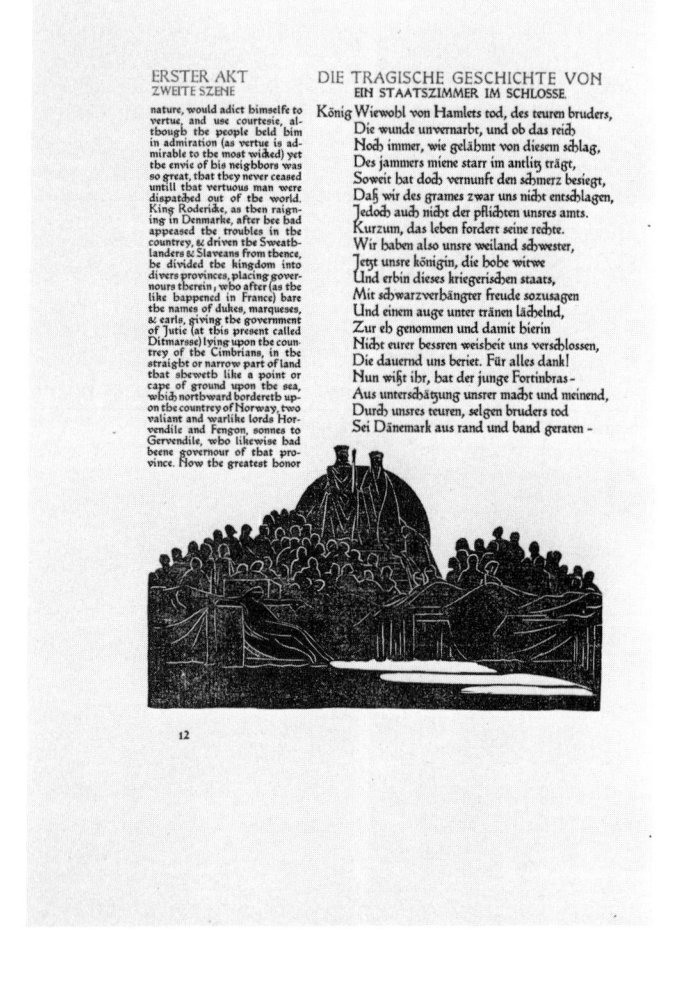

collection, includes a complete run of Kelmscott Press imprints, many printed on vellum, specially bound, or distinguished as association copies, and examples from the Doves Press, John Henry Nash, and the Grabhorn, Gehenna, Janus, and Bird & Bull presses.

Lessing Rosenwald once remarked that "an interest in books naturally leads to an interest in the development of printing." The Rosenwald Collection includes significant holdings of French type specimens, decrees governing printing and bookselling in eighteenth-century France, and printing manuals from France, England, Italy, and Germany. A 1982 acquisition by

the Rare Book and Special Collections Division of Moxon's *Mechanick Exercises* for the Rosenwald Collection affirms the continued commitment to this field.

The nucleus of the approximately 5,000 volumes in the reference collection was formed by Howard Coppuck Levis, who compiled a *Descriptive Bibliography of the Most Important Books in the English Language, Relating to the Art and History of Engraving and the Collecting of Prints* (London: Ellis, 1912). When he purchased the Levis collection in 1929, Lessing Rosenwald acquired many early and rare "books of secrets and mysteries" relating to the history of engraving: dictionaries of engravers, histories of engraving, private library and sale catalogs, and catalogues raisonnés. Some of the earlier works form part of the Rosenwald rare book collection; others are maintained as a supporting collection. There are scrapbooks of articles, clippings, trade cards, and tickets compiled by Levis. Levis interleaved his copy of the *Descriptive Bibliography,* now in the collection, with extensive additions for an unpublished revision. Lessing Rosenwald continued to add to this core collection of histories, bibliographies, and catalogs, creating a valuable resource for the study of the history of the graphic arts.

The personal papers of Lessing Rosenwald, about 28,000 items or 34 linear feet, were transferred to the Manuscript Division between 1980 and 1983. They consist of correspondence between family members and subject files covering a wide variety of his activities, including the American Philosophical Society, emigré assistance, and the early years of the Rosenbach Foundation. Files relating to individual book purchases are maintained by the Rare Book and Special Collections Division, and professional papers and files relating to prints are at the National Gallery.

The Rosenwald Collection sustains and stimulates research in the fields of bibliography, the history of printing, literature, geography, and art history. The intellectual and aesthetic significance of the books he collected was of great importance to Lessing J. Rosenwald, and his vision of their scholarly potential is being realized in this national treasure for the study of the history of books.

REFERENCES

Hindman, Sandra, ed. *The Early Illustrated Book: Essays in Honor of Lessing J. Rosenwald.* Washington: Library of Congress, 1982.

The Lessing J. Rosenwald Collection: A Catalog of the Gifts of Lessing J. Rosenwald to the Library of Congress, 1943 to 1975. Washington: Library of Congress, 1977. Includes a comprehensive listing of "Works about or Derived from the Collection" to that date.

Matheson, William. "Lessing J. Rosenwald: 'A Splendidly Generous Man.' " *Quarterly Journal of the Library of Congress* 37 (1980): 3-24.

Needham, Paul. *The Printer & the Pardoner: An Unrecorded Indulgence Printed by William Caxton for the Hospital of St. Mary Rounceval, Charing Cross.* Washington: Library of Congress, 1986.

Rosenwald and Rosenbach: Two Philadelphia Bookmen, Catalogue of an Exhibition at the Rosenbach Museum & Library from the Lessing J. Rosenwald Collection at the Library of Congress, April 30 to July 31, 1983. Philadelphia: Rosenbach Museum & Library, 1983.

United States. Library of Congress. *Special Collections in the Library of Congress: A Selective Guide.* Comp. by Annette Melville. Washington: Library of Congress, 1980. See no. 211.

❏ STONE & KIMBALL COLLECTION

A representative collection of 182 volumes from the 306 books and 3 periodicals recorded by Sidney Kramer in *A History of Stone & Kimball and Herbert S. Stone & Co. with a Bibliography of Their Publications, 1893-1905* was developed from copyright deposits in the general collections. Stone & Kimball imprints are also to be found in the unclassified collection and in the general collections of the Rare Book and Special Collections Division and the Library's general collections.

❏ YUDIN RUSSIAN COLLECTION

In 1903 Alexis V. Babine, Slavic specialist at the Library of Congress, went to Russia to view the private library offered for sale by Gennadii Vasil'evich Yudin (1840-1912), a Siberian merchant and bibliophile. Babine had been sent by Librarian of Congress Herbert Putnam, to whom he reported his findings in coded letters sent from Moscow. After lengthy negotiations over the purchase price, the collection was bought and arrangements concluded for the transport of over 80,000 volumes across Russia to Washington. The original handwritten inventory of these books is available on microfilm in the division.

Yudin had formed one of the finest personal libraries in the Russian

Empire through agents in Moscow and St. Petersburg. Lenin, who used the library when exiled in Siberia from 1897 to 1898, wrote that "It is a remarkable collection of books. For instance, there are complete sets of periodicals (the principal ones) dating from the end of the 18th Century up to the present day and I hope I shall be able to use them for the references necessary for my work." The Yudin Collection has for the most part been dispersed throughout the general collections, where it forms the core of the Library's strong Slavic holdings. The fields of Russian bibliography, history, local history, genealogy, and literature are very well represented by monographs, annals, indexes, and periodicals. Siberian imprints and books on Siberian history, ethnography, description, and travel are special strengths of the collection.

Rare materials from the Yudin Collection are maintained as a special collection within the Rare Book and Special Collections Division. Approximately 1,300 eighteenth-century imprints, the finest collection outside the Soviet Union, document the deliberate effort by Peter the Great to bring Russia into the West and the role played by books in this modernization effort. Before 1698, when the Dutch received printing privileges, the only press was at the court and the only alphabet was that of the Church. The first book in secular type appeared in 1708; the first press in the new city of St. Petersburg was founded in 1711. Throughout the eighteenth century, students were sent abroad to study. European books were imported and translated, and all aspects of the book trade expanded. Voltaire was the most frequently translated author, followed by Molière, Goethe, and Shakespeare. Practical works such as grammars, law books, and geographies were also widely distributed.

The most successful commercial publisher of the late eighteenth century was Novikov, a Freemason who combined the ideas and attitudes of the Enlightenment with a respect for Russian history and culture. His imprints, well represented in the collection, accounted for approximately one-third of Russian book production of the 1780s. Also present is a lengthy run of early publications of the Academy of Sciences and university and government publications. These products of a self-conscious and state-controlled campaign to bring Russia into the modern world document a fascinating chapter in the history of books.

REFERENCES

Annual Report of the Librarian of Congress, 1907: 20-24.

Babine, Alexis V. *The Yudin Library, Krasnoiarsk (Eastern Siberia).* Washington: [Press of Judd and Detweiler], 1905.

Fessenko, Tatiana, comp. *Eighteenth-Century Russian Publications in the Library of Congress: A Catalog.* Washington: Library of Congress, 1961.

United States. Library of Congress. *Special Collections in the Library of Congress: A Selective Guide.* Comp. by Annette Melville. Washington: Library of Congress, 1980. See no. 268.

Yakobson, Sergius. "An Autobiography of Gennadii Vasil'evich Yudin." *Quarterly Journal of the Library of Congress* 3, no. 2 (February 1946): 13-15.

❑ Part Two

Among the first items registered for copyright in several frontier states were local images such as photographs and city views and maps. The 1864 Colorado copyright ledger contains photographs of the Garden of the Gods, for which William Chamberlain claimed the copyright "as author." Early Copyright Records Collection, Rare Book and Special Collections Division.

3 □ Copyright Records and Deposits

□ COPYRIGHT LAWS AND
   REGISTRATION REQUIREMENTS

On May 2, 1783, before the adoption of the Constitution, the Continental Congress responded to the efforts of such authors as Andrew Law, Joel Barlow, and Noah Webster and followed the example afforded by Connecticut's "Act for the encouragement of literature and genius" by passing a resolution recommending "to the several States, to secure to the authors or publishers of any new books not hitherto printed . . . the copy right of such books." (For the text of this resolution, the individual state laws, and all federal copyright legislation through 1976, see *Copyright Enactments: Laws Passed in the United States Since 1783 Relating to Copyright,* published in 1973, and its subsequent revisions.) Within three years all the states but Delaware had passed copyright laws. These were based on the English Statute of Anne of 1710, which had broken the monopoly of the Stationers Company and recognized as the source of copyright interest the creative act of authorship, rather than the commercial, entrepreneurial act of printing or publishing. This concept, embodied in state and then in federal legislation, was essential to the development of authorship as a profession in America. (See Barbara Ringer, "Two Hundred Years of American Copyright Law," in *Two Hundred Years of English and American Patent, Trademark, and Copyright Law* [Chicago: American Bar Center, 1977], 121.)

The individual state laws were not uniform. Over half stipulated that copyright protection for an author from another state was dependent on the existence of a copyright law in that state. Some offered protection to previously printed works and others only to those "not hitherto printed." Copyright might be restricted to citizens or residents of a state or open to all. Pennsylvania's law was not to take effect until all the states had passed similar laws. The Connecticut, North Carolina, South Carolina, Georgia, and New York laws granted to the state the power to allow reprinting if the market was not sufficiently supplied by the copyright proprietor or if the price was unreasonable.

With the adoption of the Constitution, copyright legislation passed from the states to the federal government. Article I, Section 8, of the Constitution granted to Congress the power "To promote the progress of science and useful arts, by securing, for limited times, to authors and inventors, the exclusive right to their respective writings and discoveries." The first federal copyright law, the "Act for the encouragement of learning, by securing the copies of maps, charts, and books, to the authors and proprietors of such copies, during the times therein mentioned," was enacted on May 31, 1790, and provided a uniform law for all of the states. Copyrights were granted, but only to citizens or residents of the United States, for a period of fourteen years. If the author was still alive at the end of the term, renewal for another fourteen years was possible.

Copyright protection was based on registration and deposit for record prior to publication, as in the English Statute of Anne. Depending on the period covered, the records created and deposits submitted included deposit copies, title pages, published notices, record books, applications, renewals, correspondence, card catalogs, and published records. These printed and archival resources, now in the Library of Congress, document almost two hundred years of printing, publishing, and creative and intellectual activity in America. Fifteen years ago G. Thomas Tanselle described the contents of the records and their significance to bibliographers and literary, cultural, intellectual, and printing historians in "Copyright Records and the Bibliographer," *Studies in Bibliography* 22 (1969): 77–124. This remains the most detailed guide to the materials and to their potential research use.

Between 1790 and 1870, responsibility for administering the copyright law resided with the federal district court in each state. Requirements for securing copyright included the deposit of a printed copy of the title page

Photographs of "The great flood in Denver, Colorado Territory, May 19th, 1864," were entered in the Colorado copyright ledger for 1864. Early Copyright Records Collection, Rare Book and Special Collections Division.

with the clerk of the district court prior to publication, the insertion of a copyright notice in a newspaper within two months of publication, to run for four weeks, and the deposit of a copy of the work in the Office of the Secretary of State within six months of publication. In the first comprehensive revision of the copyright statute in 1831, which added prints and music as subjects of copyright, the original term was extended to twenty-eight years, the renewal privilege was extended to widows and children, and the requirement of a newspaper notice was discontinued. Statutory changes over the next forty years principally affected the number and location of deposit copies.

The Massachusetts state copyright law of 1783 had provided that two deposit copies be sent "to the library of the University of Cambridge [Harvard College], for the use of the said university," but the 1790 federal act viewed the deposits solely as items of legal record. The first effort to use the deposit requirement to enrich library collections, as Anthony Panizzi had done at the British Museum, was reflected in the 1846 act establishing the Smithsonian Institution, which provided for deposit copies to be sent to the Smithsonian and to the Library of Congress. Until 1865, when the deposit-for-use provision was reinstated after a six-year lapse, no penalties were attached to failure to deposit, and copyright proprietors routinely ignored the requirement. Approximately 20,000 deposit copies survive from about 150,000 copyright registrations made in the offices of the clerks of the district courts between 1790 and 1870 (Martin Arnold Roberts, *Records in the Copyright Office Deposited by the United States District Courts Covering the Period 1790–1870* [Washington: Government Printing Office, 1939]).

The year 1870, when copyright responsibility was centralized at the Library of Congress, marks the emergence of this institution as a comprehensive national collection of printed materials. This was precisely the goal of Ainsworth Rand Spofford, Librarian of Congress from 1864 to 1897, when he lobbied for deposit for use and strict enforcement procedures. (See John Y. Cole, "Of Copyright, Men and a National Library," *Quarterly Journal of the Library of Congress* 28: 114–36.) By 1897, when the Jefferson Building opened, over 40 percent of the 840,000 volumes and at least 90 percent of the map, music, and graphic arts collections had been acquired through copyright deposit. The enormous numerical growth of the Library in the twentieth century and its informal position as the national library of the United

States result from the operations of the copyright law. Of 1,021,601 pieces added to the Library in 1982, for example, 602,278 were acquired through copyright deposit (*Annual Report of the Librarian of Congress,* 1982 [Washington: Library of Congress, 1983], A-3, A-5).

❑ EARLY COPYRIGHT RECORDS COLLECTION

Copyright records transferred to the Library of Congress in 1870 from the district courts and the Department of State form the Early Copyright Records Collection in the Rare Book and Special Collections Division. They contain unique documentation of publication dates, publishing details, and authorship, and they provide evidence of projected works that were never published and published works that have not survived. Included are the original district court record books, in which clerks entered the names of the copyright proprietors, the full titles of the works, and the dates of deposit; an incomplete set of the secretary of state's record books beginning in 1796; published registration notices through 1831; printed title pages; the record of assignments; surviving deposit copies; and correspondence. There are gaps in the holdings: some record books may not have survived and several remain in other depositories. (See G. Thomas Tanselle, "Copyright Records and the Bibliographer," *Studies in Bibliography* 22: appendixes A and B.) Although some of the individual district court books have an alphabetical index, there is no general index.

Title pages were either pasted into the record books or filed separately. There are ninety-two boxes of loose title pages, arranged chronologically by district and, within each year, alphabetically by author. Some title pages of works by well-known authors have been pulled together in one box. For certain districts in certain years, for example, Philadelphia, 1790–1800, the title-page holdings are extensive. Although the ledger entry remains the principal record, the title pages supplement it in many ways. They were usually proof title pages with manuscript corrections, submitted before the final version was printed.

The wording on the title page may differ from the title recorded in the ledger, revealing changes that took place after the work was in the printing shop and on press. Sometimes, as in the case of Mathew Carey's *Short Account*

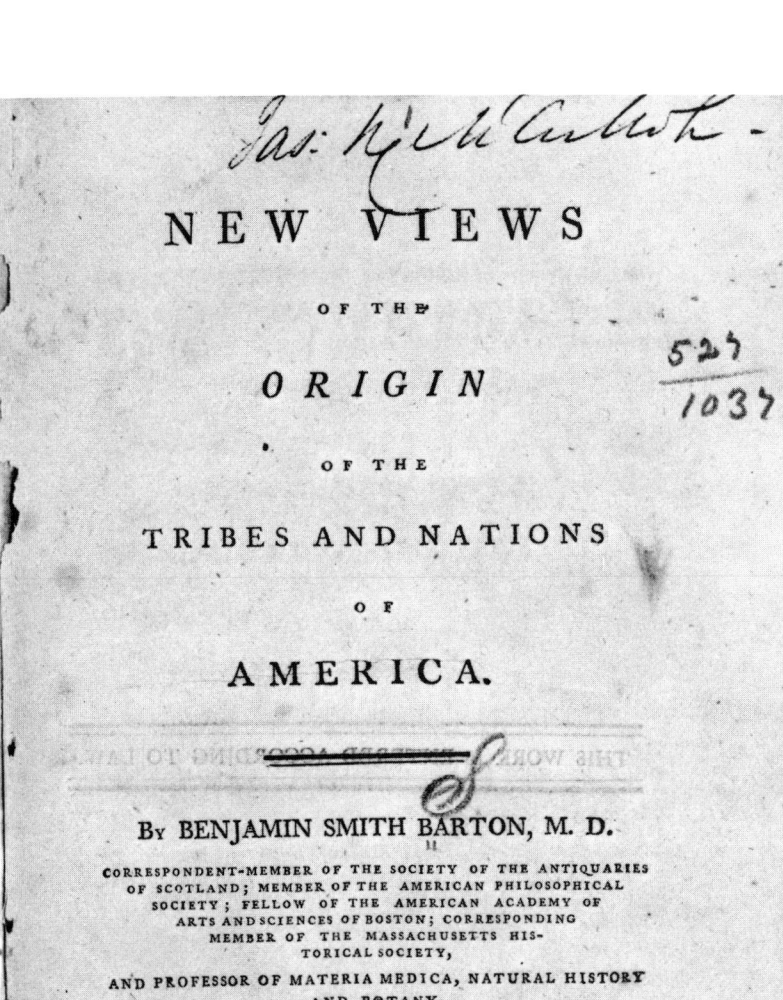

NEW VIEWS

OF THE

ORIGIN

OF THE

TRIBES AND NATIONS

OF

AMERICA.

By BENJAMIN SMITH BARTON, M. D.

CORRESPONDENT-MEMBER OF THE SOCIETY OF THE ANTIQUARIES
OF SCOTLAND; MEMBER OF THE AMERICAN PHILOSOPHICAL
SOCIETY; FELLOW OF THE AMERICAN ACADEMY OF
ARTS AND SCIENCES OF BOSTON; CORRESPONDING
MEMBER OF THE MASSACHUSETTS HIS-
TORICAL SOCIETY,

AND PROFESSOR OF MATERIA MEDICA, NATURAL HISTORY
AND BOTANY,
IN THE
UNIVERSITY OF PENNSYLVANIA.

PHILADELPHIA:

PRINTED, FOR THE AUTHOR,
BY JOHN BIOREN.
1797.

Title page for Benjamin Smith Barton's New Views of the Origin of the Tribes and Nations of America *(Philadelphia: Printed, for the Author, by John Bioren, 1797), deposited as part of the requirement for securing copyright protection under the first federal copyright law, enacted in 1790. Early Copyright Records Collection, Rare Book and Special Collections Division.*

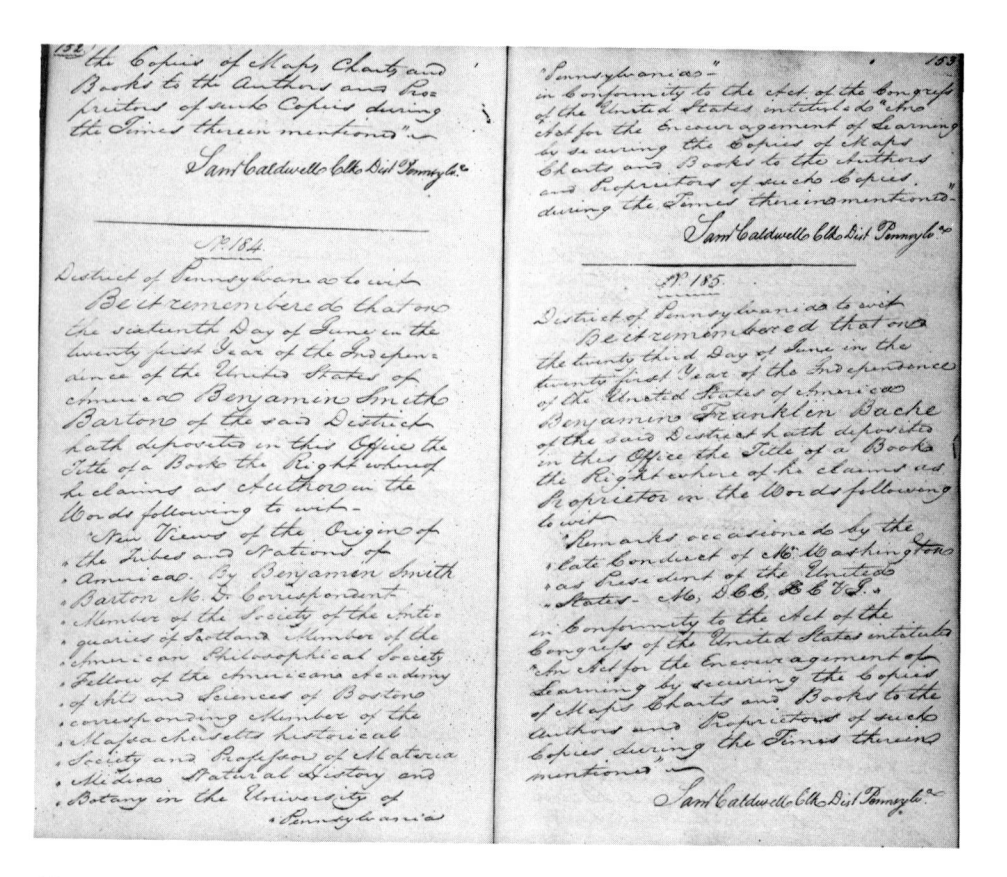

The ledger entry for Benjamin Smith Barton's New Views of the Origin of the Tribes and Nations of America *(Philadelphia, 1797), recorded by the clerk of the district court, Eastern District, Pennsylvania. Early Copyright Records Collection, Rare Book and Special Collections Division.*

of Algiers (Philadelphia: J. Parker for Mathew Carey, 1794), two entirely different settings were submitted. The page or entry number for the ledger volume is usually recorded on the verso of the title page, often with the proprietor's name. Title pages from earlier editions, with or without corrections in the title or imprint, were sometimes deposited to secure protection for a projected revision or reissue.

The title pages are of great interest as specimens of printing. They can be used to trace the use of type and paper, and they reflect the development of typographic and graphic design, stylistic similarities between printers, regional variations, and continuity and change over almost a century of American printing.

Letters that accompanied deposit copies sent to the secretary of state between 1818 and 1856 are in the Library of Congress Archives in the Manu-

script Division. Correspondence from writers and composers such as Stephen Foster, Samuel Griswold Goodrich, Washington Irving, and Noah Webster reflects the growing recognition of copyright as a valuable economic commodity. The concern of these authors for strict compliance with legal requirements to ensure copyright protection suggests that by the second decade of the nineteenth century, some authors and publishers expected to derive financial benefits from literary efforts. This marks an important development in the professions of authorship and publishing in America. Copyright was certainly not a sufficient condition for making a living from writing or publishing but it was a necessary one, as these letters reveal.

The Center for the Book in the Library of Congress is encouraging efforts to index and publish these records. A pilot project covering the decade 1790–1800 suggests the types of research that would be possible with flexible access to the complete body of data. (See *Federal Copyright Records, 1790-1800*, comp. by Carter Wills and ed. by James Gilreath [Washington: Library of Congress, in press].) Bibliographers of authors, of individual works, and of printing and publishing firms as well as biographers of authors may find here new titles and variants. The changing relationships among authors, printers, publishers, booksellers, and agents are reflected in the identity of the proprietor and the wording of imprint statements. Chronological and title indexes, access by format and genre, or access to subjects through key words will aid literary and intellectual historians. The full record of American printing and publishing will not be completed until these documents are widely available and thoroughly exploited.

❏   POST-1870 COPYRIGHT RECORDS AND DEPOSITS

Centralization of copyright responsibility in the Library of Congress in 1870 initiated a complete and uniform record of published work. The record is maintained by the Copyright Office, which was established in 1897. Access is provided through card catalogs in the Copyright Office that serve as indexes to the record books, stored in the Records Maintenance Unit. Approximately 41 million cards record owner/claimant, title, date, and registration or renewal number in various chronological and form sequences. The General Index for 1870–97 includes entries for authors, titles, and claimants in one alphabet. Cards list the registration number and author or brief title for

Wood-engraved, hand-colored title page for La Gata Blanca *(New York: D. Appleton, 1865), deposited for copyright on August 1, 1865. Early Copyright Records Collection, Rare Book and Special Collections Division.*

identification in chronological order, sometimes one entry per line and sometimes one per card. There are long sequences for material as diverse as
sewing patterns published by the Butterick Publishing Company and literary
works issued by Charles Scribner's and Sons and George Munro's Seaside
Library. Although there are no subject headings and no cross-references,
there are key-word headings such as "Medicine," represented by over 100 cards.

For the period between 1898 and 1937 there is a separate card catalog for
each class of copyrighted works and a renewal index. Claimants in the
"Books" category range from established trade publishers to news syndicates
and corporations, such as the American Tobacco Company, which issued
promotional brochures. The "Graphic Arts" claimants include Charlie
Chaplin, Thomas A. Edison, the Sanborn Map Company, and Harper &
Brothers for posters and book illustrations. Other categories were periodicals,
music, and drama. From 1938 to 1977 the Copyright Card Catalog is organized by chronological divisions, and each block of time incorporates all
classes. Starting with January 1, 1978, the records of registration, renewals,
and transfers are available online.

Each change in the copyright law altered the nature or extent of the
copyright record. The 1909 revision construed copyright to date from the
time of publication and extended protection to unpublished works designed
for exhibition, performance, or oral delivery. In 1976 the concept of auto-
matic copyright attaching upon the fixation of a work eligible for protection
in a tangible form, rather than registration, further broadened copyright
coverage. Just as the administrative changes of the 1870 law had an enormous
impact on the growth of the Library and the creation of a uniform record,
the substantive and administrative details of the law of 1891 are of great
importance to historians of American printing and publishing.

One problematic aspect of American copyright law through the late nineteenth century was the failure to protect works by foreign authors. The
resulting flood of cheap U.S. reprints of English works led to many claims by
American authors that the competition was ruinous to the native literature
that copyright was designed to encourage. Concerned authors and publishers
mounted a long campaign for international copyright that resulted in the Act
of March 3, 1891, granting U.S. copyright protection to foreign nationals
whose countries gave similar benefits to United States citizens.

Another feature of the 1891 revision was the so-called manufacturing
clause, which provided that copyrighted matter must be "printed from type

set within the limits of the United States, or from plates made therefrom, or from negatives, or drawings on stone made within the limits of the United States, or from transfers made therefrom." In the 1909 revision, the requirement for American manufacture was clarified to include type set by typesetting machines, the printing of the illustrations, and binding. Exceptions were made for books for the blind and books in foreign languages. In order to prevent illegal importation, the 1891 law also required the publication of the current record of copyright entries as the *Catalogue of Title-Entries,* later the *Catalogue of Copyright Entries.* The full record of copyright registrations has been available in published form since that time.

The procedure for establishing American manufacture of a printed item for which copyright was sought included the filing of an affidavit completed by the proprietor, agent, or printer stating "the place where and the establishment or establishments in which such type was set or plates were made . . . printing and binding were performed . . . and the date of the completion of the printing of the book or the date of publication." The manufacturing clause, now highly controversial, is still in force, and affidavits were required until 1976. These documents, created as part of the legal requirement for copyright, are excellent resources for printing and publishing history. They document book manufacturing in America and provide information about relationships among publishers, printers, typesetters, and binders. The affidavits provide addresses, frequently specify the printing process, for example electrotyping or stereotyping, and identify the method of illustration. They can also answer such questions as which publishers did their own manufacturing, how centralized was the printing trade, and were text and illustration printed in separate or combined shops.

The copyright assignment books record the transfer of copyright for a specified sum of money and additional consideration, a contractual and financial aspect of author-publisher relations of importance to the study of individual careers and the business of American publishing. Indexes to the assignment books are in several sequences. For the period 1870 to 1941 there are two files: assignor (mostly authors) and assignee (mostly publishers, often assigning rights to each other). The assignor/assignee files are combined for 1941–77. There is an assignment title index from 1928 to 1977.

The deposit copies, the physical artifacts preserved through the operations of the copyright law, are of special significance to bibliographers and historians of printing and publishing. They constitute the earliest issue of a book in

Affidavits, required as proof of American manufacture from the time of the 1891 revision of the copyright act until 1976, provide information about the book trade, specifying particular firms and documenting relationships among them. This affidavit, submitted by Benjamin Huebsch in 1917 for James Joyce's Portrait of the Artist as a Young Man, *identifies the establishments at which the edition was printed, typeset, and bound. Copyright Office Card Catalogs.*

its original form, one which often differs from the first commercially published edition. Especially at the end of the nineteenth and beginning of the twentieth century, publishers rushed to submit deposits in advance of publication to secure copyright protection. They sometimes made corrections in the text, altered or completed the binding of the edition, and added illustrations between the time of submission and publication. In some cases, the copy submitted is not from the first issue, and delayed submission reveals important facts about the book's production history, such as an unanticipated success. These variants add to our knowledge of the stages a particular work went through before publication and illuminate aspects of authorship, printing, and publishing.

Almost no deposit copies survive from the early decades of federal copyright law. Of 550 deposits of books, maps, music sheets, and prints received before 1820, only 48 were identified in a recent census. (See Roger Stoddard, "United States Deposit Copies of Books and Pamphlets Printed before 1820," *Publishing History* 13:5.) These are all in the Rare Book and Special Collections Division.

The submission and survival of deposit copies began to improve in the middle decades of the nineteenth century and, as noted above, were radically altered by the provisions of the 1870 law. Deposit copies make up the vast majority of items in the general collections. They form the core of the Geography and Map, Music, and Prints and Photographs Division collections, and transfers from the general collections continue to add acquisitions of great bibliographical importance to the Rare Book and Special Collections Division. Recent transfers include a copy of Jack London's *Martin Eden* in original wrappers, printed for copyright purposes and dated 1908, a year in advance of the first published edition of 1909, and the deposit copy of Mark Twain's *Tragedy of Pudd'nhead Wilson and the Comedy Those Extraordinary Twins* (1894), which lacks the illustrations at the end of both texts that appeared in the first published edition.

Current copyright deposits received at the Library are reviewed by selection officers for possible addition to the collections. Slightly over half of the deposits received are forwarded to divisions of the Library. Of approximately 888,000 deposits submitted in 1984, an estimated 500,000 books, periodicals, motion pictures, pieces of music, sound recordings, prints, photographs, and artworks were added to the collections. They can be identified by the Copyright Office deposit stamp. Certain categories of out-of-scope materials are automatically sent to the Copyright Office storage collections. These include, for example, computer programs and designs for wallpaper and textiles.

Dramatic works are deposited for copyright protection when first written or produced, and significant revisions are similarly protected. The deposit playscript often differs substantially from the published version, and some plays that were never published survive only in this form. The Rare Book and Special Collections Division houses deposit copies for approximately 3,000 unpublished dramatic works dating primarily from 1870 to 1930, including works by Djuna Barnes, Sinclair Lewis, W. Somerset Maugham, and Eugene O'Neill. Radio scripts and playscripts submitted for copyright by important performing artists and literary figures are also maintained in the Manuscript Division. Among the authors represented in Manuscript Division holdings are Fred Allen, Maxwell Anderson, W. C. Fields, Clifford Odets, Robert E. Sherwood, and Mae West.

Current copyright deposits for approximately five hundred living English and American authors collected by the Rare Book and Special Collections Division are automatically sent to that division. The division also receives

for selection deposit copies of limited editions of 500 copies or less and a representation of contemporary children's literature, chosen by the Children's Literature Center. The law specifies the deposit of "best edition." Sometimes a limited edition may be selected for the Rare Book and Special Collections Division and no trade edition submitted for the general collections.

Deposits not selected for inclusion in the Library's collections remain under the jurisdiction of the Copyright Office Records Management Division as a deposit for record. This copyright storage collection is housed in the Federal Record Center at Suitland and in a warehouse in Landover, Maryland. These vast collections, which are organized by registration number and retained for use in possible litigation, may be inspected for a fee of ten dollars an hour. The scholarly value of the copyright deposit storage collections has been recognized, but as yet no system for preserving or providing access to them has been devised.

In March 1983 the Copyright Office decided to retain deposit copies of published materials for five years, rather than the full copyright term, visual arts materials for ten years, and unpublished works (in accordance with the requirements of the 1976 law) for the full term of copyright. Envelopes containing "unfinished business" will be retained for thirty years rather than permanently.

Before disposal, all deposits are reviewed by selection officers, and several categories previously not selected are pulled for addition to the collections. Comic books and mass-market paperbacks (ordinarily out-of-scope for the Library), published dramatic works, and title pages are reviewed for transfer to the Rare Book and Special Collections Division, juvenile material for the Children's Literature Center, and unpublished dramatic works for the Manuscript Division. Other categories receiving special handling such as microfilming include Yiddish drama and music and unpublished lectures and dramatic works for 1900–1918. These ongoing efforts reflect a need to control an ever-growing storage problem and the desire to use the review process to identify material to add to the Library's collections.

❏ COPYRIGHT CASES

The provisions of each copyright law reflect contemporary attitudes toward authorship, printing, and publishing as professions and trades, and toward their products as intellectual and economic commodities. They also reveal the level of organized power or cultural influence available to these groups. Thus, in the 1891 law international copyright was primarily the result of lobbying efforts by authors, whereas the manufacturing clause satisfied American printers and publishers fearful of foreign competition.

As with other laws, concepts in copyright statutes are interpreted and refined and their application clarified through court cases. Decisions involving copyright law afford insights into such subjects as the evolving definition of creation, authorship, and publishing, the changing relationships and expectations among the various book trades, international book trade relations, and routine and unusual contractual and financial arrangements and trade practices.

In addition, the cases provide detailed bibliographical and technical information about the authors or works in question. *Decisions of the United States Courts Involving Copyright and Literary Property, 1789–1909, with an Analytical Index* (Washington: Library of Congress, 1980; Copyright Office Bulletins, nos. 13–16) illuminates the relationship of the law to the copyright collections in the Library of Congress and to the history of books. The index volume provides access to titles of works and subjects and the names of notable individuals mentioned in copyright and related litigation. The name index includes almost every nineteenth-century literary and publishing luminary, but cases involving small firms and unknown authors also add substantially to our knowledge of literary and publishing history.

One of several cases in which Mark Twain was the plaintiff involves subscription publishing, price fixing, and sales by agents. (See Copyright Office *Bulletin* no. 13, 651–53.) The defendants, Boston booksellers and publishers Estes & Lauriat, offered *Huckleberry Finn* in their holiday catalog at a price reduced from $2.75 to $2.25. Twain claimed that sales of the book by canvassing agents would be injured by the discount. The decision described the operations of the canvas system and the use of dummies and determined that the defendants were not party to any contractual agreement or breach that existed between Twain and his agents, against whom Twain might have a right of action.

A 1903 suit brought by Rudyard Kipling against G.P. Putnam's Sons determined, among other points, that an American publisher had the right to purchase unbound sheets from the authorized (British) publisher and copyright owner and to bind and sell the sheets here (Copyright Office *Bulletin* no. 14, 1503–10). The decision included details about the content, printing, press runs, and binding designs of the "Brushwood," Outward Bound," and "Swastika" editions. It also carefully examined and described the addition of new material to previously copyrighted material, contracts for the use of stereotype plates, and the question of whether an imprint of an elephant's head on paper covers merits protection as a trademark.

Many cases concern the definition of an act of original creation and the degree to which revisions, abridgments, adaptations, and compilations constitute copyrightable material. Illustrations, legal and scientific works, encyclopedias, textbooks, cookbooks, and trade catalogs are among the forms and genres most frequently at issue. The rights of authors and the responsibilities of publishers addressed in court cases include the relationship between serial and book publication, whether "book rights" convey serial and dramatic rights (no), whether an agreement to publish an author's works carries the necessary implication that the works must be published entirely by themselves or within separate covers (no), and whether an American firm that has the exclusive rights to work by a foreign author can obtain a copyright in its own name (yes) (Copyright Office *Bulletin* no. 16, 104–10).

A distinction between printing and publishing was articulated in a decision that "A book is not published merely by printing it and placing it in the hands of various persons under a contract restricting its use, and stipulating that it is not sold, and requiring its return to its owners" (Copyright Office *Bulletin,* no. 14, 1372–79). One decision questioned whether the arrangement of type on a printed label involved more than the expected skill of a typesetter and was thus eligible for protection as intellectual creativity or artistic merit. Numerous cases center around protection of imported sheets printed abroad, works printed abroad from type set in the United States, and the sale or use of stereotype and electrotype plates.

This retrospective compilation supplements the ongoing bulletins issued by the Copyright Office reporting current cases involving copyright and literary property. Litigation involving nonbook categories of copyright subjects—films, prints, music, dramatic compositions—was particularly prominent in the periods when these kinds of materials were first covered by

copyright. Once again today, new technologies have raised important questions about every aspect of copyright and literary property that await resolution by legislation and litigation. For every period, the copyright law, court decisions, and copyright records and deposits in the Library of Congress reveal how authors, printers, and publishers conduct their business. These archival materials, printed documents, and artifacts constitute unique resources for the historian of books in America.

REFERENCES

American Bar Association. *Two Hundred Years of English and American Patent, Trademark, and Copyright Law.* Chicago: American Bar Center, 1977.

Cole, John Y. "Of Copyright, Men, and a National Library." *Quarterly Journal of the Library of Congress* 28, no. 2 (April 1971): 114–36.

Federal Copyright Records, 1790–1800. Comp. by Carter Wills and ed. by James Gilreath. Washington: Library of Congress, in press.

Goff, Frederick R. "Almost Books." *New Colophon* 1 (April 1948): 125–33.

————. "The First Decade of the Federal Act for Copyright, 1790–1800." In *Essays Honoring Lawrence C. Wroth* (Portland, Me.: Anthoensen Press, 1951), 101–28.

Quarterly Journal of the Library of Congress 28, no. 2 (April 1971), celebrating the centennial of the 1870 revision.

Roberts, Martin Arnold. *Records in the Copyright Office Deposited by the United States District Courts Covering the Period 1790–1870.* Washington: Government Printing Office, 1939.

Schreyer, Alice D. "Copyright and Books in Nineteenth-Century America." Forthcoming.

Stoddard, Roger E. "Lost Books: American Poetry before 1821." *Papers of the Bibliographical Society of America* 76 (1982): 11–41.

————. "A Provisional List of U.S. Poetry Copyrights, 1786–1820, and a Plea for the Recovery of Unlocated Copyright Registers." *Papers of the Bibliographical Society of America* 75 (1981): 450–83.

————. "United States Copyright Deposit Copies of Books and Pamphlets Printed before 1820." *Publishing History* 13 (1983): 5–21.

————. "United States Dramatic Copyrights, 1790–1830: A Provisional Catalogue." In *Essays in Honor of James Edward Walsh* (Cambridge, Mass.: The Goethe Institute of Boston and The Houghton Library, 1983), 231–54.

Tanselle, G. Thomas. "Copyright Records and the Bibliographer." *Studies in Bibliography* 22 (1969): 77–124.

United States. Courts. *Decisions of the United States Courts Involving Copyright, 1909–1914.* Washington: Government Printing Office, 1928. (Copyright Office Bulletin, no. 17, 2d enl. ed.)

————. *Decisions of the United States Courts Involving Copyright, 1909/14.* Washington: Library of Congress, 1972–. (Copyright Office Bulletin.)

————. *Decisions of the United States Courts Involving Copyright and Literary Property, 1789–1909, with an Analytical Index.* Washington: Library of Congress, 1980. (Copyright Office Bulletins, nos. 13–16.)

United States. Laws, statutes, etc. *Copyright Enactments: Laws Passed in the United States Since 1783 Relating to Copyright.* Washington: Library of Congress, 1973. (Copyright Office Bulletin no. 3, rev.); Pub. L. 93–573, 88 Stat. 1873, 17 U.S.C. (1974); Pub. L. 94–553, 90 Stat. 2541, 17 U.S.C. (1976).

A SPECIMEN of the TYPE and PAPER, with CONDITIONS annexed, for re-printing by Subſcription, an American Edition of

COMMENTARIES

ON THE

LAWS

OF

ENGLAND.

BY

WILLIAM BLACKSTONE, Esq.

VINERIAN PROFESSOR OF LAW,

AND

SOLICITOR GENERAL TO HER MAJESTY,

IN FOUR VOLUMES.

REPRINTED FROM THE LONDON COPY,
PAGE FOR PAGE
WITH THE LAST EDITION.

A M E R I C A:
PRINTED FOR THE SUBSCRIBERS,
BY ROBERT BELL, Bookſeller, and American Publiſher of ROBERTSON'ſ HISTORY OF CHARLES THE FIFTH, which may now be purchaſed, Three Volumes for Three Dollars, at the late Union Library, in Third-ſtreet, PHILADELPHIA. MDCCLXXI.

Prospectus for the first American edition of William Blackstone's Commentaries *(Philadelphia: Robert Bell, 1771–72), which became the most famous colonial American law book. Over 1,557 sets were ordered by more than 840 subscribers. William Blackstone Collection, Law Library.*

4 □ Law Library

The founders of the Library of Congress sought to provide a comprehensive collection of laws and legal materials for the use of American legislators. In 1790, Elbridge Gerry proposed to the House of Representatives a congressional library consisting of:

> Laws of the several States, laws relating to the trade and navigation of the several nations of Europe with whom the United States may have treaties, laws of Ireland and Scotland, laws of Canada, British statutes at large, militia system of Switzerland, the Russian and Frederician codes, sundry authors on the laws of nature and nations, sundry authors on the privileges and duties of diplomatic bodies, a collection of parliamentary books, sundry books on the civil and common law, etc., etc.

With the purchase of Thomas Jefferson's library in 1815, the scope of the Library's collection was broadened far beyond this proposal, but the primary responsibility of the Law Library has remained to provide to Congress reference service in American law and both reference and research service in foreign, international, and comparative law. The present Law Library collection serves this function and supports research in legal history and many other scholarly disciplines.

In 1832 a separate law library was established within the Library of Congress, under the control of the justices of the Supreme Court, with 2,011

books segregated from the general collections. In 1897, when the Library of Congress moved to its new building, the Law Library remained in the Capitol, but by 1901 its 80,000 volumes had far exceeded the available space, and in 1905 law books were kept in six different locations in the city. Over the next two decades the law collection was moved to the Library of Congress. A branch of the Law Library is still maintained in the Capitol for the use of members of Congress. Until 1935, when the Supreme Court moved into its own building, the Law Library served the Supreme Court as well as Congress.

During the first 100 years of the Law Library's existence, the collections grew steadily, especially in the area of Anglo-American materials, through copyright deposit, gift, purchase, and exchange. In the early 1930s the American Bar Association participated in the effort to secure support to develop the collection. A "New Program of Development" written in 1934 articulated the shift from a government reference center to a more general legal research center and set as goals "the gradual acquisition of all the works in the sphere of law proper and in closely related fields which reflect the genesis of the science of law from the XIIth to the XXth century" and filling "the gaps in the collection of original sources of law that have played an important part in legal history (ordinances, statutes, codes, court reports) from the earliest times to the present" (*Annual Report of the Librarian of Congress,* 1934:94).

Fifty years later, the Law Library's collection of close to 2 million volumes, including legal literature from all countries, historical periods, and legal systems of the world, constitutes a comprehensive resource for legal research. Its holdings of constitutions; codes, compilations, and revisions of laws; commentaries on and indexes to laws, codes, and rules and regulations; court decisions and reports; digests, citations, and indexes of decisions and reports; and legal periodicals, monographs, and reference works will support the intensive study of all laws relating to book production and distribution. Areas of the law significant in the history of books include licensing, libel and sedition, freedom of the press, copyright and intellectual property, regulation and restraint of trade, customs, excise, taxation, postal service, and public printing. Sources in the Law Library thus enable book historians to study the political, economic, and social context of authorship, printing, publishing, and distribution.

Approximately 25,000 volumes (including over 300 incunabula) are separately maintained in the Law Library Rare Book Room, and there are legal

materials in the Rare Book and Special Collections Division as well. These historical resources demonstrate the relationship between law and society and the role of printed books in the development of legal systems, legal education, and the legal profession. This chapter focuses on some special collections in the Law Library that illustrate this connection and suggest research opportunities.

❏ ROMAN AND CANON LAW

The revival of Roman and canon law theory and practice in the three centuries preceding the invention of printing resulted in the systematic codification and exegesis of both systems. Within the first decades after Gutenberg, all the major Roman and canon law texts were published in several editions and circulated widely throughout Europe in standardized form. The combined holdings of legal incunabula in the Law Library and the Rare Book and Special Collections Division, representing a considerable percentage of the products of the principal incunabular presses, enable book historians to examine the effect of printed laws on the development of national legal systems.

"Roman" or civil law refers to the system that prevails in those countries that derive their judicial theory and practice from the collections of laws compiled by the Emperor Justinian in 528–34 known as the Corpus juris civilis. These include countries in Latin America and the Near East, Japan, Indonesia, a large part of Africa, and all of Europe except the United Kingdom. The twelfth-century renaissance of legal studies was based on Justinian's collections, and Roman law was refined and developed by the writings and decisions of church or canon lawyers.

The 15,000-volume collection of sources of Roman law and literature about it in the Law Library includes 1,600 rare items, of which over 70 are incunabula. The library of Prof. Paul Krüger of Bonn, acquired in 1930, brought 4,700 items to this collection, which contains extensive holdings from every century and is very strong in early editions of the individual parts of the Corpus juris civilis. Justinian had directed a commission of jurisconsults to classify and arrange the varied precepts of Roman law, which was done in four parts: the *Institutiones,* an elementary textbook; the *Digesta,* or writings of jurists; the *Codex,* or statutes; and *Novellae,* or new statutes. The four parts

were not published together under the title *Corpus juris civilis* until 1583, when they were edited and annotated by Denis Godefroy. *Institutiones cum glossa* (Mainz: Peter Schoeffer, 1468) is the first edition of any of the four texts and contains the first eulogy on the invention of printing (Lessing J. Rosenwald Collection 36, Rare Book and Special Collections Division).

By the time Justinian's collections were printed, the work of two schools of commentators was available for inclusion. A school of "glossators" founded at Bologna under Irnerius in the twelfth century had added interlinear and marginal notes or glosses clarifying and interpreting the text. The glosses in the 1468 Mainz edition of the *Institutiones* are attributed to Franciscus Accursius and Accursius glossator, the last of the prominent glossators, who collected approximately 96,000 existing glosses in *Glossa ordinaria.* The Law Library collection is strong in early editions of the scholastic commentators or "post-glossators" of the thirteenth and fourteenth centuries, whose systematic compilation and analysis of the *Corpus juris civilis* adapted it to the legal, social, and economic conditions of the time. Over 85 of the commentaries in the Law Library are by Bartolus de Saxoferrato; others are by his student, Baldo degli Ubaldi. Bartolus's *Super authenticis* [Milan: Joannes Antonius de Honate], 1480, went through thirteen editions before 1500 in this collected form and in parts. The collection is especially rich in the works of Guillaume Budé, the sixteenth-century humanist interpreter of Roman law, Greek scholar, diplomat, and royal librarian whose *Altera editio annotarium in pandectus,* printed by Estienne in 1535, earned him the title of the first legal historian.

Just as Justinian's compilation of earlier law, revived and revised from the twelfth century on, formed the basis for civil law, the twelfth-century collection known as the *Decretum Gratiani* provided the basis for canon, or ecclesiastical, law. Gratian, an Italian monk and educator, coordinated and synthesized approximately 3,800 diverse and often contradictory legal texts that had developed in the Roman Catholic church through conciliar decrees, papal decretals, and the writings of the church fathers. The *Decretum,* completed about 1140, sought to provide one systematic, definitive, and complete source for ecclesiastical law. Although it was never officially endorsed by the Church, the *Decretum* formed the basis for the teaching and study of canon law in the West for centuries. Gratian's disciples, known as "decretists," added glosses and *summae* (doctrinal statements appearing apart from the text). Later official collections included the decretals of Gregory IX (1234), the *Liber sextus decretalium* of Bonifacius VIII (1298), and the *Constitutiones*

of Clemens V (1314). These, together with the *Decretum Gratiani,* make up the *Corpus juris canonici,* completed in 1437 and expanded by two collections of *Extravagantes* published in 1500 by John Chappuis. A group of sixteenth-century correctores Gratiani revised Gratian; early editions often printed the original work with that of the decretists and the correctores.

The 2,800 volumes in the canon law collection provide evidence of the profound influence of canon law and lawyers on the development of political theory in early modern Europe. The collection is especially strong in the works of seventeenth- and eighteenth-century church figures and early editions of the sources of ecclesiastical law. The glosses of Johannes Andreae appeared in many early editions of the *Constitutiones* of Clemens V, beginning with the first edition, also the first printed law book ([Mainz]: Johann Fust and Peter Schoeffer, 1460; Lessing J. Rosenwald Collection 30, Rare Book and Special Collections Division) and of the *Liber sextus decretalium* of Bonifacius VIII, including the edition published in Mainz by Johann Fust and Peter Schoeffer in 1465 (Lessing J. Rosenwald Collection 33, Rare Book and Special Collections Division) and that in Mainz by Peter Schoeffer in 1473 (Lessing J. Rosenwald Collection 43, Rare Book and Special Collections Division). Andreae's glosses also appeared separately in many Latin and German editions of the *Super arboribus consanguinitatis.* An edition that contained both the *Liber sextus decretalium* and the *Constitutiones* with Andreae's glosses (Basel: Johann Froben and Johann Amerbach, 1500) was edited by Sebastian Brant. Among the later editions of the *Decretum* in the Law Library are one of five surviving copies of the Venice, 1514 edition. Other material in the canon law collection includes collections of decisions handed down by the Rota Romana, a high ecclesiastical court, beginning with the editions published in Rome by Georgius Lauer in 1475 and in Mainz by Peter Schoeffer in 1477 and continuing through the eighteenth century.

Two genres of legal literature that combined Roman and canon law were *coutumes* and *consilia.* The *coutumes,* medieval laws of provincial central and northern France, fused Germanic rules, Roman law, canon law, and local usage. Originally unwritten local customary laws, they had been compiled in writing in numerous private works by the thirteenth century, and Charles VII ordered the preparation of a systematic collection in 1453. The process of codification was only completed in 1804 with the promulgation of the Napoleonic Code, in which the predominant influence was the coutumes. The Law Library collections include 700 volumes of coutumes from France and more than 100 from other European countries. These constitute the largest

A copy of the coutumes *of Paris, printed in 1513 by Guillaume Eustace and Jehan Petit, displays on its title page the printer's mark of Guillaume Eustace.* Coutumes Collection, Law Library.

collection of coutumes outside France and include the "Coutumes de Normandie," a magnificent fifteenth-century illuminated manuscript copy of the "Grand coutumier de Normandie," of about 1254–58. The *Coutume de Paris* served as a model for the national codification of provincial coutumes. *La Somme rurale de Boutillier*, compiled sometime after 1383 by Jean Boutillier, a citizen of Tournai, was written in French for the common man. His summary of all the customary law of the fourteenth century was printed in Bruges by Colard Mansion in 1479 (Thacher Incunabula, Rare Book and Special Collections Division). Coutumes were printed in the region covered by the laws and provide examples of the best typographic efforts of French provincial printers. In addition to their historical importance for the develop-

ment of modern legal systems, coutumes provide a lively and detailed portrait of daily life in medieval France.

Consilia, legal opinions rendered by jurists or lawyers at the request of a judge or a private individual, evolved in connection with the revival of Roman law studies in the thirteenth century and were issued until the eighteenth century. They show the fusion of theories derived from Roman and canon law with local customary practice, a process which led to the development of the civil law and thus to modern European legal codes, whose formation made consilia unnecessary. The biographical sketches and detailed statements of the facts of the case sometimes included in consilia make them important sources for social and intellectual history.

The Law Library contains close to 1,000 volumes of consilia representing some 260 authors. Among the incunabular editions are the *Consilia* of Johannes and Gaspar Calderinus (Rome: Adam Rot, 1472). There are several fifteenth and many sixteenth-century editions of the consilia of the civil law commentators Baldo degli Ubaldi and his teacher, Bartolus de Saxoferrato. The Law Library has sponsored a forthcoming bibliography of consilia in its own collections and other major U.S. collections. In a survey of the collection in preparation for this work, several nonlegal items were discovered, including contemporary book dealer cards.

❑ NATIONAL LAW CODES

In the codification of national legal systems, practical rules governing local usage merged with the theoretical teachings of Roman and canon law. Canon law writings contributed to the refinement of civil law principles and to the concept of lawmaking in government. The Law Library contains comprehensive holdings of national law codes that reflect these developments and shed light on the role of printed law books in the process.

The 130,000-volume Hispanic law collection includes 1,200 rare items ranging from early editions of ancient and medieval Spanish codes to legal documents related to the Spanish colonies in America. The first printed edition of the *Breviary of Alaric* (506), the earliest extant Spanish code, appeared in 1550. *Las siete partidas,* initiated by Alfonso X of Castille in 1256 and completed in 1265, was the first body of law in the Spanish vernacular. The Law Library has the first printing of the first edition (Seville: Meinardus

Ungut and Stanislaus Polonus, 1491). The authors of the *Partidas* were influenced by ecclesiastical and civil law, regional fueros, and Spanish ordinances. *Las siete partidas* remained the national code for several centuries and was included in later codifications. The *Partidas* was brought to the New World by Spanish colonists. Some of its concepts influenced legal codes adopted in Texas, California, the Philippines, Puerto Rico, and Louisiana, as described in *The Laws of Las Siete Partidas, Which Are Still in Force in the State of Louisiana,* translated by L. Moreau Lislet and Henry Carleton (New Orleans: James M'Karaher, 1820).

A collection of 500 volumes of statuta contains the laws prevailing in Italian city-states until the eighteenth century. Early statuta include those from Bologna (1475), Brescia (1490), Milan (1498), Parma (1494), Venice (1477), and Verona (1475). A process of romanization and codification took place in Germany during the fifteenth and sixteenth centuries as the laws of local tribes and territories were compiled into local law codes for city-states. Examples of these Reformationen or Stadtrechte in the Law Library include codes from Nuremberg (1503) and Freiburg im Breisgau (1520).

The 27,000-volume collection of sources and literature of Russian law in the Law Library is almost equally divided between prerevolutionary and Soviet material. It contains many rare items and legal volumes from the personal library maintained by Tsar Nicholas II at the Winter Palace, Tsarskoe Selo, including finely bound and miniature editions and many works printed on special paper or parchment.

The first law book printed in Russia did not appear until 1649, almost a hundred years after the introduction of printing in 1564. The second law book printed in Russia was the *Kormchaia Kniga* or *Nomokanon* (Rudder or Pilot book), a collection of ecclesiastical and civil law compiled in ninth-century Byzantium for the use of church authorities. The work was printed in 1650, but before it was distributed a schism in the Russian church led to a general revision of all ecclesiastical books. The Law Library has a 1653 edition.

Peter the Great ordered that Church Slavonic no longer be used for nonecclesiastical works. The first law book printed in the specially designed type that evolved into the modern Russian alphabet was the naval code *Instruktsii i artikuly voennye nadlezhashchii k rossiiskomu flotu* (Moscow, 1710). Nineteenth-century reforms of the Russian legal system are well represented in the collection, many in copies owned by the Romanov family, including

volumes recording the transactions of the committees called to prepare the law for the abolition of serfdom enacted in 1861 by Alexander II.

The Czechoslovakian codes of 1564, 1579, 1583, and 1627 cover a critical period in Czech history and reflect the transition from autonomy and self-government to the triumph of the German language and culture. The 1564 code secured the highest autonomy for the Czechs and sought to fuse resolutions passed in the national parliament and rules of customary law with the privileges granted by the king to the gentry and cities. The *Obnovené zřízení zemské* or "Revised Code" of 1627, enacted after the defeat of the Czech gentry in 1620, reveals the shift to centralization and Germanization. The complete text is printed in German and only a part (up to leaf 135) in Czech, the remainder being in manuscript. (See Vladimir Gsovski and Jindrich Nosek, "Some Rare Legal Acquisitions," *Quarterly Journal of the Library of Congress* 9, no. 1, November 1951, 14–19.)

Legal codes published in Romania from the seventeenth to the nineteenth century are excellent sources for the study of the development of the Romanian language. During the seventeenth century, Church Slavonic books began to be replaced by works in Romanian, using the Cyrillic alphabet in combination with letters reproducing the sounds of the non-Slavic Romanian. Over the next two centuries, Cyrillic was gradually replaced by the Latin alphabet and the necessary new presses were obtained despite Russian opposition. In 1859 Latin characters were ordered to be used in the official gazette, although twenty years later signs of Cyrillic characters can be found in publications issued in other plants. An early work that displays the special form of Cyrillic is the *Carte Românescă de învătătură, pravile inpărătesti* (Jassy, 1646), the first legal code completely in the Romanian language. Nineteenth-century books printed in a mixture of Latin and Cyrillic alphabets include *Comentariile dreptului penalu* (Bucharest, 1857), a commentary on the 1851 penal code. These books document the stages by which Romania moved toward Western Europe in law and language, culture and civilization. (See Raoul Gheorghiu, Dean M. A. Murville, and Vladimir Gsovski, "Rare Rumanian Legal Literature," *Quarterly Journal of the Library of Congress* 16, no. 1, November 1958, 1–6.)

Works of general and international law reveal a close connection between law and other fields such as philosophy and political theory. A collection of maritime customs and ordinances, *Capituli et ordinatione di mare e di mercantie* (Rome: Ant. de Bladi de Asola, 1519), was followed in cities along the

Mediterranean Coast and influenced the development of Anglo-American law. The Law Library's holdings of treatises on the law and theory of war range from Giovanni da Legnano's 1360 work *De bello, repressaliis et duello* (Pavia: Christophorus de Caibus, 1487) to the first printing of Hugo Grotius's *De jure belli ac pacis libri tres* (Paris: Apud Nicolaum Buon, 1625) and many later publications by Elzevier or Blaeu.

❏   ## ANGLO-AMERICAN COMMON LAW AND LEGAL LITERATURE

The development of English common law, on which the American legal system is based, can be traced in the year books, or medieval reports which began in the thirteenth-century reign of Edward I and continued until that of Henry VIII. Intended as practical textbooks for the use of serjeants or barristers, rather than for citation in court, the year books reported pleadings in law French rather than the Latin of the contemporary court records. Cases in the year books involve every social class and record medieval life, language, and law in fresh and vivid detail.

The first year books were printed by John Lettou and William de Machlinia seven or eight years after the introduction of printing in England. Their editions of 35 and 36 Henry VI (ca. 1482) were printed from manuscript approximately thirty years after the hearings of the actions reported and thus recorded contemporary law. Richard Pynson, the first systematic English law book printer, issued approximately 50 year book editions; Richard Tottell, who made them profitable and popular during the forty years from 1552 to 1593, while he had a patent to print law books, was responsible for almost 250 year book editions. Year book printing ended with the "Standard edition" in eleven parts of 1678–80, which brought together year books previously printed in separate editions for the reigns of Edward III through Henry VIII. During this period, approximately 445 separately printed issues of years or groups of years had appeared.

Printed year books, taken from different manuscripts and frequently reprinted, are textually unreliable and bibliographically complex. The legal historian Frederic Maitland called them "that hopeless mass of corruption" and Charles C. Soule, in his "Year-Book Bibliography" (*Harvard Law Review* 14 [1901]: 557–87) urged close examination and comparison of copies to identify reset texts, signatures of one edition bound with remainders of an-

other, and other variants. The Law Library collection of over 300 bound volumes, which dates to the purchase of the library of William V. Kellen in 1905, contains 11 editions printed by Pynson, almost 200 by Tottell, and all parts of the standard edition. The Law Library has a collection of law book catalogs, beginning with the second edition of Thomas Bassett's *Catalogue of the Common and Statute Law-Books of This Realm* . . . (London, 1682), enabling scholars to reconstruct the distribution and availability of these texts.

During the sixteenth century, printing effected significant changes in the systems of legal reporting and public proclamation of laws. The discursive, private notes taken by a reporter for his own use were soon recognized to be of immense practical value to the legal profession. Printed reports, which soon included abstracts, digests, and indexes, reflect the change from a system of oral to written pleading and a gradually higher standard of accuracy and detail.

A similar transition occurred in the practice of proclaiming official laws of the land. As Katharine F. Pantzer demonstrated in "Printing the English Statutes, 1484–1640: Some Historical Implications" (in *Books and Society in History,* ed. Kenneth E. Carpenter [New York: R.R. Bowker, 1983], 69–114), the introduction of printing in England immediately altered the way in which statutes were proclaimed: "The ultimate distinction of 'public' up to this time was not so much the content of an act but its selection for transformation into law French, for only such acts formed the statute of the session and did not require special pleadings in the law courts. From 1490 the essential distinction was no longer the language but rather the appearance of acts in print" (p. 70).

The Law Library's holdings of early English statutes, abridgments, session laws, decisions, and treatises are recorded in a marked copy of Joseph Henry Beale's *Bibliography of Early English Law Books* (Cambridge: Harvard University Press, 1926). They include many editions of individual and collected statutes such as *Magna carta, Abbreviamentum statutorum* (London: John Lettou and William de Machlinia, ca. 1482), Rastell's *Statutes,* and Ferdinand Pulton's *An Abstract of All the Penall Statutes Which Be Generall, in Force and Use* . . . (London: Richard Tottell, 1577). Anthony Fitzherbert's *La Graunde Abridgement* and Littleton's *Tenures* are present in many early law French and English printings. Thomas Littleton's work on real property, *Tenores nouelli* (London: John Lettou and William de Machlinia, ca. 1482), was the earliest printed treatise on the English law. It had gone through over seventy editions by 1628, when Edward Coke's edition and commentary, *The*

First Part of the Institutes of the Lawes of England; Or, a Commentarie upon Littleton . . . (London, Printed for the Societie of Stationers, 1628), was published. Writs governing complaints brought into court were an essential part of legal procedure from the late thirteenth to the early eighteenth century. Printed treatises on this topic in the Law Library begin with the rare *Natura brevium* (London: Richard Pynson, ca. 1494). (See *Quarterly Journal of the Library of Congress* 12:189–90.)

The Law Library has a good collection of manuals or handbooks for justices of the peace, who exercised judicial and administrative duties in their counties. Their power grew during the fifteenth century as the English system of local government evolved and, because they rarely had legal training, manuals were needed for their guidance. *The Boke of Justices of Peas,* first printed in 1505 or 1506 by Richard Pynson and reprinted thirty-one times before 1580, and Anthony Fitzherbert's *Loffice et auctoryte des Justyces de peas* (1538) were the principal sixteenth-century texts, until the appearance of William Lambarde's *Eirenarcha,* first published in 1581 and substantially expanded in 1588 and 1592, and Richard Crompton's 1583 revision of Fitzherbert.

The most influential legal work of the seventeenth century, Michael Dalton's *The Countrey Justice,* first appeared in 1618 and was reprinted at least twenty times over the next one hundred years. Many later treatises plagiarized from this work and adopted its alphabetical arrangement of the section on administrative powers, which ranged from "alehouses" to "weights and measures." Dalton also wrote *The Office and Authoritie of Sherifs* of which the Law Library has his 1628 abridgment, a manual for the office responsible for the growth and stability of royal power through revenue, military, police, jails, courts, execution of writs, and other orders.

English manuals for justices of the peace, brought with the colonists or imported by them, were immediately adopted by the local officials who governed colonial America. Michael Dalton's *The Countrey Justice* was as popular in seventeenth-century America as it was in seventeenth-century England. The first manual printed in America was *Conductor Generalis; or The Office, Duty and Authority of Justices of the Peace* . . . (Philadelphia: Andrew Bradford, 1722), based on William Nelson's *The Office and Duty of a Justice of the Peace* (1704). Revised editions were published by Benjamin Franklin and David Hall in Philadelphia and James Parker in New York in 1749. Later editions in the north continued to abridge popular English manuals, but the

development of the genre was substantially different in the south, where the first native justice of the peace manual appeared. Much of the text in George Webb's *The Office and Authority of a Justice of Peace* (Williamsburg: William Parks, 1736) was taken from Dalton and Nelson, but each title was annotated to include references to Virginia statutes and material specifically relating to local concerns such as Indians, servants, slaves, and tobacco. Similar works were written by William Simpson in South Carolina (1761) and James Davis in North Carolina (1774). These editions were necessary because of the new responsibilities and increased independence acquired by southern justices in the eighteenth century. (See Larry M. Boyer, "The Justice of the Peace in England and America from 1506 to 1776: A Bibliographic History," *Quarterly Journal of the Library of Congress* 34:315–26.)

Legal literature of great interest to social and political historians is contained in the American and English Trials Collection. The confessions of individuals and accounts of trial proceedings cover murder and commercial and political crimes, some involving royalty and state officials such as Charles I, Queen Caroline, or assassinated American presidents. Among the British trials represented is that of John Lilburne, the leader of the Levellers. *The Trial of Mr. John Lilburn . . .* (London, 1653) was a landmark in English criminal law procedure because it established the right of an accused to obtain for examination a copy of the indictment against him. A group of late eighteenth-century pamphlets relate to prosecution of the Quakers in ecclesiastical and other courts for conscientious objection to payment of tithes and forced contributions to the maintenance of ministers of the Church of England.

Pamphlets and books reporting fugitive slave cases and other cases concerning slavery found in the Law Library's Trials Collection and elsewhere in the Library of Congress are recorded and summarized in Paul Finkelman's *Slavery in the Courtroom: An Annotated Bibliography of American Cases* (Washinton: Library of Congress, 1985). The Law Library's extensive collection of American criminal trial accounts is recorded in Thomas M. McDade's *Annals of Murder: A Bibliography of Books and Pamphlets on American Murders from Colonial Times to 1900* (Norman: University of Oklahoma Press, 1961). As McDade notes, these materials are part of legal, social, political, economic, and local history, although "The publication of a murder trial was more indicative . . . of the development of printing in the community than of the prevalence of homicide" (p. xviii). The crimes range from famous

ones like those of Lizzie Borden or the Molly Maguires, assassinations, the military massacre in Boston in 1770, and the Haymarket case of 1886 to obscure episodes of individual or collective personal violence, mutiny, piracy, and race riots.

By the middle of the eighteenth century, English common law had developed into a mass of precedents which had neither been formalized into basic principles nor expressed comprehensively and comprehensibly to laymen and lawyers. All of these tasks were accomplished by William Blackstone, whose influence has been compared to that of Justinian on Roman law. (See Walter H. Zeydel, "Sir William Blackstone and His *Commentaries,*" *Quarterly Journal of the Library of Congress* 23:302–12.)

Blackstone's *Commentaries on the Laws of England* was the first legal treatise to present the principles, precedents, and decisions that constituted English common law in a logical arrangement and clear language. This first attempt to teach law systematically grew out of a series of lectures given at All Souls College, Oxford. At the inaugural lecture Blackstone stated that it was the responsibility of every English gentleman to acquire a knowledge of "the guardian of his natural rights and the rule of his civil conduct." The first edition of the *Commentaries* (Oxford, 1765–69) was published by the Clarendon Press, where Blackstone had once served as delegate and taken an active interest in the mechanics of printing and the deficiencies of printing presses and current business methods.

The immediate success and far-reaching influence of the *Commentaries* are apparent in the piracies, reprintings, and translations recorded in Catherine Spicer Eller, *The William Blackstone Collection in the Yale Law Library: A Bibliographical Catalogue* ([New Haven]: Yale University Press, 1938). The Law Library has 37 of 45 English and Irish editions published between 1765 and 1876, including three sets of the first edition, over half of 55 listed American editions, 20 American editions Eller does not describe, and 2 copies of the first American edition (Philadelphia: Robert Bell, 1771–72). Over 1,500 copies of this edition were subscribed. Among those named in the list of subscribers are booksellers like James Rivington, who ordered 200 copies; colonial governors of Virginia, New Jersey, and the Bahamas; sixteen signers of the Declaration; and many nonlawyers. The Law Library has an eight-page prospectus for this edition, *A Specimen of the Type and Paper, with Conditions Annexed, for Re-printing by Subscription, an American Edition of Commentaries on the Laws of England,* as well as the *Proposals for Publishing an*

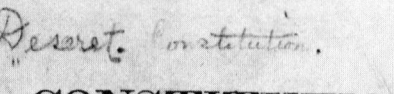

Deseret Constitution.

CONSTITUTION

OF THE

STATE OF DESERET,

WITH THE

JOURNAL

OF THE CONVENTION WHICH FORMED IT,

AND THE

PROCEEDINGS OF THE LEGISLATURE CONSEQUENT

THEREON.

KANESVILLE,

PUBLISHED BY ORSON HYDE,

1849.

"Deseret," or "land of the honey bee," was the name given to the provisional state formed by the Mormons in 1849. One year after the printing of this Constitution of the State of Deseret (Kanesville [Council Bluffs]: Orson Hyde, 1849), Congress contracted the State of Deseret to the confines of the present states of Utah and Nevada, organized it as the Territory of Utah, and appointed Brigham Young as the first territorial governor. American-British Law Division, Law Library.

American Edition of Blackstone's Commentaries . . . by St. George Tucker (Philadelphia: W.Y. Birch and A. Small, [1797?]) for the edition published in 1803 that came to be known as the "American Blackstone."

Until the late eighteenth century, most law books in American lawyers' and gentlemen's libraries were imported manuals of practice, form books, case reports, and statutory compilations. Herbert Alan Johnson, in *Imported Eighteenth-Century Law Treatises in American Libraries, 1700–1799* (Knoxville: University of Tennessee Press, 1978) observed that treatises were added after these utilitarian holdings had been acquired. The legal titles in Thomas Jefferson's library (one-quarter of the total) include classic common law commentaries, treatises, abridgments, digests, and English and colonial statutes. The widespread assumption that America relied on England for legal works well into the nineteenth century remains to be tested against surviving titles.

Early American statutory materials in the Law Library comprise comprehensive holdings of colonial, state, territorial, and U.S. session laws, codes and compilations, all but one of the editions of session laws of both the Provisional and Confederate governments, laws of American Indian tribes in English and the Indian vernacular, and congressional publications. Among the earliest colonial imprints in the Library of Congress for each state are legal titles printed by William Parks in Virginia and William Bradford in Pennsylvania, New York, and New Jersey. (See Roger J. Trienens, *Pioneer Imprints from Fifty States* [Washington: Library of Congress, 1973].) Territorial material includes the *Constitution of the State of Deseret* (Kanesville [Council Bluffs]: Orson Hyde, 1849) given to a convention of Mormons for the territory out of which Utah was carved. Codes were enacted immediately in mining districts to create a lawful government. *Laws and Regulations of the Miners of the Gregory Diggings District* . . . (Denver, 1859), a broadside, one of two recorded copies of which is in the collections, was the first non-newspaper printed in Colorado. (See Peter C. Schanck, "Of Gregory, Gold, and Greeley," *Quarterly Journal of the Library of Congress* 26:226–33). *The Pah-Ranagat Lake Silver Mining District of Southeastern Nevada* (New York, 1866) contains the mining code and descriptions of the location, terrain, and accessibility of the mine. These illustrate how an orderly government was created where none had existed and how printing was used to establish the law of the land.

The growth of a distinctly American body of law and legal precedent was made possible by a 1785 Connecticut statute requiring judges of the state superior and supreme courts to file written reports. Within the next five years, regular printed law reports began to be issued by the states, in 1798 by the Supreme Court, and in 1817 by Congress. Original American legal text-books and treatises developed from a similar need to create a native body of law distinct from English law. In the first decade of the nineteenth century, several specialized areas were covered in texts, including forms and pleadings in court cases.

The appearance of James Kent's four-volume *Commentaries on American Law* (New York: O. Halsted, 1826–30) began a period of great growth in original American treatises and paralleled the significance of Blackstone in England, although Kent did not model his work on Blackstone. Based on lectures delivered at Columbia College, the *Commentaries* covered the American common law in six parts devoted to the law of nations, U.S. government and jurisprudence, the sources of municipal law, the rights of persons, personal property, and real property. Over the remainder of the nineteenth century, American treatises grew in number and authority. Many covered new areas of law that developed in response to social and economic change. These included works on the law of railways, telegraphs, taxation, electricity, contracts, and corporations.

Contemporary legal publishing is as specialized as the profession itself. Lawyers and law students rely on printed texts, treatises, digests, dictionaries, codes, and reporters. The Law Library's collection exemplifies the relationships among law, society, and printed books as it serves practicing lawyers, legislators, legal scholars, and historians of society and culture.

REFERENCES

The Law Library of the Library of Congress: Its History, Collections, and Services. Ed. and comp. by Kimberly W. Dobbs and Kathryn A. Haun. Washington: Library of Congress, 1978.

Library of Congress. *The Canon Law Collection of the Library of Congress: A General Bibliography with Selective Annotations.* Comp. by Dario C. Ferreira-Ibarra. Washington: Library of Congress, 1981.

United States. Library of Congress. European Law Division. *The Coutumes of France in the Library of Congress: An Annotated Bibliography.* By Jean Caswell and Ivan Sipkov, with the editorial assistance of Natalie Gawdiak. Washington: Library of Congress, 1977.

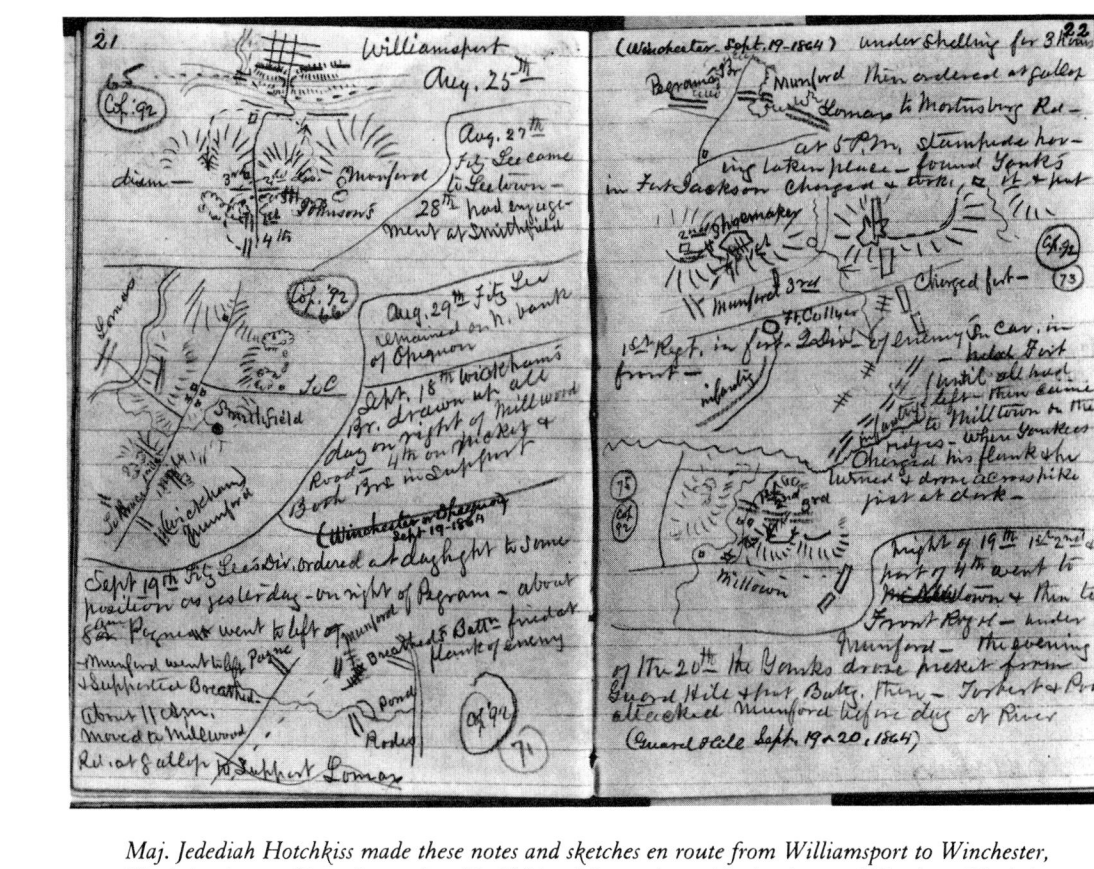

Maj. Jedediah Hotchkiss made these notes and sketches en route from Williamsport to Winchester, Virginia, August 25 to September 19, 1864, while serving with the Army of Northern Virginia. Many of the Civil War maps first drawn by Hotchkiss from horseback in his field notebooks were later published in the Atlas to Accompany the Official Records of the Union and Confederate Armies, 1861-1865 (Washington: U.S. Government Printing Office, 1891–95). The maps were printed by Julius Bien, who was the major printer and publisher of geographical and geological reports and maps for the federal government in the late nineteenth century, though he is better known today for his chromolithographic edition of Audubon's Birds of America. Jedediah Hotchkiss Collection, Geography and Map Division.

5 □ Geography and Map Division

Traditional map research focuses on the information carried by maps and the light they shed on the state of geographical knowledge, military strategy, urban development, and genealogical inquiry. In the last decade increasing attention has been paid to maps as physical objects and as products of a unique production network. Two distinct areas of cartobibliographic research have emerged: map printing processes, which are part of developments in other graphic arts, and the roles of mapmaker-cartographer and printer, which parallel author-printer-publisher relationships. The need for research in these areas was articulated in a group of essays edited by David Woodward in *Five Centuries of Map Printing* (Chicago: University of Chicago Press, 1973), based on a series of lectures in the history of cartography at the Newberry Library. The Geography and Map Division provides scholars with the resources to explore these and many other lines of inquiry in the fields of map printing, publishing, distribution, and influence.

The special requirements of map printing include the need to accommodate lettering on the image, large plates, tone and color, fineness of line, and frequent revision. Woodcut dominated map printing, especially in northern Europe, until it was superseded by copperplate engraving by the middle of the sixteenth century. Lithography, transfer and color lithography, and photographic reproduction each in turn revolutionized map production: with each new printing technology, the cartographer achieved increasing autonomy from the map printer.

Maps, charts, and atlases have been included in the collections of the Library of Congress since 1800. A separate hall of Maps and Charts was created in 1897 to house the collection of 47,000 maps and 1,200 atlases. The holdings grew rapidly through copyright deposit, gift, purchase, and transfer from other federal agencies. The Geography and Map Division now holds some 3.7 million maps and charts, of which over 2 million are set or series maps; 44,000 atlases; 8,000 reference works; over 300 globes; 2,000 three-dimensional plastic relief models; and materials in other formats. It is the largest and most comprehensive cartographic collection in the world, spanning all dates, all geographic areas, and all subjects.

The Geography and Map Division has a long tradition of encouraging cartographic scholarship. The Bibliography of Cartography, maintained since 1878, is a comprehensive analytical index to the literature of maps, mapmaking, and mapmakers. In 1973, 92,000 cards, representing entries through 1971, were reproduced in five volumes by G.K. Hall. A two-volume, 22,000-entry supplement, published in 1980, provides a thesaurus of special headings and a list of regularly analyzed publications. Approximately 3,000 cards are added to the Bibliography of Cartography each year.

Bibliographies and publications based on the collections, many of which are now standard references, appeared from the beginning of the twentieth century. Philip Lee Phillips, the first chief of the division and an active force behind its organization, compiled a *List of Maps of America in the Library of Congress,* published in 1901. This high level of scholarship and publications activity has been maintained by the division, where reference librarians provide access to over 1 million uncataloged maps acquired before 1969 and filed by area in a "title collection," organized by geographical area and by date. The historian of books is especially well served by the special collections and specialized catalogs in the division, which organize groups of maps and atlases into cohesive and accessible units.

❏   EARLY ATLASES

The atlas as a book form and as an influence in society were the themes of an international symposium, "Images of the World: The Atlas through History," jointly sponsored by the Center for the Book and the Geography and Map Division in October 1984, papers from which will be published. The

conference called attention to the outstanding atlas collection, which is enriched by the atlases in the Rare Book and Special Collections Divison, particularly in the Rosenwald and Thacher collections. The card catalog of the atlas collection provides access to cataloged holdings by cartographer, title, and engraver or lithographer. Over 18,435 atlases are described in great detail, with tables of contents provided for many, in *A List of Geographical Atlases in the Library of Congress with Bibliographical Notes,* compiled by Philip Lee Phillips. Four volumes were published between 1909 and 1920; four supplementary volumes compiled by Clara Le Gear were published from 1958 to 1974; and a ninth volume, a combined author list compiled by Clara Le Gear, is in press.

Several groups of fifteenth- and sixteenth-century atlases suggest the nature of potential research. There are 45 printed editions, in 93 copies, of Ptolemy's *Geography,* including 3 copies of the Rome, 1478 edition. (The first edition, Bologna, 1477, is lacking.) The printer of the 1478 edition, Arnold Buckinck of Cologne, explains in the dedicatory letter that his partner Conrad Sweynheym of Mainz had begun to prepare plates for this Rome edition as early as 1474. Thus although the Bologna printers succeeded in completing their edition first, the 1478 edition probably contains the earliest maps to be engraved on copper. The text was stamped on the plates. In the Florence, 1480? edition (Phillips 352), text as well as image was engraved. The Library has five copies of the Ulm, 1482 edition (Phillips 353 and Rosenwald 88), the first with woodcut maps and the first in which the design and execution of the maps are assigned to a known cartographer. Sixteenth-century editions of Ptolemy represent a period of experimentation in the printing of illustrations. In the Venice, 1511 edition (Phillips 358) the text is printed in black and red from type fitted into the block, and the woodcuts are printed on both sides of the sheet except in the new map of the world. The map of Lorraine in the Strasbourg, 1513 edition is the earliest example of printing in three colors. The Ptolemy holdings in the division have not yet been systematically studied. The bibliographic and graphic variants within each edition and between editions reveal the progress of science and the course of discovery in this period, in which Ptolemaic geography and cartography based upon it were of immense influence.

The concept of publishing a bound set of maps engraved according to a common format and issued with a title page and table of contents is usually attributed to Abraham Ortelius, a promoter and distributor of maps who was

trained in Antwerp as a map colorist. He spent ten years gathering maps of several European countries printed on separate sheets. The result, *Theatrum orbis terrarum,* published in 1570, was a great success. The Library also has four impressions of the second edition, published that same year. Forty editions of Ortelius's atlas were published by 1612. The text of the Library of Congress's copy of the 1579 edition (Phillips 386), the first printed by Christopher Plantin, contains many manuscript notes that were incorporated into later editions.

Christopher Saxton's *Atlas* of English counties (1579) was based on original surveys that introduced new standards of accuracy. In addition to their historical, geographic, and cartographic importance, Saxton's maps, by various engravers, are of great artistic and decorative significance. There are four copies of the atlas in the Library: two in the Geography and Map Division (Phillips 2913 and 8109) and two in the Rosenwald Collection (Phillips 8107 and 8108 and Rosenwald 1248), of which one is the only known copy on vellum and has the earliest impression of the frontispiece portrait of Queen Elizabeth engraved by Remigius Hogenberg.

Unlike Ortelius, who acted as a publisher and distributor, Gerardus Mercator was a geographer and cartographer whose teaching and writing contributed substantially to the geographical knowledge of his day. The 1595 edition of his *Atlas sive Cosmographicae meditationes de fabrica mundi et fabricati figura* (Phillips 5918), published one year after his death, used the term *atlas* for the first time. The first part of the *Atlas* had appeared in 1585, the second part in 1589; the Library has each of these parts, as well as the complete editions of 1595 and 1602 and a representative number of later editions.

Examples from the mid-sixteenth century illustrate the change from woodcut to engraving for map printing and the concurrent shift in cartographic leadership from south and central Europe to the Low Countries, where the "Golden Age" of Netherlands cartography coincided with the greatest period of Dutch painting. The seventeenth century was not a time of innovation in cartographic technique, but the consistent level of technical excellence has won it deserved recognition, as the work of the Blaeus and other seventeenth-century publishers represented in the division's holdings reveals. By the end of the seventeenth century, the "reformation" of cartography had brought an era of scientific measurement. In the work of eighteenth-century map publishers such as Jaillot, De Lisle, and the two Robert de

A hand-colored, engraved frontispiece portrait of Queen Elizabeth I by Remigius Hogenberg, from Christopher Saxton's Atlas of English counties *(1579), an early national survey that introduced new standards of accuracy in mapping. Atlas Collection, Geography and Map Division.*

Double-page plate from Vincenzo Coronelli's Libro de' globi *(In Venetia: Gli Argonauti, 1693 [i.e., not before 1697]). The plate depicts one of a pair of manuscript globes constructed by Coronelli, a Venetian globemaker, for Louis XIV of France. These great globes, each fifteen feet in diameter, were presented to the king in 1683. In Libro de' globi, Coronelli brought together a record of all the globes he had made. Geography and Map Division.*

Vaugondys, it is possible to study the transition from speculative cartography to exact observation and from decorative to utilitarian mapmaking: for example, unexplored regions are no longer filled up with Indians and wild animals but are left blank. This decline in artistic embellishment marks the beginning of modern cartography.

In the period during which copperplate engraving dominated map production, certain practices were common, including the reuse of plates over extremely long periods of time and the use of the same plates by several publishers. Publishers revised plates, recut the incised lines, cut plates up, masked them, and added new ones. Consequently, detailed bibliographical analysis of printed maps will increase our understanding of the structure of the map trade and how it was related to the book and other graphic arts trades. Evidence from watermarks and offset, for example, reveals simultaneous printing of maps and prints in sixteenth-century Italian engraving shops; and maps of mixed geographical origins in composite atlases suggest migration of plates or prints.

The early atlas collection is supplemented by thousands of separate maps, filed by area in the division's map collection, which provide a survey of changes in cartography and map printing for particular geographical areas. The first topographic survey of an entire country was begun in 1669 by Giovanni Domenico Cassini and was completed over one hundred years— and four generations of Cassini family—later. The Geography and Map Division holdings are particularly strong in official cadastral surveys and topographic set and series maps and charts that provide international coverage of the development of geographic knowledge and cartographic technique.

❏   EARLY AMERICAN CARTOGRAPHY

The collections of the Geography and Map Division are rich in maps of outstanding historical significance relating to the period of American discovery and exploration. Most of these are in manuscript or facsimile form, such as the Johann Georg Kohl Collection, maps received from Henry Harrisse, and the study collection formed by Woodbury Lowery of maps relating to former Spanish possessions within the United States. Several important

printed maps of the colonial period present opportunities for bibliographical analysis. The Library has five of the ten variants of John Smith's map of Virginia issued between the first printing of 1612 and 1632, and one of five known copies of Augustine Herrman's map of Virginia and Maryland, printed in 1673. Also in the collection are nineteen of twenty-one impressions of John Mitchell's *Map of the British and French Dominions in North America* (1755), used in negotiations at Paris. These include seven English, two Dutch, ten French, and two Italian pirated versions. The division has a nearly unbroken sequence of the issues of Lewis Evans's *General Map of the Middle British Colonies in America* (1755) and several editions of the accompanying *Analysis,* printed in Philadelphia by Benjamin Franklin. Each of these maps was copied and adapted by subsequent mapmakers. The Library's comprehensive holdings make it possible to analyze the complex bibliographical relationships among them.

Manuscript and printed maps relating to the French and Indian War and the American Revolution were among the earliest purchases of the Library of Congress. The Faden Collection of 101 maps and plans, more than half in manuscript, was acquired from E. E. Hale in 1864. Faden, geographer to King George III and a leading British map publisher of the late eighteenth century, worked for Thomas Jefferys, the publisher of an atlas of America used by both sides in the Revolution, and succeeded to Jefferys's business. The maps in the Faden Collection, acquired by him in the course of "his duty of engraving for the English government," and the Peter Force collection, purchased three years later, provide remarkable insights into the mapmaking and publishing practices of Faden and his contemporaries.

Multiple copies and variant editions of many items in the Faden and Force collections invite the historical cartographer to compare multiple editions, states, and impressions, to examine different cartographic styles, and to follow a map from manuscript to printed versions and foreign derivatives. A manuscript map of the Battle of Brandywine (Sellers and van Ee, *Maps and Charts,* 1336; Force 234) served as the printer's copy for Faden's 1778 edition (Sellers and van Ee, *Maps and Charts,* 1337) and bears extensive annotations in his hand. A printed copy of the second state of this edition (Sellers and van Ee, *Maps and Charts,* 1338) was the printer's copy for another, probably unpublished, edition. Large sections of the map have been cut out, new pieces in manuscript pasted in, the imprint changed, and the word "Rebels" crossed out and replaced by "Americans" in several places.

Such sequences exist for several important eighteenth-century maps of

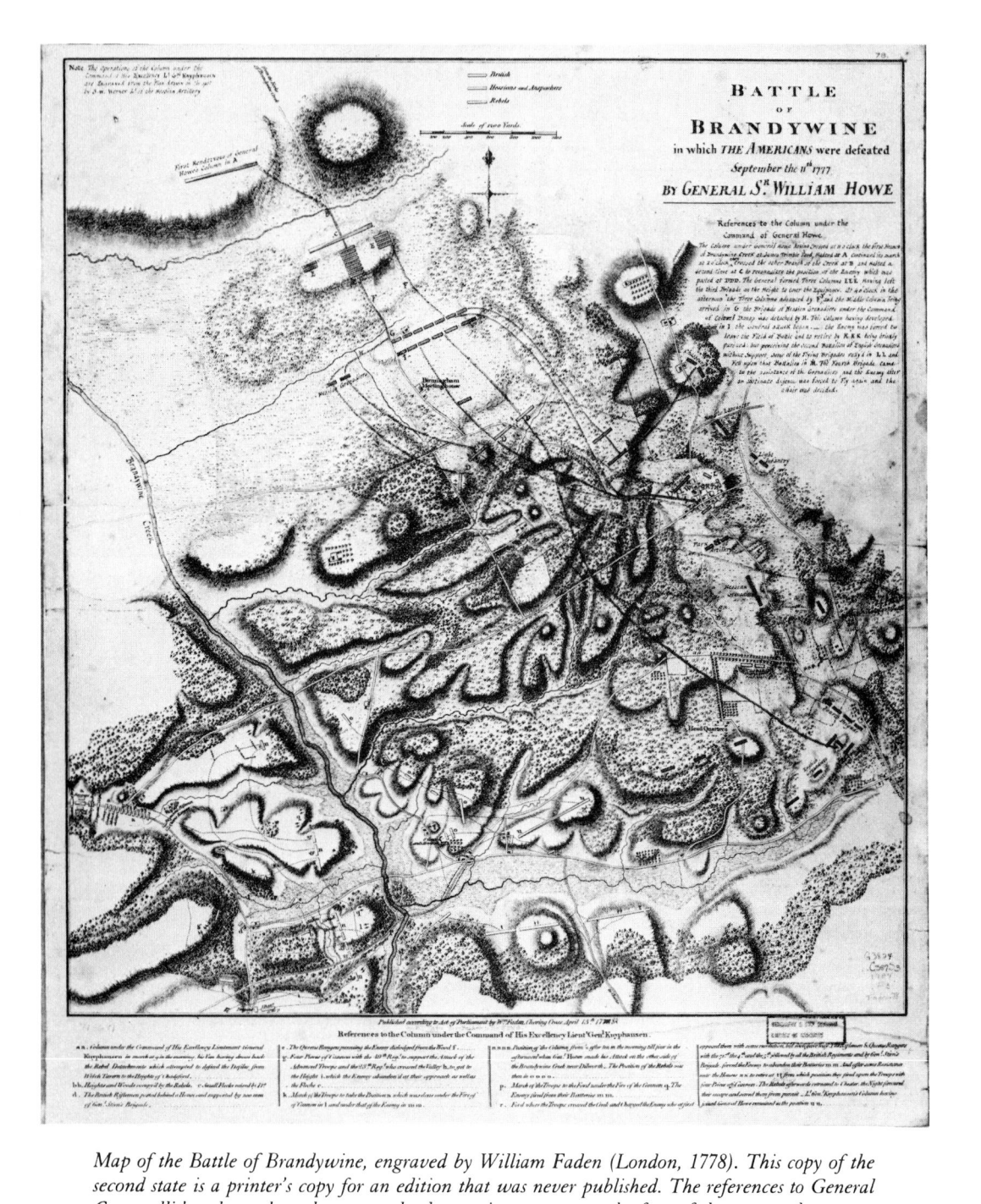

Map of the Battle of Brandywine, engraved by William Faden (London, 1778). This copy of the second state is a printer's copy for an edition that was never published. The references to General Cornwallis's column have been completely rewritten, some on the face of the map and some on attached pieces. The imprint has been altered, and the word "Rebels," which appeared four times in the references, has been crossed out and "Americans" written above. William Faden Collection, Geography and Map Division.

PROPOSALS FOR PUBLISHING

A

S U R V E Y

OF THE

R O A D S

OF THE

United States of America.

By CHRISTOPHER COLLES, of New-York.

C O N D I T I O N S.

1. THAT the work shall be neatly engraved upon copper, each page containing a delineation of near 12 miles of the road upon a scale of about one inch and three quarters to the mile, and parti-

2. That a set of general . . . . upon a small scale with references from . . . . to the par-ticular page where the description of any road is to be found; these maps will then answer as an index and will be found more convenient than any other index that can be made.

3. That each subscriber shall pay one quarter dollar at the time of subscribing (to defray several inci-dental charges necessary for the work) and one eighth of a dollar upon the delivery of every six pages of the work: but such gentlemen as are willing to advance one dollar will be considered as patrons of the work, and will not be entitled to pay any more till the value thereof is delivered in.

4. That subscribers shall pay 20 cents for each of the general maps and three cents for each sheet of letter press in the alphabetical lists or other necessary explanation of the drafts.

5. That each subscriber shall be considered as engaging to take 100 pages.

6. That non-subscribers shall pay three cents for each page of the work.

These surveys are made from actual mensuration, by a perambulator of a new and convenient construc-tion, invented by said Colles, and very different from any hitherto used, which determines the number of revolutions of the wheel of a carriage to which it is fixed, and is found by experiment to ascertain the distance to a much greater degree of accuracy than could be expected; the direction of the road is determined by a compass likewise affixed to the surveying carriage.

Account of the Advantages of these Surveys.

A traveller will here find so plain and circumstantial a description of the road, that whilst he has the draft with him it will be impossible for him to miss his way: he will have the satisfaction of knowing the names of many of the persons who reside on the road; if his horse should want a shoe, or his car-riage be broke, he will by the bare inspection of the draft be able to determine whether he must go backward or forward to a blacksmith's shop: Persons who have houses or plantations on the road may in case they want to let, lease, or sell the same, advertise in the public newspapers that the place is mark-ed in such a page of Colles's Survey of the roads; this will give so particular a description of its situation that no difficulty or doubt will remain about it. If a foreigner arrives in any part of the Continent and is under the necessity to travel by land, he applies to a bookseller, who with the assistance of the index map chooses out the particular pages which are necessary for his direction. It is expected many other en-tertaining and useful purposes will be discovered when these surveys come into general use.

. Subscription papers will be sent to most of the Booksellers on the continent.

Proposal for publishing by subscription Christopher Colles's Survey of the Roads of the United States of America *(New York, 1789). This set of maps by one of America's earliest engineers, published in parts, was one of the first private map-publishing ventures in this country. Geography and Map Division.*

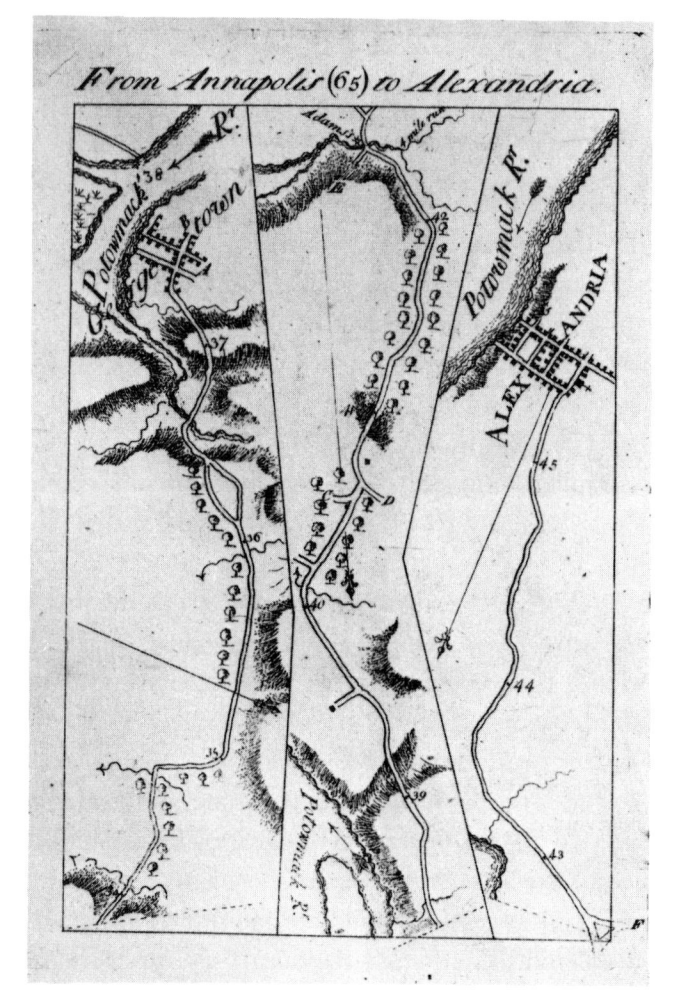

Map of the road between Annapolis, Maryland, and Alexandria, Virginia, from Christopher Colles, A Survey of the Roads of the United States of America (New York, 1789). Geography and Map Division.

British America, in addition to nineteen sets, comprising 1,369 plates, of *The American Neptune,* published by Joseph Frederick Wallet Des Barres for the use of the British Royal Navy between 1774 and 1784. Coastal charts before *The Atlantic Neptune,* such as *The English Pilot: The Fourth Book,* the most popular guide to navigation in North America throughout the eighteenth century, were rarely based on actual surveys. Des Barres, a British engineer and surveyor sent to America to assist in the war effort, had been trained in the latest surveying techniques. He returned to England in 1774 to edit and publish his findings. The navy was so desperate for accurate information that many of the charts were printed before they were finished. More than 100 were issued over the course of fourteen years and most exist in several states. The sets have been disbound and the charts filed by area, bringing together variants of each plate for comparative study.

Late eighteenth-century American materials in the Geography and Map

Division illustrate the relationship between cartography and the growth of the new nation. American cartography emerged during the Revolution to meet military needs. After the treaty of peace, the industry was stimulated by boundary questions, the construction of transportation routes, and westward expansion. Christopher Colles, an Irish immigrant who was one of America's earliest engineers, published the first American road guide. Based on his own surveying and mapping experiences during the Revolution and on those of George Washington's geographers and surveyors-general Robert Erskine and Simeon De Witt, Colles's *Survey of the Roads of the United States* (New York, 1789) was one of the first private map-publishing ventures in this country. The small maps, published by subscription and issued in parts, record roads between Albany, New York, and Yorktown, Virginia. Churches, houses, taverns, and blacksmith shops are among the buildings depicted. The project was an economic failure, like all of Colles's forward-looking ideas, and despite a warm endorsement from the postmaster general, Congress declined to supply funds to support it. The two copies in the Geography and Map Division (one from Peter Force and one from Thomas Jefferson) are among the most complete sets known of this historical record and cartographic innovation and were used to compile the facsimile edition edited by Walter W. Ristow (Cambridge, Mass.: Belknap Press of Harvard University Press, 1961).

Following the Revolution, states appointed surveyors such as William Blodget in Vermont, Simeon De Witt in New York, and Nicholas King in the City of Washington, whose official or quasi-official efforts were engraved and printed by commercial firms. This was a uniquely American situation; the enterprising individuals who responded to a need the states were financially unable to meet created a new profession, American commercial cartography. The techniques and procedures developed by these resourceful mapmakers and printers contributed significantly to the growth of nineteenth-century printing and graphic arts.

One of these commercial cartographers was John Melish, the first American publisher to specialize in geographic and cartographic works. He issued the first edition of *Map of the United States with the Contiguous British & Spanish Possessions* in 1816. Six revisions were dated 1816 and twenty-five variants have been identified dating from 1816 to 1823. The early editions were printed from six copperplates engraved by John Vallance and Henry Tanner. Henry Tanner, trained as an engraver along with his brother Benja-

min, expanded his cartographic activities to include compilation, engraving, printing, and publishing. His *New American Atlas* was first published in its complete form in 1823. The work and careers of Melish, Tanner, and their contemporaries—including Mathew Carey, Anthony Finley, and Fielding Lucas—may be studied in depth in the Geography and Map Division.

Maps were covered by the first federal copyright law, and the nucleus of the division's American holdings was formed by copyright deposit, which ensured the survival of many rare maps. Titles were submitted just as they were for books, and in some instances letterpress "title pages" were printed for maps that were to be engraved. The few extant title pages are separately maintained in the division. Several ghosts for maps that were never published have been identified, along with some copyright claimants whose role stood outside the printer-publisher relationship. The vast majority of the deposit holdings are from the mid-nineteenth century and later, although there are a few from the 1790s.

❑ NINETEENTH- AND TWENTIETH-CENTURY AMERICAN MAPS AND ATLASES

In the first four decades of the nineteenth century, surveying and mapping expanded dramatically as a result of historical and technological factors. Both altered the nature of the product, the relationship between the cartographer and the printer, and the distribution of maps and atlases to an ever-growing market. These trends may be studied in several groups of commercially produced maps in the Geography and Map Division that have been the subject of theme, area, or subject bibliographies and in the comprehensive holdings of set and series maps and charts issued by federal agencies.

The introduction of lithography into the United States in the mid-1820s coincided with a period of great activity in railroad construction that continued through the pre-Civil War decades. Lithography made it possible for the first time to print large runs of maps at a low unit cost. Later in the century, improved color printing, high-speed power presses, and photography were applied to map printing.

The 5,000 railroad maps in the Geography and Map Division serve as a model of the rapid application of technical improvements to commercial cartography. The earliest railroad map in the collection, James Hayward's

Plan of a Survey for . . . Boston, 1828, was one of the first products of the Smith and Arnim firm, which established in that year the Senefelder Lithographic Company of Boston, taken over in 1830 by William and John Pendleton. Lithographic procedures were firmly established by this time, but railroad maps reveal that earlier techniques continued in use and were combined with lithography, especially before the transfer technique came into wide use in the 1840s. Zincography, which was adaptable to the rotary steam press introduced by P. S. Duval in Philadelphia, was first used by him in 1849. Color printing was used by the 1850s to indicate networks, regions, and administrative divisions. Over 30 percent of the railroad maps in the division were produced by the firm of J. H. Colton, established in 1831. Other important firms represented in this collection include Julius Bien, Duval, James T. Lloyd, and the Pendletons.

During the Civil War, surveyors and cartographers were diverted to official mapping for military purposes. Maps in the Jedediah Hotchkiss Collection demonstrate Civil War mapmaking techniques. Major Hotchkiss, a topographical engineer who served with the Army of Northern Virginia, was a brilliant draftsman. He made detailed battle maps used by Generals Lee and Jackson, and he filled field notebooks with finished drawings of maps he had first sketched on horseback. After the war, over 120 of these maps were supplied to the editors of the *Atlas to Accompany the Official Records of the Union and Confederate Armies, 1861–1865* (Washington: Government Printing Office, 1891–95), issued in thirty-seven parts printed in color by Julius Bien. For some maps it is possible to compare the on-the-spot sketch, finished drawing, and printed version.

In the postwar decades, commercial map production accelerated, along with rapid urban development. The Library's large collection of approximately 1,500 land ownership maps illustrates how lithography enabled the surveyor to compile data without regard to limitations imposed by the engraving process. Most maps are so large they were lithographed in four parts and mounted on one piece of cloth five- to six-feet square. They were popular wall decorations in mid-nineteenth-century America. By the mid-1860s, multisheet atlases had begun to replace hand-colored and varnished wall maps.

By this time, too, private map publishers were no longer able to meet the land survey demands of a rapidly growing country. Federal involvement in mapping had begun with the Rectangular Land Survey under Thomas Hutchins in 1785. At the very beginning of the nineteenth century, Thomas

Jefferson and other supporters of federal expansion authorized maps of newly acquired lands west of the Mississippi. Nicholas King, an English cartographer who was surveyor of the City of Washington, compiled maps before and during the Lewis and Clark expedition that were the first official geographical record of the trans-Mississippi West. By the 1840s, maps were produced in sets or series based on systematic mapping programs, and in 1879 the U.S. Geological Survey was established to coordinate geographical and geological efforts. Coastal charting followed a similar course. The first navigational charts were published by commercial firms in the first decade of the nineteenth century, and Jefferson established the Coast Survey in 1807. The first American nautical chart, a lithograph of New York Bay, appeared in 1839. The first copperplate chart, of New York Harbor and vicinity, was printed on six plates in 1844. By 1900 the U.S. Coast and Geodetic Survey was well established.

These official products form an essential part of the history of map printing in the United States from the nineteenth century to the present, which may be constructed from the division's exhaustive holdings. The fifty-four plates in the first *Statistical Atlas of the United States Based on the Result of the Ninth Census,* compiled by Francis Amasa Walker and published in 1874, were printed in color by Julius Bien. Bien was the major printer and publisher of geographical and geological reports and maps for the federal government until his death in 1909. He contributed as much to the development of scientific cartography as he did to the lithographic trade. No bibliography of Bien's vast map output exists, but the Geography and Map Division holdings provide a solid basis for such a project. Copperplate engraving persisted in government map printing long after it had been superseded by lithography for commercial work. The Coast Survey imported chart paper, copperplates, and master engravers from Europe during the mid-century. Among the draftsmen trained at the Coast Survey was James McNeill Whistler. The finely engraved and elegant maps and charts issued by the federal government during the nineteenth century stand in sharp contrast to their commercial contemporaries. The resources in the Geography and Map Division for comparative work in this area are unparalleled.

One branch of commercial cartography that flourished well into the twentieth century was the fire insurance map, originally prepared for fire insurance companies and underwriters. The Geography and Map Division has custody of the largest collection of fire insurance maps in the United

States, including more than 700,000 separate sheets covering some 12,000 towns and cities issued by the Sanborn Map Company beginning in 1867. These maps, which constitute a superb record of urban areas for geographers, historians, urban planners, and architects, form a cartographic archive spanning a period of over one hundred years and illustrating many technical improvements in mapmaking.

The late-Victorian panorama map was closely tied to developments in chromolithography. These colorful bird's-eye views of urban and industrial areas in post-Civil War America were popular wall hangings, usually drawn (with painstaking care) and published by the same person. Cities were portrayed as if viewed from above at an oblique angle. Street patterns, individual buildings, and landscape features were depicted in perspective, although not to scale. The Geography and Map Division has a large and representative collection that includes 224 of 301 panoramas drawn and published by Thaddeus Mortimer Fowler, one of the most prolific panoramic map producers. Fowler said of his career: "I was on the Road as Publisher and Canvasser ever since the [Civil] War." Albert Ruger issued many panoramas under the Ruger or Ruger & Stoner imprint; 198 of these are in the collections, along with works by Lucien Burleigh, Henry Wellge, and Oakley Bailey.

A nineteenth-century development of great interest to printing historians was cerography, or wax-engraving, which did not significantly affect mapmaking until more than thirty years after it was invented. Sidney Edwards Morse, the son of geographer Jedidiah Morse and brother of inventor Samuel F. B. Morse, announced the new engraving process in the *New-York Observer* of 1839 and named it cerography. In *The Cerographic Atlas,* issued as a supplement to the *New-York Observer* (1842), Morse explained that several years and much money had gone into developing "a new method of engraving, which should combine, in a good degree, the peculiar advantages of each of the old methods, viz. *the facility in preparing the plate for the press* of Lithography; *the clear, fine, flowing line* of Copperplate Engraving; and the *durability under the Press, and rapidity in the printing,* of Wood Engraving." He provided cost figures to illustrate "the value of Cerography in furnishing the Community with *cheap* maps" and concluded by assuring his audience that the present specimens did not reveal the finest work that could be produced from cerographic plates. Examples of Morse's work in the Geography and Map Division enable the printing historian to study what David Woodward has called the "experimental period" of this process.

Wax-engraving was developed in response to the need for a map-printing process that began with a material soft enough to engrave and produced a relief printing plate strong enough for use in a power steam press. The invention of electrotyping made the manufacture of such a plate possible and beginning in 1850 type was set directly into the plate. Morse did not patent his process until 1848, and it was apparently a secret trade for another two decades. Rand McNally began to issue atlases reproduced by cerography in 1872. Between 1870 and 1930, wax-engraving was the technique by which the vast majority of American commercial maps and atlases were produced. Cerographic specimens in the Geography and Map Division reveal that the product lost in fineness and clarity what it gained in economy, and in the period between 1930 and 1950, it was gradually replaced by other techniques. With the application of photo-offset lithography, maps could be compiled photomechanically, plates produced photochemically, and huge editions printed on rotary presses at great speed. Future developments in printing technology will continue to make map production increasingly efficient. These are the final stages in a five-hundred-year effort to find a reproductive graphic process to meet the special requirements of map printing.

Several acquisitions in the past decade reflect the commitment of the Geography and Map Division to resources that document the relationship between printing processes and cartographic products. These include approximately 10 copperplates used to print maps and charts published by the federal government from the mid-nineteenth to the early twentieth century. They show revisions over several decades and may be compared with the full run of printed copies of each set in the division's collections. Gores, or sections the shape of orange peels, are printed on flat surfaces and put together to form a globe. A set of gores for the 1688 edition of Vincenzo Coronelli's globe pieced together as a flat circle clarifies the engraving process. The division's copy of Coronelli's compilation *Libro dei globi* (Venice, 1693) documents the dissemination of his up-to-date geographical information and brilliant cartographic technique.

A remarkable recent acquisition is the engraved copperplate of a map showing the Province of San Diego in New Spain in 1682, signed Antonio Ysarti. The map appeared in Baltasar de Medina's *Chronica de la Santa Provincia de San Diego de Mexico . . .* (Mexico: Juan de Ribera, 1682; Rare Book and Special Collections Division), and it is considered the first signed and

The copperplate used to print a map showing the Province of San Diego in New Spain in 1682, signed by Antonio Ysarti. The plate has been revised for a new edition, of which no known copy survives. The map, which shows the ecclesiastical centers of New Spain, is considered the first signed and dated copper engraved map of the New World. It appeared in Baltasar de Medina's Chronica de la Santa Provincia de San Diego de Mexico *(Mexico: Juan de Ribero, 1682). Geography and Map Division.*

dated copper-engraved map of the New World. The plate has been revised for a new (apparently unpublished) edition of the map. On the verso is part of an engraved broadside commemorating the ordination or ascension of a priest. Such recycling testifies to the shortage of copper that resulted in most engraved plates being melted down for reuse. The imprint of the broadside is almost gone, but stylistic similarities between it and Ysarti's frontispiece for Medina's work invite research. This artifact suggests the interdependence of materials—and of craftsmen, too, perhaps—in the graphic arts and serves as a striking example of how the Library's collections complement and enhance one another.

Mapmaking has never taken place in a vacuum: new techniques have

facilitated incorporating lettering and color on the image, ease of revision, large plates and editions, and fineness of line. Research into the printing, publishing, and distribution of maps and atlases will establish strong links to the history of books, printing, and graphic arts as it takes account of the unique nature of mapmaking. Some studies are overlapping: the use of paper as evidence in dating or biographical and biobibliographical studies of printers and publishers, for instance. Others are more specialized: how and by whom the information in a map was compiled and how it was transmitted from compiler to printer, the life of a particular plate ("plate history" or "cartogenealogy"), and the development of graphic styles in mapmaking. Maps and atlases in the Geography and Map Division may be studied as physical objects, as products of a particular technological, economic, and intellectual network, and as forces of great cultural and historical influence. They are, in fact, an integral part of the study of the history of books.

Fragment of the copperplate used to print a broadside commemorating the ordination or ascension of a priest. The shortage of copper resulted in the frequent reuse of plates; this one was cut and the verso was used for Antonio Ysarti's 1682 map of San Diego in New Spain (opposite). We can estimate the full size of the broadside, no known copy of which is extant, from this surviving portion, which shows a young priest holding a complete copy of the broadside. Geography and Map Division.

REFERENCES

Colles, Christopher. *A Survey of the Roads of the United States of America, 1789.* Ed. Walter W. Ristow. Cambridge, Mass.: Belknap Press of Harvard University, 1961.

Hale, Edward Everett, comp. *Catalogue of a Curious and Valuable Collection of Original Maps and Plans of Military Positions Held in the Old French and Revolutionary Wars . . . .* Boston: [J. Wilson] 1862. (Catalog of the William Faden Collection.)

Library of Congress. Geography and Map Division. *Panoramic Maps of Cities in the United States and Canada: A Checklist of Maps in the Collections of the Library of Congress, Geography and Map Division.* Comp. by John R. Hebert. 2d ed., rev. by Patrick E. Dempsey. Washington: Library of Congress, 1984.

Lowery, Woodbury. *The Lowery Collection: A Descriptive List of Maps of the Spanish Possessions within the Present Limits of the United States, 1502–1820.* Ed., with notes by Philip Lee Phillips. Washington: Government Printing Office, 1912.

Melville, Annette. *Guide.* See United States. Library of Congress. *Special Collections in the Library of Congress: A Selective Guide.*

Modelski, Andrew W. *Railroad Maps of North America: The First Hundred Years.* Washington: Library of Congress, 1984.

Ristow, Walter W. "Aborted American Atlases." *Quarterly Journal of the Library of Congress* 36 (1979): 320–45.

————. *Maps for an Emerging Nation: Commercial Cartography in Nineteenth-Century America.* An Exhibition at the Library of Congress. Washington: Library of Congress, 1977.

————. "Theatrum Orbis Terrarum, 1570–1970." *Quarterly Journal of the Library of Congress* 27 (1970): 316–27.

————, comp. *A la Carte: Selected Papers on Maps and Atlases.* Washington: Library of Congress, 1972.

Sellers and van Ee. *Maps and Charts.* See United States. Library of Congress. *Maps and Charts of North America and the West Indies, 1750–1789.*

Stephenson, Richard W. "Maps from the Peter Force Collection." *Quarterly Journal of the Library of Congress* 30 (1973): 183–204.

United States. Library of Congress. *Maps and Charts of North America and the West Indies, 1750–1789: A Guide to the Collections in the Library of Congress.* Comp. by John R. Sellers and Patricia Molen van Ee. Washington: Library of Congress, 1981.

————. *Special Collections in the Library of Congress: A Selective Guide.* Comp. by Annette Melville. Washington: Library of Congress, 1980. See the list in the appendix, pp. 401–2.

United States. Library of Congress. Geography and Map Division. *The Bibliography of Cartography.* 5 vols.; Boston: G.K. Hall, 1973. Suppl., 2 vols., 1980.

————. *Civil War Maps: An Annotated List of Maps and Atlases in Map Collections of the Library of Congress.* Comp. by Richard W. Stephenson. Washington: Library of Congress, 1961.

————. *Fire Insurance Maps in the Library of Congress: Plans of North American Cities and Towns Produced by the Sanborn Map Company.* A checklist comp. by the Reference and Bibliography Section, Geography and Map Division; intro. by Walter W. Ristow. Washington: Library of Congress, 1981.

————. *Land Ownership Maps: A Checklist of Nineteenth Century United States County Maps in the Library of Congress.* Comp. by Richard W. Stephenson. Washington: Library of Congress, 1967.

————. *Library of Congress Acquisitions: Geography and Map Division.* Washington: Library of Congress, 1983–.

————. *Panoramic Maps of Anglo-American Cities: A Checklist of Maps in the Collections of the Library of Congress, Geography and Map Division.* Comp. by John R. Hébert. Washington: Library of Congress, 1974.

————. *Railroad Maps of the United States: A Selective Annotated Bibliography of Original 19th-Century Maps in the Geography and Map Division of the Library of Congress.* Comp. by Andrew M. Modelski. Washington: Library of Congress, 1975.

United States. Library of Congress. Map Divison. *The Hotchkiss Map Collection: A List of Manuscript Maps, Many of the Civil War Period, Prepared by Major Jed. Hotchkiss, and Other Manuscript and Annotated Maps in His Possession.* Comp. by Clara Le Gear, with a foreword by Willard Webb. Washington: Library of Congress, 1951.

————. *A List of Geographical Atlases in the Library of Congress, with Bibliographical Notes.* Vols. 1–4 comp. under the direction of Philip Lee Phillips; vols. 5–8, 9 (in press) comp. by Clara Le Gear. Washington: Library of Congress, 1909–.

————. *List of Maps of America in the Library of Congress.* Comp. by Philip Lee Phillips. Washington: Library of Congress, 1901.

————. *United States Atlases: A List of National, State, County, City, and Regional Atlases in the Library of Congress.* Comp. by Clara Le Gear. 2 vols. Washington: Library of Congress, 1950–53.

Woodward, David. *The All-American Map: Wax Engraving and Its Influence on Cartography.* Chicago: University of Chicago Press, 1977.

————. *Five Centuries of Map Printing.* Chicago: University of Chicago Press, 1973.

A vignette from the sheet music for "The Maid of the Rock," lithographed by Henry Stone in Washington, D.C., ca. 1823. Stone was one of the first lithographers in the United States. Henry Stone Collection, Music Division.

6 ▢ Music Division

The history of printed music reveals a continuous search for an economical and aesthetically satisfactory solution to the complex requirements of music printing. The pattern is not of successive but of concurrent processes, applied to different types and styles of music, in different contexts and for different purposes: sacred and secular music; monodic and polyphonic; serious and popular; and music for performance, theory, and instruction. Separate publishing and distribution practices developed for typographic and engraved music, the former with links to the book trade, the latter more closely allied to the development of graphic arts such as maps and prints. Music bibliography also requires a specialized approach: separately published or sheet music is typically undated, creating a need for reliance on external evidence such as paper, plate marks, publishers' catalogs, and the graphic characteristics of engraving tools to establish the date of publication. A vigorous oral musical tradition and the wide circulation of music in manuscript continued to flourish after the invention of printing. These aspects of musical culture as well as the growth of public performance, first in concert and then in broadcast and recorded form, affect what we mean by the term *published music*.

As in other areas of book history, research in the field of music printing and publishing depends on diverse examples and multiple copies to trace and analyze trends. During the years between the purchase of Thomas Jefferson's library in 1815—the source of the first volumes of music and music literature

acquired by the Library of Congress—and the opening of the Thomas Jefferson Building in 1897, close to 200,000 musical compositions were received. A separate division was created that year, and from the start the broadest and most comprehensive geographical and chronological scope was envisioned. In his annual report for 1898, Librarian of Congress John Russell Young wrote: "Music in its best sense is a science belonging to all ages, as well as to all nationalities and conditions of men, and the Library of Congress should contain its earliest as well as its latest and most complete expression . . . a complete embodiment of the history as well as of the science of music." Four years later Oscar George Theodore Sonneck was appointed chief of the Music Division and began a determined and successful effort to develop a research collection of international prominence.

The collections of the Music Division now number approximately 8 million pieces of music, 300,000 books and pamphlets, and 500,000 nonmusic manuscripts, photographs, and scrapbooks. Manuscript sources include autograph scores and letters by master composers and musicians such as Bach, Beethoven, Berg, Brahms, Britten, Haydn, Koussevitzky, Liszt, Mendelssohn, Mozart, Rachmaninoff, Schoenberg, and Stravinsky. The superb American manuscripts range from the autograph music book of Francis Hopkinson, a signer of the Declaration of Independence who is considered the first native-born American composer, to extensive holdings of works by Samuel Barber, Amy Cheney Beach, Leonard Bernstein, Elliott Carter, Aaron Copland, Vernon Duke, George Gershwin, Victor Herbert, Ulysses Kay, Edward A. MacDowell, Sigmund Romberg, Ruth Crawford Seeger, John Philip Sousa, Deems Taylor, and Harry von Tilzer. Gifts from several foundations continue to enrich these collections. The Elizabeth Sprague Coolidge Foundation, the Heineman Foundation, the Serge Koussevitzky Music Foundation, and the Gertrude Clarke Whittall Foundation provide funds for acquisitions, performances, and commissioning new works. Copyright deposits account for the largest source by far of past and present acquisitions in the Music Division, but material is also received through purchase, gift, exchange, and transfer.

Material in the Music Division is organized according to a system devised by Sonneck, which separates Music (M), Music Literature (ML), and Music Theory (MT). A classed catalog provides subject access to the cataloged musical compositions. Material in the vast numbers of uncataloged "M" items, largely twentieth-century copyright deposits, is classified by genre or performance medium and alphabetized by composer. For some time periods the

arrangement is by copyright registration number. The organization and con-
tents of the American holdings are clearly set forth in the entry for the
Library of Congress in *Resources of American Music History,* edited by Donald
Krummel et al. (Urbana: University of Illinois Press, 1981).

❏　　EARLY MUSIC PRINTING

The printing of music presents complex problems for the typefounder, compositor, and printer. Music printing requires an exact correlation of staves,
notes, and text in vertical alignment, the representation of changes in time
and intervals in pitch by spacing or other means, and the printing of two or
more notes on two or more staves at once. The printed music in fifteenth-
century books in both the Music Division and the Rare Book and Special
Collections Division reveals a range of innovative if imperfect solutions to
these technical difficulties. Printing from movable type preceded the use of
woodblocks. In the earliest book known to contain printed music, Johannes
Gerson, *Collectorium,* 1473 (Music Division, Goff G-199), the notes were
stamped or printed with inverted capitals and the lines or staves filled in by
hand. In the first printed example of secular music and mensural notation,
Franciscus Niger's *Grammatica,* Venice, 1480 (Music Division and Rare Book
and Special Collections Division, Goff N-226), the notes were printed from
metal type and the lines filled in by hand. The first printing of music from
woodblock appeared the same year, in the earliest book dealing entirely with
music, also the first book printed in Naples to include woodblocks:
Franchino Gaffurio's *Theorica musicae* (general rare book collection and
Lessing J. Rosenwald Collection, Rare Book and Special Collections Division, Goff G-5). In the Basel, Wenssler, 1485 edition of Niger (Rare Book and
Special Collections Division, Goff N-227), each row is cut on a single woodblock. Such combinations and experiments reflect the pattern that developed
during the incunabula period. Of the approximately 250 fifteenth-century
liturgical books with monodic music, most were printed from movable type
in two impressions, the stave lines in red and the notes in black. Books of
theory or instruction, of which only about 20 are known, used wood (or
sometimes metal) relief blocks to print short polyphonic musical quotations
or examples.

Polyphonic music is much more difficult to print than liturgical plain-

song, which is one reason why Ottaviano dei Petrucci, who achieved great aesthetic excellence with a triple-impression process, has been (mistakenly) called the Gutenberg of music printing. Petrucci was, however, the first to devise a process for printing polyphonic music from movable type: staves, notes and other musical signs, and texts were printed separately. Petrucci's skill may be studied in one of five known copies of *Harmonice musices Odhecaton A* (Venice, 1504), a selection of secular compositions, in the Music Division. Because of the technical difficulty of triple-impression printing, Petrucci had few successors or successful imitators. A less complex and therefore more economical process of music printing was introduced in France in the second quarter of the sixteenth century, probably by Pierre Attaingnant, the royal music printer. This single-impression process has remained the basic method of musical typography. Its early stages are represented in depth in the Music Division in works printed by the Ballard family. Their monopoly, maintained through the eighteenth century, prevented other French typefounders, including Pierre Simon Fournier, from introducing their own systems.

Theoretical details of the most successful eighteenth-century single-impression process, developed by Johann Gottlob Immanuel Breitkopf of Leipzig, are contained in his correspondence with Pierre Simon Fournier and in Fournier's *Traité historique et critique sur l'origine et les progrès des caractères de fonte pour l'impression de la musique* (1765). By the 1750s Breitkopf had perfected a single type-unit, now known as mosaic type, which was more suited to the chords of the florid contemporary music styles. These developments may be studied in the many Breitkopf and (from 1795 on) Breitkopf & Härtel imprints in the Music Division, for example the first edition of Haydn's *Die Jahreszeiten* (Leipzig: Breitkopf & Härtel, 1802) with a title page engraved by Amadeus Wenzl.

Despite Breitkopf's efforts and similar developments in the field of single-impression typographic music printing—in the Netherlands by the Enschedé firm and in England by Caslon—the system never achieved the elegant appearance and continuity of line for which engraved music had created a demand. The difficulty of composition and presswork and the large size of music fonts (Breitkopf's was over 300 matrices, but Fournier reduced the number in his *Essai d'un nouveau caractère,* 1756, to approximately 160) also restricted the use of movable type to large collections of printed music.

Information about many aspects of late eighteenth-century music print-

ing, publishing, and distribution is contained in publishers' catalogs, of which the Music Division has approximately 1,000. Catalogs bound into musical works or printed on back paper covers of volumes are listed by publisher in the "ML" catalog along with separately published catalogs, and there are in addition uncataloged holdings. Most publishers of engraved music issued single-sheet catalogs which, bound into editions, provide evidence for dating and distinguishing issues. Among the English publishers well represented in this group are John Bland, Robert Birchall, Robert Bremner, Broderip & Wilkinson, and Longman & Broderip. The coexistence of manuscript, engraved, and typographic music is documented in the thematic catalogs issued by Breitkopf between 1762 and 1787. Breitkopf issued catalogs for the Leipzig fairs that were in length and arrangement much like book trade lists of the time. The thematic catalogs, arranged by musical incipit, reveal the prevalence of copy manuscripts and engraved music in the Breitkopf inventory.

When copperplate engraving was first applied to music in Italy at the end of the sixteenth century, established engraving techniques were easily adapted to printing polyphonic music. The two musical examples in Vincenzo Galilei's *Dialogo* (Florence: Giorgio Marescotti, 1581) were printed from copperplates. Engraved music was used next in England, in the 1612/13 edition of *Parthenia or the Maydenhead of the First Musicke That Ever Was Printed for the Virginalls,* of which the Huntington Library has the only known copy. There is a copy of the second edition, engraved by William Hole for Dorethie Evans and printed in London by G. Lowe [ca. 1615], in the Music Division. One of the composers whose songs were collected in *Parthenia* was William Byrd, who held a monopoly on English music printing until 1596. A first edition of Byrd's *Psalmes, Sonets, & Songs of Sadnes and Pietie* . . . (London: Thomas Este, [1588]), the third book of English songs known to be published, is also in the division.

Engraved music, exempt from the monopoly that governed typographic music, gained steadily in popularity in England and on the Continent over the course of the seventeenth century. Works published by John Playford between 1651 and 1684 were printed from type, first by Thomas Harper and later by William Godbid. Some of those published by Playford's son were engraved by Thomas Cross, who dominated the field between 1683 and 1733 and popularized the single sheet. An early and superb example of Cross's work is the Music Division copy of Henry Purcell's *Sonnata's of III Parts: Two Viollins and Basse* . . . (London: Printed for the author, 1683).

Publishers' catalogs, such as this list of works printed and sold by Longman, Clementi & Co. bound into Haydn's New Grand Sonata for the Piano Forte *(London: Longman, Clementi & Co., ca. 1800)*, are used by music bibliographers in dating engraved sheet music. Music Division.

Music engraving formed a specialized trade, and when Jean-Benjamin de La Borde arranged for the production of his extravagant four-volume *Choix de chansons* (1783) he engaged both the foremost music engraver and the leading illustrator in Paris. J. M. Moreau designed and engraved the illustrations for the first volume (two copies of which are in the Lessing J. Rosenwald Collection, Rare Book and Special Collections Division, and one in the Music Division), and the music was engraved by Mlle Vendôme. A dispute between La Borde, the composer-compiler-publisher, and Moreau, the illustrator-engraver, ended the collaboration. The remaining volumes were illustrated by several artists. This deluxe effort displays the elegance of engraved music at its best: it is an extreme example of how well traditional engraving was suited to the needs of music printing and why it resulted in such an expensive product.

At the beginning of the eighteenth century, two changes occurred in the music-engraving process. A method was developed to soften the copper, and this soon led to its replacement by plates made from pewter, an alloy which was cheaper and easier to engrave. At about the same time, freehand cutting of the impression gave way to a system of stamping or punching with steel punches. Punching is a quicker and easier process than freehand work and results in a more uniform product. Although engravers were often required for delicate work, the punching and stamping could be turned over to less skilled craftsmen. Prices began to drop, and as a result of increased demand, the output, especially of single sheets, rose substantially. By the late eighteenth century, the techniques of single-impression printing from movable type and punched and stamped engraved plates were fully developed. The musical culture and trade they sustained provide a context within which to consider the influence of the third important music printing process, lithography, and the American materials in the Music Division of the Library of Congress.

❏   MUSIC PRINTING AND PUBLISHING IN AMERICA

The appearance of Oscar Sonneck's *Bibliography of Early Secular American Music (18th Century)* in 1905, revised and expanded by William Treat Upton (1945; Da Capo Press reprint, 1964), was the first step toward a comprehensive bibliographical record of early American musical imprints. The coverage

and span of the work begun by Sonneck have been extended by Richard J. Wolfe in *Secular Music in America, 1801–1825: A Bibliography* (New York: New York Public Library, 1964), catalogs of sheet music holdings in the Newberry Library (Boston: G.K. Hall, 1983) and the University of Virginia (computer-produced, 1977), and Irving Lowens in *A Bibliography of Songsters Printed in America before 1821* (Worcester, Mass.: American Antiquarian Society, 1976). Lyrics to patriotic and political songs published in colonial newspapers have been inventoried by Gillian Anderson in *Freedom's Voice in Poetry and Song* (Wilmington, Del.: Scholarly Resources, 1977). The forthcoming *Bibliography of Sacred Music through the Year 1810 Published in America* by Lowens, Allen P. Britton, and Richard Crawford (Worcester, Mass.: American Antiquarian Society) is creating a record of early American sacred music.

Music copyright registrations in the district court record books in the Rare Book and Special Collections Division, especially for the period following 1831—when music was named as a separate subject—are an essential resource for a comprehensive bibliography of American musical imprints. Beginning in 1891, the published *Catalogue of Title-Entries* (called after 1906 the *Catalogue of Copyright Entries*) serves as a complete record of American music deposited for copyright. The formidable task of compiling a record of music published in America during the intervening six decades remains. It is necessary for scholars to begin to extend the bibliographical record, and the historical analysis derived from it, based on the resources that Oscar Sonneck shaped. Between 1830 and 1890 music played a significant role in cultural and political events and was closely linked to the other graphic arts through lithography and stereotyping. Historians of nineteenth-century America and music bibliographers will find Music Division holdings for this period extraordinarily rich and diverse.

Studies of the printing and publishing of early American music and the role of music in early American life have been stimulated by bibliographical research and conducted by the principal compilers. Richard J. Wolfe examined technology and trade during the period covered by his bibliography in *Early American Music Engraving and Printing* (Urbana: University of Illinois in cooperation with the Bibliographical Society of America, 1980). Cultural and economic factors were explored by Richard Crawford and Donald Krummel in an essay on "Early American Music Printing and Publishing," published in *Printing and Society in Early America,* edited by William L. Joyce et al. (Worcester, Mass.: American Antiquarian Society, 1983).

The printing trends documented in these studies echo developments in Europe. The first music in America, printed from relief cut, appeared in the ninth edition of the Bay Psalm Book (1698). Freehand engraving dominated music printing in America until the end of the eighteenth century, when stamped and punched engraved plates and typographic music were introduced. The concurrent use of engraved plates to print sheet music and movable type for book-length collections prevailed into the twentieth century, although lithography had a brief period of success in the second quarter of the nineteenth century.

A full analysis of early American music publishing will account for the fact that of the approximately 650 hymnals and 5,000 pieces of sheet music printed before 1825 in the collections of the Music Division, almost none are copyright deposit copies. The district court record books in the Rare Book and Special Collections Division confirm that during this period only a very small number of musical compositions were registered or deposited, although two composer-compilers, William Billings and Andrew Law, were among the first to seek copyright protection from the states, and music was protected by the first federal law in 1790. We need to establish, for example, what percentage of the total musical output of the pre-1825 period the copyright records represent, and how this compares with registered books and maps. Other questions include: what kind of music was printed here and what was imported; whether plates for music that was printed in America were engraved here or imported; how much of the music printed here was original and how much derivative; and how much competition there was.

The most fundamental but perhaps the most elusive aspect of early American music publishing centers around the division of responsibility for compiling, composing, engraving, printing, publishing, and selling printed music. In the period before 1800, tune-book compilations routinely included a typographic preface of a theoretical nature followed by engraved music. This combination suggests close cooperation between engravers and letterpress printers, combined facilities, or a third party who played a coordinating and entrepreneurial role. Internal and external evidence suggests that the composer-compiler arranged for printing, publishing, and financing. Musical imprints, for example, introduce significant evidence but are not always sufficient to document the individual roles of the multiple parties named or to discount the participation of others. Among the engravers of early American music was Paul Revere, named on the title page of Josiah Flagg's *A Collection*

of the Best Psalm Tunes . . . (Boston: Printed and sold by [Revere] and Josiah Flagg, 1764). The typographic preface calls attention to the fact "That however we are oblig'd to the other side of the Atlantick chiefly, for our Tunes, the Paper on which they are printed is the Manufacture of our own Country." Flagg and Revere are the only contributors named. The division of financial, intellectual, and technical responsibility is not clear.

Revere also engraved the frontispiece for William Billings's *The New-England Psalm-Singer* . . . (Boston: Edes and Gill, 1770), the first complete collection of music entirely by an American composer. Clarence Brigham, Revere's bibliographer, assumed that he was also responsible for the music engraving, despite the absence of an entry for it in the Revere record books. Billings's biographers, David McKay and Richard Crawford, disagree. Looking at stylistic similarities, they concluded that Josiah Flagg, listed along with Revere and Billings as a seller of *The New-England Psalm-Singer,* engraved the music. Graphic analysis must be used to supplement other evidence. A manuscript note by William Holroyd of Providence in the Music Division copy of *The New-England Psalm-Singer* records the purchase of the book from the composer, Billings, for nine shillings on June 12, 1776, suggesting that the "remainder" of an edition might be held by the composer-compiler for sale in later years.

The bibliographical complexities of Andrew Law's major compilations (recorded by Richard Crawford in his biography, *Andrew Law, American Psalmodist* [Evanston, Ill.: Northwestern University Press, 1968]) indicate a rather cavalier attitude toward the integrity of editions and issues on the part of tune-book compilers. Parts were issued separately and bound together in later years with title pages that provided scanty or unreliable imprint information. The Music Division has one of two known copies of the 1778 edition, which Crawford terms "preliminary," of Law's *Select Harmony.* On the typographic title-page advertisement Law notes that "The times being such, that it is impossible to get plates cut for all the musick at first proposed, there will be an addition made as soon as they can be done . . . ." No printer is named in this or the first edition of 1779 (printed in New Haven by Thomas and Samuel Green). The printer of the three parts of Law's *The Art of Singing,* first brought together in 1794–96, was his brother William Law, who is named on several of the half titles and from whom there is a receipt in the Andrew Law Papers at the William L. Clements Library, dated ca. 1790, for over 5,000 copies printed of *Select Harmony.*

An edition of Law's *Select Harmony* probably from 1784, pirated by Daniel Bayley in Newburyport, Massachussetts, and the freedom with which Isaiah Thomas borrowed from Law demonstrate the inability of state laws to provide copyright protection even to compilers who sought it. The federal law of 1790 remedied this problem, but the number of music copyrights for the following decades remained very low. In the late 1780s musical output and trade competition began to expand, and over the next century copyright became the central issue for a group of composers, compilers, and publishers who revolutionized the music trade with the help of its protection.

Three important late eighteenth-century developments in the technology of music printing in America had, as Crawford and Krummel note, significant effects on the cultural and economic aspects of music printing and publishing, paving the way for this growth. Beginning with the first edition of Isaiah Thomas's *Worcester Collection* (1786), printed at one impression from imported Caslon music type, the role of the printer in the compilation and financial processes was expanded, the cost of tune-books fell, and the output increased. By the first decades of the nineteenth century, technological and trade mechanisms were in place for an explosion in the production of sacred and secular tune-books, typographically printed and promoted by their compiler-printer on a scale unimaginable in Thomas's time.

The second development was the replacement of freehand engraving by punched and stamped engraved plates in the early 1790s. John Aitken, a Philadelphia engraver and metalsmith who first used the technique, imported tools similar to those used by metalsmiths, bookbinders, and typefounders. Donald Krummel has shown how the distinctive characteristics of particular tools can be used to date punched and stamped sheet music when, as in the case of the output of a publisher such as George Blake of Philadelphia, they can be assigned to music engraved within a specific span of years. Dating by "graphic analysis" can be misleading, however, because publishers often used engraving shops where work was done simultaneously for several publishers.

Unlike typographic music, engraved music required little capital investment, enabling composers such as James Hewitt or members of the Carr family to publish their own works in sheet form. Small editions were printed from undated plates and reprinted as demand or other circumstances required. The first appearance of Francis Scott Key's poem "Defence of Fort McHenry" under the title "The Star Spangled Banner" with the music from

A page from the account book of music publisher Simeon Wood, showing the number of copies of The Star of Bethlehem *printed, deposited for copyright, sold, and given away from April to September 1821. Miscellaneous Manuscripts, Music Division.*

the tune "Anacreon in Heaven" was engraved by Thomas Carr in Baltimore in 1814. A second issue was printed from the same plates in the last months of that year to correct a misprint in the original subtitle, "A Pariotic Song." Both issues are undated. The division's comprehensive collection of early printings of the national anthem includes each of these as well as the first broadside printing without music that preceded them.

Systematic plate numbering, devised by European publishers as a means of retrieving plates for reprinting, provides bibliographers evidence for dating sheet music. A system of retrieval became necessary, however, only when an inventory of cleaned and stored plates was sufficiently large. Most publishers of early American sheet music did not routinely number or letter their plates. The problem of dating sheet music is complicated by the tendency of purchasers to bind their collections into volumes. Domestic and imported sheets are bound together in the Gansevoort Collection in the Music Division, comprising 193 songs and pieces for the pianoforte and violin, published for the most part in the United States between 1795 and 1838, and collected and used by the daughter of Brig. Gen. Peter Gansevoort. The Eleanor Parke Custis and Mrs. James A. Gary Collections are among over 280 albums (M1.A15) that afford valuable insights into the musical taste of the time.

Title page for The Easy Instructor, *deposited by Edward Stammers and William Little for copyright registration in the Southern District of Philadelphia on June 15, 1798. The earliest extant edition of the work, which introduced the shape-note system of musical instruction, is dated 1802. Music Division.*

One of the few extant original resources relating to the publication of early American sheet music is the account book of Simeon Wood (d. 1822) in the Music Division. This twenty-two-leaf manuscript (published as Appendix A in Wolfe's *Early American Music Engraving and Printing*) confirms many conclusions previously based upon internal evidence alone. Wood, a musician who went into the publishing business, neither operated his own store nor did his own printing. He sent out the plates he engraved to be printed and sold or let printed titles out on consignment to music sellers. The account book, covering the years 1818–21, records the sizes of his approximately thirty editions, the dates of printing and sale, and the arrangements for reprinting. The migration of engraved plates was common in this period, and inventories were absorbed following the bankruptcy or death of a small music publisher. After Wood's death, Gottlieb Graupner of Boston acquired some of Wood's plates for a collection, as did Edwin W. Jackson (these were later reprinted by Firth and Hall in New York).

The third late eighteenth-century development in music printing was the shape-note system, a method of teaching sight reading through individual shapes for each syllable. The typographic title page in the Music Division for *The Easy Instructor,* which announced the system, was deposited in the Southern District of Philadelphia by Edward Stammers and William Little

on June 15, 1798. An 1802 engraved edition, published in Philadelphia, is the earliest extant copy. Irving Lowens has studied engraved editions of *The Easy Instructor* published between 1802 and 1808 and typographic editions issued from 1808 through 1822. Numerous other shape-note systems were devised in the late eighteenth and early nineteenth centuries, including one by Andrew Law probably based upon Little's.

In order to succeed, a music printing process has to satisfy several criteria, of which technical feasibility is only one. Aesthetic considerations, for example, stimulated the invention and development of lithography, but ultimately contributed to its defeat as a music printing process. Alois Senefelder related that he was first inspired to experiment with relief etching and printing on stone by a specimen of poorly printed music in a prayer book. Senefelder's association and partnership with the composer Franz Gleissner strengthened his interest in the musical applications of his invention, and when lithography was perfected during the first decade of the nineteenth century it was used to print Gleissner's music.

One of the first lithographers in the United States was Henry Stone, an Englishman active in Washington, D.C., between 1823 and 1826. The Music Division has an undated and unbound collection of music lithographed by Stone, which Richard Wolfe has dated [1823?]. The lettering of titles and song texts closely resembles an engraved hand; the notes are regularly shaped but blurred. The title vignettes were also lithographed by Stone.

By the late 1820s music lithography was widely used in America, although the difficulty of drawing directly on stone and lack of clarity in the printed music were severe obstacles to acceptance by the trade and the public. These were both overcome by the introduction in the 1840s of transfer copies, whereby proofs taken from a punched, engraved plate were transferred to a lithographic stone for printing. The process, requiring an engraver to create the plate and a lithographic printer to reproduce it, results in a crisp impression without the labor of inking and cleaning the engraved plate for each pull. Today it remains the ideal process for printing sheet music and has been adapted to new techniques. Photolithography, facsimiles of the composer's autograph manuscript, special typewriters, and computers can be used to produce a plate that is still termed by the trade "engraved" and is printed by offset lithography.

Although lithography did not replace engraving as the predominant method of music printing, the process was highly successful for the illustra-

tion of music and thus had a lasting influence on the format and appearance of sheet music. Unlike earlier decoration on a page of music or on the title page of a collection, lithographed "covers" of American sheet music are actually pictorial title pages. Publishers embraced their promotional potential. Some, like J. H. Bufford, who had trained as an illustrator in the Boston lithographic shop of the Pendleton brothers, operated large and profitable establishments that issued lithographed popular prints and maps as well as sheet music covers. In the 1850s Bufford and other firms such as Childs and Inman, Nathaniel Currier, and Sarony and Major employed draftsmen and fine artists—Winslow Homer drew for Bufford, Fitz Hugh Lane and James McNeill Whistler for Sarony and Major. Their striking images captured the fancy of the buying public and created an enthusiastic and enormously expanded market for sheet music.

Copyright deposit title pages and cover titles in the Music Division for the period 1800–1870 have been indexed by title. Several thousand covers of special artistic distinction or visual interest have been transferred to the Prints and Photographs Division. A survey of sheet music covers from the mid-nineteenth through the mid-twentieth century in the Music Division reveals a relationship between trends in musical culture, promotion and distribution, and the graphic arts. By the 1890s, when the poster was attracting attention as an art form and as an advertising medium for which lithography was superbly suited, music covers had declined in quality of design and production. Photographic reproduction and, more recently, computer-assisted processes replaced lithography for printing sheet music covers. The most innovative designs for music are now in the field of poster and record jacket design or are used for contemporary avant-garde scores. As the percentage of income music publishers derived from the sale of sheet music declined in comparison to money earned from performance rights and records, there was a dramatic shift in advertising and promotional techniques within the music industry.

Approximately 14,000 copyright deposit pieces of sheet music published between 1820 and 1860 are cataloged and classed together in the Music Division. The division also has approximately twice this number of cataloged nondeposit copies of single sheets from this period and 10,000 uncataloged sheets bound in volumes by collectors. A dramatic increase in sheet music output, which began immediately following the Civil War, continued unabated until record sales began to dominate in the middle of this century. Tens

of thousands of post-1860 sheet music deposits are classified by performance medium or genre and alphabetized by composer. A vast amount of American popular music from the periods 1890–1929 and 1939–1940 is arranged by copyright registration number. Among the separately classed categories are Civil War songs, Spanish-American War songs, World War I songs, state and city songs, ethnic and emigré songs, college songs, patriotic and political songs, and songs of trade, professional, occupational, and other groups. Historians of American music can trace in these songs the growth of a popular tradition encompassing influences from spirituals, gospels, minstrel shows, and many other genres, as well as the work of individual composers such as Stephen Foster. They are also a rich source of information and documentation on many aspects of public and private life for the social and cultural historian.

This vast collection of nineteenth- and twentieth-century sheet music provides evidence of changes in the relationship between printed and performed music and the impact of these changes on printing, publishing, and distributing musical compositions. During the nineteenth century, music was still widely circulated in manuscript or printed in small quantities (approximately 200 copies) in every town across the country for educational or performance use. Sheet music in the Music Division often bears physical evidence of distribution mechanisms: a seller's stamp, a composer's autograph (in facsimile or original, from sessions like modern book-signing parties), the notice "for professional use only," and, increasingly toward the end of the century, copyright deposit stamps.

In a case study by Dena J. Epstein of the mid-nineteenth-century Chicago music publishing firm of Root & Cady, copyright records proved less helpful than might have been expected. Many publications were reissues of popular hits and thus ineligible for registration. Music and book publishers were inconsistent about deposits before the enforcement provision passed in 1867. Two later changes in the copyright law significantly increased depository compliance. The 1891 Copyright Act, which also instituted the *Catalogue of Title-Entries* as an aid to customs collectors in detecting illegal imports, was one. Next, the 1909 revision, which continued common law protection for unpublished musical works, inserted performance rights, established by Congress in 1898, in the law, and stipulated that copyrighted music could not be performed "publicly . . . for profit" without the permission of the copyright

owner. Once linked to the increasingly remunerative right to regulate performance as well as copying, securing copyright became of paramount importance to music publishers. By the end of the nineteenth century, musical
deposits, arriving at the rate of approximately 15,000 per year, vastly out-
numbered every other subject category, and they continue to do so.

One perspective on late nineteenth- through mid-twentieth-century sheet
music publishing is afforded by copyright deposits in the Music Division
submitted by "song sharks," the musical trade equivalent of vanity publishers. Song sharks, who thrived in Washington, D.C., and New York City,
exploited the desire of composers to see their work published and their will-
ingness to pay to do so. They printed a very small number of copies, deposited one for copyright, and sent the author most of the remainder. No effort
at distribution or sale was made. The copyright deposit copies at the Library
of Congress may be the most abundant evidence of this fraudulent but flour-
ishing element in music publishing, and they merit further study. The compilation of imprint lists for these firms is complicated by the fact that although published music is registered for copyright under the firm as
copyright proprietor, song sharks entered compositions under the composer's
name. Among the firms well represented in the division are H. Kirkus
Dugdale, active at the turn of the century; Gotham Attucks, one of the first
successful black publishers in the 1890s, who sold out to a song shark; and
Nordyke imprints, from the 1940s and 1950s.

The explosive surge in American music publishing during the mid-
nineteenth century was not confined to sheet music. The application of stereotyping to music printing by the middle of the century enabled printers to
store plates for future use. Music publishers began to build inventories, increase output, and lower prices to meet growing demand. Firms such as the
Oliver Ditson Company, which issued its first imprint in Boston in 1835 (and
was absorbed in 1931 by the Theodore Pressler Company), expanded dramatically by purchasing the rights to individual titles or complete catalogs of
firms. Sacred hymnals formed the bulk of this trade, but secular songbooks
issued in similar oblong format were becoming more popular. Two figures
who dominated the mid-century scene and whose careers illuminate it are
Lowell Mason and William Batchelder Bradbury.

Mason was a musical educator and hymn-writer. The first edition of his
first compilation, *The Boston Handel & Haydn Society's Collection of Church*

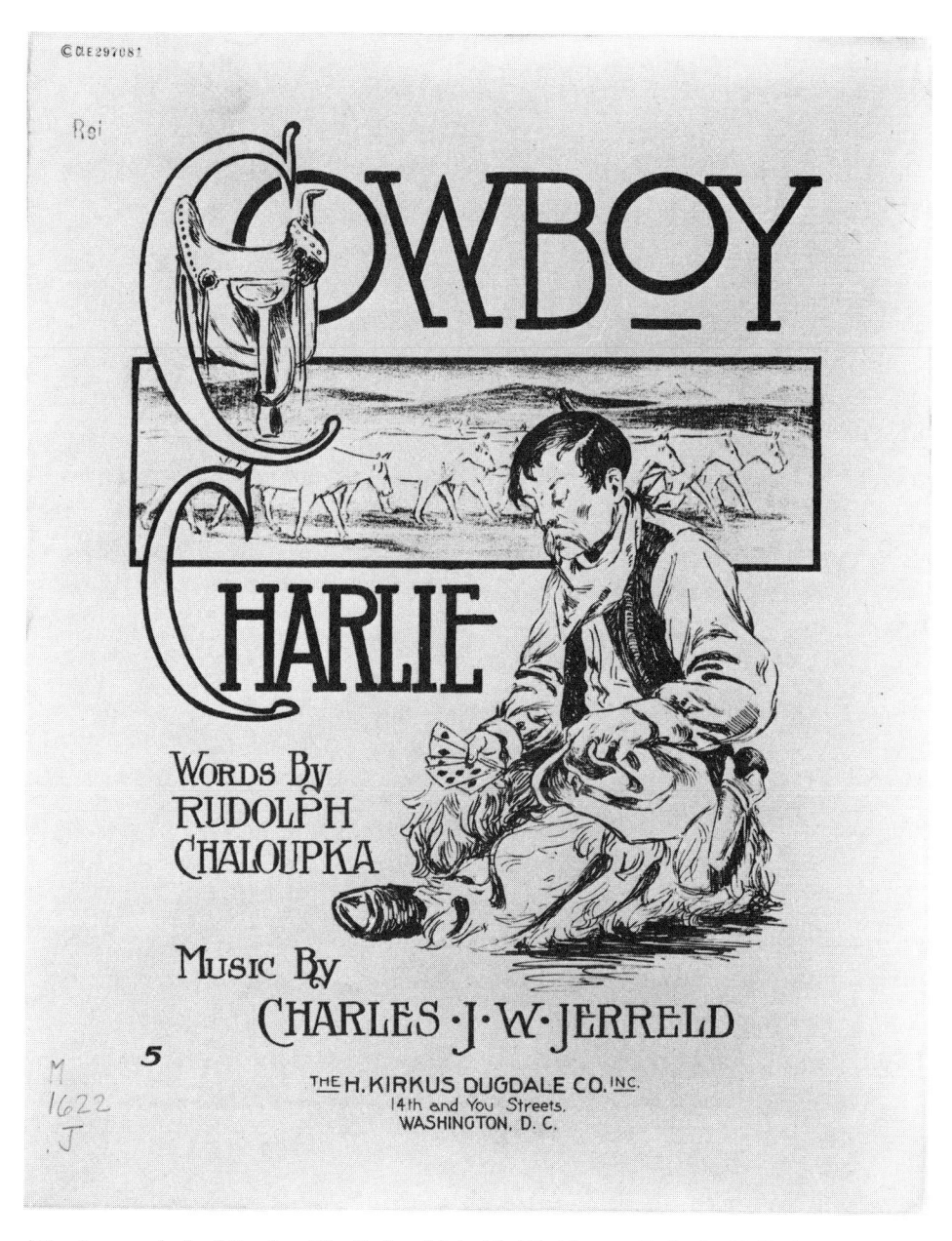

The sheet music for "Cowboy Charlie," published in Washington, D.C., by H. Kirkus Dugdale, a song shark or vanity music publisher, and deposited for copyright registration in 1912. Music Division.

Music, was published in 1822 without his name because he did not want to be known as a musician. It was immensely successful and went through many versions and editions, among the most popular entitled *Carmina Sacra.* Copyright deposits of the first two editions are dated June 19 and October 9, 1841. The identical front covers record the numerous music publishers and sellers who had agreed to purchase a sufficient number of copies to appear in the imprint. The continued success of Mason's compilation is evident from the frequency with which editions of *Carmina Sacra* and its successor, *New Carmina Sacra,* appeared. The Music Division has an incomplete set of revised and unrevised first and second proofs of the first edition of *Carmina Sacra* and comprehensive holdings of this and others of Mason's nearly 50 publications, including secular collections such as *The Odeon.* In a manuscript of a speech dated 1878, Mason asked "how may legislation be secured which shall make music a study in our public schools." His efforts to introduce the teaching of music in public schools may be his most lasting contribution; it surely enhanced his commercial success, as many of his collections were designed for school use.

Relations among music publishers are forcefully evoked by a stern letter from Mason to William Batchelder Bradbury, dated October 10, 1861. Bradbury was a pupil of Mason's who had gone on to great popular success, which his former teacher viewed as cheapening or sweetening the sacred repertoire. Mason forwarded a copy of his latest collection, *Asaph,* with a caveat regarding "copy-right property, by which I understand the rights (both legal & moral) which one has in that which originates in his own mind. . . . This property extends both to music and to words or poetry." Mason claimed that much was original in both words and music in *Asaph* and that he would allow no "separation between them." Mason assured Bradbury that he sent the same warning to George F. Root, another music teacher and prolific songbook compiler and sometime collaborator of Mason's, and that his son and present collaborator William Mason and his publisher approved of his message.

A letterpress book by William Batchelder Bradbury, covering the years 1861–62, in the Music Division reveals the care with which songbook compilers guarded their copyrights and documents many other trade practices of this period. Bradbury wrote in response to numerous requests for permission to use his music in schools and religious assemblies or conventions, naming prices such as $100 for the use of twelve of his most popular tunes, half of the money down. Perspectives on pricing and promoting, advertising, and dis-

tributing are afforded by letters to booksellers in which Bradbury offered new works at special rates and the addition of the bookseller's name to the imprint for an order of 1,000 copies. Bradbury's distribution efforts were very successful: one of the works he promoted vigorously was *The Golden Chain,* of which 2 million copies were sold.

Two issues with which music publishers were concerned throughout the nineteenth century were copyright infringement and price cutting. Although the trade was still quite decentralized, large firms were expanding and increasing their monopoly through the absorption of failing firms. An attempt by William Hall & Son in New York to cut prices on noncopyright music—a standard practice in the book trade—resulted in the formation of a musical board of trade by the twenty-one major firms and the publication in 1870 of a *Complete Catalogue of Sheet Music and Musical Works Published by the Board of Trade of the United States of America* (reprint, 1973). This trade catalog, arranged by musical category, records publisher and price and serves as a bibliographical record of music in print. It is, however, very incomplete (even though the stock of these large firms incorporated the inventory of many smaller ones whose catalogs they had bought) and lacks composer, title, or imprint indexes.

The catalog reveals many aspects of musical culture in America, including the continued popularity of imported music in certain categories. Thus when the first international copyright law was passed on March 3, 1891, in order to ensure an adequate supply of imported music at reasonable cost, Librarian of Congress Ainsworth Rand Spofford expressly and deliberately exempted music from the manufacturing clause, which required that an item be printed in this country to qualify for protection. European music publishers could deposit copies of musical compositions printed abroad, although foreign book publishers now had to reprint works for copyright protection. The board of trade, led by Oliver Ditson, fought for the extension of the manufacturing clause to cover music and lost. As a result, imported music became an increasingly important part of the American music publishing trade. In the years following the 1891 Copyright Act, American publishers formed close alliances with European firms, acting as and appointing agents or opening foreign offices.

The Arthur P. Schmidt Company Archive in the Music Division provides an outstanding example of this trend. The firm, which was started by Arthur Paul Schmidt as a music store in Boston in 1876, became one of the largest

music publishing and importing firms in the United States, with offices in Boston and Leipzig. It published the works of many distinguished composers of the so-called New-England School, including John Knowles Paine, George Chadwick, Arthur Foote, Horatio Parker, and Mrs. H. H. A. Beach, as well as popular works. The collection (gift of the Summy-Birchard Company, the successor to A. P. Schmidt, 1959) spans the period 1891–1951 and comprises over 20,000 musical manuscripts and approximately 100,000 items of correspondence with composers, printers, engravers, and foreign publishers, copyright renewals, catalogs, and financial records. These resources document the increasingly international nature of American music printing and publishing as well as the influence a commercial firm had on the development of American music by using its popular successes to support the publication of serious musical works. (See the *Quarterly Journal of the Library of Congress* 15, no. 1, November 1957, 27; and Melville, *Guide,* no. 218.)

The pattern of subsidizing the publication of serious music with revenues from popular hits persists in contemporary music publishing, although it represents a minute fraction of the activity—and expenditures—of this industry. Contemporary music publishing is dominated by several large firms with catalogs of tens of thousands of publications, offices in foreign countries, and an appointment as the U.S. agent for a foreign firm. These companies— such as Boosey & Hawkes, Carl Fischer, C.F. Peters, and G. Schirmer— sometimes act jointly to publish serious, experimental, or avant-garde works. The classics are a major source of income to music publishers through record sales and performance rights royalties on works to which they own the copyright. Publication of contemporary music is a form of investment in a future catalog.

When performance rights and mechanical device royalties were included in the 1909 revision of the copyright law, they covered such events as concerts, dance halls, and cabarets. Over the next few years, broadcasting dramatically increased the income derived from these sources and led to the organization of performing rights societies (ASCAP, BMI, SESAC) to collect and distribute royalties of music in copyright. Because royalties are split between composer and publisher, successful composers like Irving Berlin form their own companies to publish new songs and buy back the copyrights on established hits. The development of the record industry and more recent technologies led to provisions in the 1976 revision of the copyright law such as mandatory licensing of cable and the statutory (rather than common law)

coverage of unpublished compositions, which can now be deposited in tape form. The effect of these changes on the music trade can be observed in statistics for copyright deposits: of over 100,000 musical compositions now received annually, approximately one-fifth are published and an even smaller fraction are printed.

Scores composed using traditional musical notation are printed principally to meet the needs of performers and the educational and religious markets. Popular songs are printed as souvenirs or after they have achieved success, a situation that has encouraged the development of quick and inexpensive printing processes, primarily the "blue print" process, to meet demand for a popular work before it dissipates and to justify production of a small number of copies for a specialized market. New technologies are being used to meet the needs of composers working in contemporary musical styles not easily adapted to traditional notation. The "short-run" technique, recently developed by C.F. Peters, incorporates IBM technology. Contemporary music publishers thus continue to search for an ideal printing process, at the same time as they thrive on a variety of activities and income sources of which printing is an ever-diminishing part.

REFERENCES

Anderson, Gillian, comp. *Freedom's Voice in Poetry and Song*. Wilmington, Del.: Scholarly Resources, 1977.

Board of Music Trade of the United States of America. *Complete Catalogue of Sheet Music and Musical Works Published by the Board of Trade of the United States of America*. New introd. by Dena J. Epstein. New York: Da Capo Press, 1973.

Breitkopf und Härtel. *The Breitkopf Thematic Catalogue: The Six Parts and Sixteen Supplements, 1762–1787*. Ed. and with an introd. and indexes by Barry S. Brook. New York: Dover, 1966.

Crawford, Richard, and D. W. Krummel. "Early American Music Printing and Publishing." In *Printing and Society in Early America,* ed. William L. Joyce et al., 187–227. Worcester, Mass.: American Antiquarian Society, 1983.

Epstein, Dena J. *Music Publishing in Chicago before 1871: The Firm of Root & Cady, 1858–1871*. Detroit: Information Coordinators, 1969.

Fisher, William Arms. *One Hundred and Fifty Years of Music Publishing in the United States* . . . . Boston: Oliver Ditson, 1933; St. Clair Shores, Mich.: Scholarly Press, 1977.

Goff, Frederick R. *Early Music Books in the Rare Books Division of the Library of Congress*. Washington: Library of Congress, [1949].

King, A. Hyatt. *Four Hundred Years of Music Printing*. London: Published by the Trustees of the British Museum, 1968.

Krummel, Donald W. "Graphic Analysis: Its Application to Early American Engraved Music." *Music Library Association Notes,* 2d ser., 16, no. 2 (1959): 213–33.

Lichtenwanger, William. "The Music of 'The Star-Spangled Banner' from Ludgate Hill to Capitol Hill." *Quarterly Journal of the Library of Congress* 34 (1977): 136–70.

———— "Late 18th Century French Music Publishers' Catalogs in the Library of Congress." *Fontes Artis Musicae* 7, no. 2 (1960): 61–64.

Lowens, Irving. *A Bibliography of Songsters Printed in America before 1821.* Worcester, Mass.: American Antiquarian Society, 1976.

———— "Copyright and Andrew Law." *Papers of the Bibliographical Society of America* 53 (1959): 150–59.

———— *Music and Musicians in Early America.* New York: W.W. Norton, 1964.

Lowens, Irving, Allen P. Britton, and Richard Crawford. *Bibliography of Sacred Music through the Year 1810 Published in America.* Worcester, Mass.: American Antiquarian Society, forthcoming.

Melville, Annette. *Guide.* See United States. Library of Congress. *Special Collections in the Library of Congress: A Selective Guide.*

The Newberry Library, Chicago, Illinois. *The Newberry Library Catalog of Early American Printed Sheet Music.* Comp. by Bernard E. Wilson. 3 vols. Boston: G.K. Hall, 1983.

Resources of American Music History: A Directory of Source Materials from Colonial Times to World War II. Comp. by D. W. Krummel et al. Urbana: University of Illinois Press, 1981.

Sonneck, Oscar George Theodore. *A Bibliography of Early Secular American Music (18th Century).* Rev. and enl. by William Treat Upton. Washington: Library of Congress, 1945; New York: Da Capo Press, 1964.

United States. Library of Congress. *Catalogue of Early Books on Music (before 1800).* By Julia Gregory; prepared under the direction of O. G. Sonneck. Washington: Government Printing Office, 1913. *Supplement (Books Acquired by the Library 1913–1942).* By Hazel Bartlett, with a List of Books on Music in Chinese and Japanese. Washington: Government Printing Office, 1944; New York: Da Capo Press, 1969.

———— *The Music Division: A Guide to Its Collections and Services.* Washington: Library of Congress, 1972.

———— *Special Collections in the Library of Congress: A Selective Guide.* Comp. by Annette Melville. Washington: Library of Congress, 1980. See the list in the appendix, pp. 410-11.

———— Copyright Office. *Catalogue of Title-Entries.* 47 vols. 1 July 1891–June 1906; *Catalogue of Copyright Entries.* July 1906–.

University of Virginia. *Computer Catalog of Nineteenth-Century American-Imprint Sheet Music.* Comp. by Lynn T. McRae. Charlottesville: University of Virginia, 1977.

Wolfe, Richard J. *Early American Music Engraving and Printing.* Urbana: University of Illinois in cooperation with the Bibliographical Society of America, 1980.

———— *Secular Music in America, 1801–1825: A Bibliography.* New York: New York Public Library, 1964.

Pencil-and-gray-wash drawing by Felix Octavius Darley for James Fenimore Cooper's The Pilot:
A Tale of the Sea *(New York: W.A. Townsend & Co., 1859). The novel, first published in 1823,
appeared with these illustrations by Darley as part of a collected edition of Cooper's works. The
illustrations were reused in several later editions, including a cheap reprint issued by D. Appleton
Co., 1872–73. The electrotype blocks used to print the illustrations are also in the collections.
Cabinet of American Illustration, Prints and Photographs Division.*

7 □ Prints and Photographs Division

The role of visual images in the diffusion of culture through printed materials and the interaction between words and images are important areas of inquiry for the historian of books. Topics for research include the technology and trade by which separately issued prints and book illustrations were produced and distributed, their relationship to book printing, book publishing, and the book trade, and the uses and influences of pictorial images.

Although distinctions between the fine and applied arts are difficult to draw, they provide a useful perspective from which to view the history of printing processes in the graphic arts and their connection to developments in book printing. The artist using a reproductive process for original artistic expression bases his choice of a medium on its special graphic qualities. Book illustrators and reproductive printmakers consider other factors: the faithfulness of the reproduction to the original; the autographic quality of the process, or the absence of the need for a craftsman to interpret the image onto a printing plate; the compatibility of the process with type, or the ability to print images along with words; and the capacity to produce large numbers of images from the printing plate. Solely on the basis of these criteria, photography is the ideal solution for applied graphic arts printing. In the history of graphic reproduction, however, increased economy and speed are not always the determining factors.

The Prints and Photographs Division, a collection devoted to all forms and uses of the graphic arts, grew out of a separate Division of Prints organized in 1897, the year the Thomas Jefferson Building opened. The collection then consisted of over 50,000 items that had been housed in the Capitol, acquired primarily through copyright deposit. By 1901 the holdings had grown to over 100,000 images, mostly through copyright, and over half of these were photographs. Over 90 percent of the 10 million items now in the Prints and Photographs Division are documentary photographic prints or negatives.

The division holds in addition a fine print collection of approximately 110,000 woodcuts, engravings, etchings, and lithographs by significant artists from the fifteenth through the twentieth centuries, arranged by century and by artist; a master photograph collection of more than 4,000 images by noted photographers; over 600,000 items related to architecture, design, and engineering; approximately 150,000 examples of popular and applied graphic art, including historical and popular prints, drawings for book and magazine illustrations, cartoons and caricatures, and commercial labels and printed advertisements; and over 80,000 posters.

Before World War II, reproductive and commercial prints and photographs received through copyright deposit continued to accumulate. During the 1940s, the war demonstrated the importance of pictorial images for intelligence work and as documentation. Archibald MacLeish, Librarian of Congress (1939–44), also served as assistant director of the Office of War Information. Through his efforts the huge Farm Security Administration/Office of War Information photographic archive was transferred to the Library of Congress in 1944. That same year the division was renamed the Prints and Photographs Division, reflecting the shift to the acquisition of visual documentation of American life, past and present.

To handle huge numbers of photographs the division developed the concept of *lotting,* or batching pictures in groups. The lots are listed in the divisional catalog. There are separate catalogs for material receiving item-level cataloging, such as fine prints, posters, and political prints. The division is building a comprehensive special subject index that will provide access to a wide range of images through terms derived from the item's origin, context, or content. The index now contains approximately 65,000 entries covering various collections and formats. Application of the Library of Congress Optical Disk Pilot Program to several collections in the division has demonstrated

the potential of this technology to facilitate the use and preservation of this vast pictorial archive.

The division acquires images of artistic and historic significance through copyright deposit, exchange, gift, transfer, and purchase. The collections of the Prints and Photographs Division are huge, varied, and uneven, and in some cases difficult to use. Their outstanding strength is in American material, and in particular, documentary photographs, but by virtue of size and breadth they offer opportunities for research in the development of the graphic arts, typography, book design, and illustration and in pictorial documentation of printing, book production, libraries, and reading.

❏   FINE PRINTS AND GRAPHIC ARTS PROCESSES

The graphic arts—the processes by which pictorial images or designs are mechanically reproduced and multiplied—preceded the typographic. Pictures and patterns were printed on textiles, playing cards, and prints from wood relief blocks in northern Europe during the fourteenth and fifteenth centuries. Popular prints flourished by the middle of the fifteenth century, reaching a large and mostly nonliterate audience who purchased them on pilgrimages and pasted them on walls or inside boxes, incorporating the graphic image and its didactic message into everyday life.

During the second half of the fifteenth century, professional woodcutters replaced the monks who, during the manuscript period, had produced religious prints for pilgrims. Examples of secular subjects and instructional themes in formats clearly intended to be posted on walls survive, for example, the anonymous "A Warning to Usurers" in the Fine Print Collection. Religious prints by far predominated, and their range and characteristics are evident in the work of Lucas Cranach the elder in the Prints and Photographs Division.

Intaglio printing also preceded printing from movable type. The earliest date on a line engraving is 1446. The origins of the engraver's art are to be found in metalwork and goldsmithing. Because engravings could not be printed along with type, the craft of engraving remained independent of book printing. Prints by Martin Schongauer reveal the fine and formal quality of the engraved line. Intaglio and relief techniques come together in the work of Albrecht Dürer. Individual prints by Dürer in the Prints and Photo-

graphs Division supplement the holdings of the Lessing J. Rosenwald Collection in the Rare Book and Special Collections Division and span Dürer's work in woodcut, engraving, and etching on religious themes and his secular portraits.

Early masters in the Fine Print Collection, the core of which was received with the Gardiner Greene Hubbard Collection in 1898, include Dürer's follower Hans Sebald Beham. The development of the ornamental print is reflected in the work of the "Little Masters" Heinrich Aldegrever and Albrecht Altdorfer. The beginnings of reproductive engraving can be studied in engravings by Marcantonio Raimondi after paintings by Raphael.

By the middle of the sixteenth century, the engraving trade had expanded to meet the increased demand for plates to be used as book illustrations. Woodcut was principally used to illustrate street or popular literature where economy took precedence over refinement—broadsides, almanacs, and chapbooks—until the revival of wood engraving by Thomas Bewick at the end of the eighteenth century. A vast number and variety of engravings were produced in this period, including topographic, portrait, religious, and political prints, of which the Fine Print Collection has representative examples. Jacques Callot experimented with tools and ground for etching. The spontaneity of the etched line distinguishes portraits by Anthony Van Dyck and portraits and other prints by Rembrandt in the collection. Callot's student Abraham Bosse published a manual of engraving and produced the first detailed prints of artisans. Wenceslaus Hollar, working in England, issued a wide range of prints (many served as book illustrations and are in the Rosenwald Collection) covering topography, architecture, portraiture, and costume.

The chiaroscuro process, in which several broadly cut blocks are printed with a "key" or line block to achieve tone in woodcuts, was in use by the late fifteenth century. The Prints and Photographs Division is particularly strong in exemplars of this technique by Cranach, Ugo da Carpi, Andrea Andreani, and others. In the eighteenth century, intaglio tonal processes were developed, including aquatint, stipple engraving, and mezzotint. Stipple engravings by Francesco Bartolozzi and mezzotints by Valentine Green demonstrate the popularity of these techniques in England. Francisco Goya, whose *Los Caprichos* (Madrid, 1799) is in the Prints and Photographs Case Collection, used aquatint and drypoint to achieve haunting results in his satiric plates.

29.

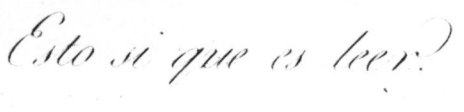

"They Call This Reading," a satiric view of book learning by Francisco Goya, from Los Caprichos (Madrid, 1799), a series of caricatures in etching and aquatint. Prints and Photographs
Division.

Graphic artist and book illustrator Joseph Pennell at his etching press, photographed by William S. Ellis in 1922. Pennell (1857–1926) experimented with a wide range of graphic techniques throughout his career. Joseph Pennell Collection, Prints and Photographs Division. LC-USZ62-2562

Because so much of the finest graphic work of the eighteenth century, especially in France, was done for book illustration, study of this period properly focuses on the Rosenwald Collection (see pp. 75-81). The rise of social and political satire, which dates to the seventeenth and eighteenth centuries, will be considered with resources for the study of popular graphic arts.

In a 1926 bequest from graphic artist and book illustrator Joseph Pennell (1857–1926), the Library received works executed by Pennell, works collected by him and his wife, Elizabeth Robins Pennell (1855–1936), including material relating to James McNeill Whistler, whose biography the Pennells wrote, and a fund to purchase Whistleriana and "original prints by modern artists of any nationality living or who have produced work within the last one hundred years." The personal papers of the Pennells and the Pennell-Whistler collection are found in the Manuscript Division. Cookbooks collected by Elizabeth Robins Pennell are in the Rare Book and Special Collections Division.

The Pennell bequest included a superb group of nineteenth-century prints by engravers who had influenced Pennell, among them Jean Baptiste Camille Corot, Félix Hilaire Buhot, Frank Duveneck, Seymour Haden, and Whistler. Pennell worked successfully as an etcher and lithographer and experimented with graphic techniques throughout his career. His published graphic work comprises some 1,885 prints, of which approximately one-third are lithographs. He executed drawings for series on English cathedrals, French cathedrals, the Panama Canal, the Yosemite Valley, and industrial scenes in Europe and America. He illustrated works by William Dean Howells, Washington Irving, Henry James, and others. The collection includes a complete file of the prints, several hundred original drawings (including the watercolor design for his Liberty Loan poster), the artist's press and tools, copies of books he illustrated, and works from his library. This record of Pennell's career reveals a printmaker and book illustrator who combined artistic and technical skills with sensitivity to the requirements for working in reproductive media.

With the receipt of the Joseph and Elizabeth Robins Pennell Fund, the Prints and Photographs Division began to build a collection of the finest examples of nineteenth- and twentieth-century printmaking. This effort, which continues to this day, has brought to the division examples of the international vitality of traditional printmaking processes in a photomechanical age. Acquisitions focus on post-1870 American prints, but images by late

nineteenth- and twentieth-century European artists have also been purchased, especially in the early years of fund acquisitions, such as examples of the graphic work of Paul Cézanne, Ernst Ludwig Kirchner, Henri Matisse, Pablo Picasso, Camille Pissarro, Henri de Toulouse-Lautrec, and Edouard Vuillard. The special vigor of Mexican and Eastern European printmakers is reflected in recent acquisitions. The American prints, some in multiple states, include aquatints by Mary Cassatt, etchings by John Taylor Arms, wood engravings by Fritz Eichenberg, and lithographs by George Bellows and Charles Sheeler. Contemporary artists have experimented with traditional and innovative graphic processes, sometimes in combination. Chuck Close, Jim Dine, Roy Lichtenstein, Robert Motherwell, Larry Rivers, and Frank Stella are among the twentieth-century artists who have used the graphic arts to create original images that have reached a broad, if not mass, audience.

❑ APPLIED GRAPHIC ART

Printed images that record or satirize current events or personages or attempt to persuade the viewer to support a cause or purchase a product are examples of applied graphic arts, so defined because they are intended for a particular, identifiable purpose. Our contemporary environment is substantially shaped by products of the applied graphic arts, and we can look at past and present forms from the perspective of the changing role of the graphic arts in society. Technological developments and design elements that increased edition size, cut cost, and enhanced visual impact provide an opportunity to study the effect of new printing processes like chromolithography and photography on the production, distribution, and influence of pictorial images.

Beginning in the seventeenth century, current events, issues, and controversies were frequently satirized by graphic artists. Although they worked in a great hurry, before the subject lost its topicality and often against a daily deadline, the level of graphic skill these artists attained is very high. The Prints and Photographs Division has an extraordinary international collection of social, political, and personal satires, cartoons, and caricatures. In addition, the division holds original drawings for several thousand cartoons spanning three centuries and a dozen countries that afford superb insights into the creation of these vivid and incisive graphic images.

The collection of over 8,000 English caricatures from 1630 to 1832 is chronologically arranged according to the *British Museum Catalogue of Personal and Political Satires.* There are in addition 1,000 images not recorded in these volumes. Early nineteenth-century caricaturists are particularly well represented, with over 700 works by James Gillray and over 500 by George Cruikshank, 280 by Henry W. Bunbury, and over 100 each by Isaac Cruikshank and Isaac Robert Cruikshank.

The Swann Collection of Caricatures and Cartoons comprises over 3,000 original drawings. Social satires by nineteenth-century French artists Henry Monnier and Paul Gavarni for *La Caricature* and *Le Charivari,* political cartoons by Louis Raemaekers, Miguel Covarrubias, and Richard Hess, and comic strips by Arthur Burdett Frost and Edward Koren indicate the range of this collection. Arthur Getz, William Steig, and Charles Saxon are among the artists represented in 1,200 cartoons and cover drawings for *The New Yorker.* Approximately 4,000 American Cartoon Drawings from the late 1850s to the present include works by Homer Davenport, Walt Kelly, Rollin Kirby, and Gary Trudeau. The division is actively developing this area in which art and politics intersect.

Art and politics also come together in prints that depict historical events. Prints produced during the American Revolution represent contemporary events with a sharp bias, as we can see in the division's examples, predominantly by French and British artists. Approximately 400 American political prints from 1798 to 1876, chronologically arranged, reflect a lively tradition of using pictorial and satirical prints to communicate a clear personal statement about political events and issues to a wide and probably sympathetic audience. Among the nineteenth-century publishers especially well represented in this group are John Childs, Henry Robinson, and Thomas Strong.

The earliest print deposited for copyright is dated 1803, and the division is not especially strong in early American popular graphic art. Representative examples of portrait and historical plates by early engravers such as Amos Doolittle and Benjamin Tanner supplement the work of these versatile printmakers for books, maps, and music in other Library divisions. A study collection formed by James T. Mitchell and formerly identified as the Stauffer Collection comprises approximately 4,000 late eighteenth- to mid-nineteenth-century books, illustrations, bank notes, certificates, scientific plates, portraits, and title pages. Among the artists included are Asher B. Durand, J. B. Neagle, Charles Willson Peale, John Sartain, Benjamin Tanner, and Cornel-

ius Tiebout. Six original watercolor sketches of genre and landscape scenes were drawn as bank-note vignettes by Henry Inman, Richard Dodson, and John Casilear in the 1830s.

Commercial printmaking expanded enormously with the development of chromolithography in the third decade of the nineteenth century. The Prints and Photographs Division has approximately 36,000 images of nineteenth-century American popular graphic art, received through copyright deposit, with comprehensive holdings of all the major lithographic print publishers. During this period, chromolithographs could be found in homes across America. Chromolithography influenced the production of maps, sheet music, and book illustrations, but nowhere is the link between printing technology and print culture stronger than in the popular print.

The output of the major early firms—J. H. Bufford, Childs and Inman, P. S. Duval, the Pendletons—reveals a great range of subjects and applications for chromolithographs. Portraits were popular from the beginning; city views and panoramas, landscapes, views of factories, commercial establishments, railroads, genre scenes, sporting prints, and historical events were all soon favorites of lithographic artists. There are superb examples of the prints of Charles Parsons, who worked for the Endicotts of New York and for Currier and Ives, including the watercolor drawing for the *Wason Manufacturing Company of Springfield, Mass.,* printed by Endicott & Co., New York, [1872], in the collections. Parsons became the superintendent of the art department for Harper's, where he employed Edwin Austin Abbey, Joseph Pennell, Howard Pyle, and others. Pennell observed that "the growth of real and vital American art started in the department of Mr. Parsons in Franklin Square."

Two firms epitomize the remarkable commercial and cultural spirit—and influence—of nineteenth-century American popular graphic art. The division's collection of approximately 3,000 prints published by Currier and Ives, almost one-half of the firm's output, is the largest in the country and contains specimens of every period and style. The ability of Nathaniel Currier and James Ives to dominate the popular print market for over half a century can be attributed to their high-volume production and low sale price. From the 1850s to the end of the century, the firm turned out an enormous number of prints, including "rush stock" images of newsworthy events and people and "stock prints" covering historical and contemporary subjects. These "Popular Cheap Prints" were precisely that—sold in an elaborate

Watercolor sketch by Charles Parsons for a lithograph of the Wason Manufacturing Company of Springfield, Massachusetts (New York: Endicott & Co., 1872). Manufacturers of railroad locomotives and machine and tool works eagerly commissioned lithographic advertisements, which often depicted the product with great detail in a highly decorative composition. Popular and Applied Graphic Art Collections, Prints and Photographs Division.

retail store in New York, from pushcart peddlers, and by agents across the country and abroad at prices well within the reach of middle-class Americans. Currier and Ives issued religious, sentimental, and humorous prints, views of Mexican and Civil War land and naval battles; panoramic views of cities and scenes of farm and country; railroad, fire, and sporting scenes, portraits, and political cartoons. Their success was based upon a vast market for pictorial images that were exactly in tune with contemporary values and taste, for Currier and Ives attempted to influence neither. Nor did they experiment with new technologies. Only after Nathaniel Currier retired in 1880 were the firm's "Colored Engravings" printed "in oils," or chromolithographed, and the firm probably never used a steam press.

Louis Prang's approach to the popular print and chromolithography contrasts sharply with Currier and Ives's conservative and traditional ideas of culture and technology. Prang deposited over 10,000 chromolithographic prints, business cards, and greeting cards for copyright between 1870 and 1903. The division has a strong collection of these and several of Prang's progressive proof books. Prang's output included book illustrations, portraits, and historical prints in black-and-white and tinted lithography, but his financial strength was based on his greeting card business. He used chromolithography to reproduce or imitate, not create, works of original art for mass distribution. Prang was controversial among his contemporaries and is an important figure in any study of graphic art and culture. He purchased paintings from many fine artists of his day—Asher B. Durand, Martin J. Heade, Eastman Johnson, Thomas Moran—and used photographs such as Carleton E. Watkins's views of Yosemite Valley to produce his "fine art chromos." Comparisons between Currier and Ives and Prang prints of similar subjects in the collection—such as views of Central Park or Civil War battles—reveal the fresh and straightforward quality of the original designs by Currier and Ives artists and the heavy-handed, romanticized tone of Prang reproductive prints.

Prang sought to raise the level of "public taste and public appreciation of the beautiful" and believed that exposure to a reproduction would, inevitably, lead to an appreciation of the original. From the beginning there was opposition to this theory, and the debate continues vigorously in our day. By the 1880s chromolithography as a printmaking process was falling victim to its own wild successes of the previous decades. The reproductive print was increasingly attacked on aesthetic and even moral grounds by critics who felt that they deceived viewers into believing they were the real thing. Copyright deposits submitted between 1880 and 1920 and stored in the division, some sorted by subject or format, show the stylistic excesses and poor technical standards to which commercial chromolithography had declined by this time.

Although the poster as we know it today was closely linked to chromolithography in the beginning, the continued vitality of this graphic art form depended on the expanding role of commercial graphic design and its ability to adapt style and process to promotional goals. Typographic and woodcut posters—often composed of many blocks—were used increasingly during

the nineteenth century to advertise circus, minstrel, and other theatrical events, political activities, and commercial products. In fact, the line between broadside, popular print, and poster is often hard to draw in this period. Beginning in the 1890s, first in France and soon after in England and America, artists were stimulated by color lithography to experiment with commercial work. Early poster design was influenced by Art Nouveau, the Arts and Crafts movement, and the Japanese woodblock print. Out of this grew a distinctive poster art that combined pictorial image, color, and typography in innovative and effective ways. These designs were so enormously popular that a poster craze (no less pervasive than the chromo craze) swept France, England, and America. Public spaces were covered with posters, people collected posters and held poster parties, and critics railed against the fad. Fad it may have been, but only of degree, for since the 1890s posters have been part of our visual environment and serve as a stunning example of the degree to which the applied graphic arts now shape the look of our world and influence what we buy and how we think.

The Poster Collection in the Prints and Photographs Division is extraordinary in size and scope. Over 80,000 posters—of which approximately 20,000 are American—span the period from the 1870s to the present and include comprehensive holdings for every major poster artist and every significant cause for which the poster has been employed. Several American poster artists of the 1890s were active in the book arts. Will Bradley, trained first as a printer, was a book designer, typographer, and publisher. Edward Penfield and Maxfield Parrish had successful careers as book illustrators. The collection is rich in the works of these artists and includes representative examples of their English and European contemporaries such as Aubrey Beardsley, the Beggarstaff brothers, Pierre Bonnard, Jules Chéret, Eugène Grasset, Alphonse Mucha, Théophile Steinlen, and Henri de Toulouse-Lautrec.

The artistic poster of the 1890s advertised books, magazines, exhibitions, and some luxury commercial products such as bicycles, chocolates, and liqueurs. The division also has thousands of advertising posters for everyday articles, mostly unsigned, deposited for copyright between 1870 and 1910 by major commercial publishers like Strobridge. Over 7,000 American circus, minstrel, magic, specialty act, legitimate theater, and motion picture posters dating from 1856 to the present document the development of the perform-

Poster artist and illustrator Louis J. Rhead designed this lithographic advertisement for Ault & Wiborg, makers of lithographic printing inks (New York: Ault & Wiborg, 1896). Poster Collection, Prints and Photographs Division.

ing arts. Posters produced under the U.S. Works Progress Administration between 1936 and 1941, many for government-supported art exhibitions and plays, evoke these years in striking silkscreen and lithographic designs.

Every war and political movement of the twentieth century has been aided by poster artists who use powerful—sometimes shocking—graphic images to stir public opinion and enlist support. Several thousand World War I and World War II posters in the collection were produced for recruiting, finance, food programs, the Red Cross, security, and propaganda. Among the World War I posters are examples of lithographs by Frank Brangwyn, Howard Chandler Christy, James Montgomery Flagg, and Théophile Steinlen. Many World War II artists used photographic techniques to create vivid images, but others like Ben Shahn continued to use lithography. Over 100 posters produced by TASS (Telegraphic Agency, USSR) by a crude stencil process were displayed in Russian cities after the Nazi invasion in 1939. Approximately 3,000 German posters from 1914 through 1945 include commercial advertisements and Nazi political propaganda by Lucien Bernhard, Ludwig Hohlwein, and others.

Several late twentieth-century political and cultural trends have infused new vigor into poster design. Psychedelic posters of the late 1960s, primarily produced for Bill Graham's Fillmore West, have had a significant influence on graphic design in the last decade, including book and record jackets. Political protest movements of the last twenty years have inspired a tremendous outpouring of political propaganda posters. Over 3,000 posters and other materials in the Gary Yanker Collection demonstrate the continued power of printed ephemera to inform and persuade.

Despite a recent trend toward producing posters in smaller editions and formats (to be framed and hung indoors like prints), traditional poster art flourishes here and abroad, especially in Japan and Switzerland. Poster artists seek new ways to incorporate pictorial and typographic (or calligraphic) matter into a design that will reproduce effectively, and the public continues to respond to these images. The "democratic art" of the chromolithograph has found its true form in the poster.

The graphic design profession emerged in the late nineteenth century with expanding commercial applications of new printing technologies. The development of commercial design is documented in several collections in the Prints and Photographs Division. Approximately 85,000 trademarks and 40,000 labels (now in storage) were received at the U.S. Patent Office be-

tween 1870 and 1920 and transferred to the Library. Advertising labels deposited for copyright protection include some 1,000 tobacco labels, arranged by subject. Other product labels in the division include those for patent medicines and several groups under headings related to printing supplies, for example, ink, paper, and type. A collection of contemporary book jackets retained for two decades beginning in the mid-1960s has recently been transferred from the Library to the Rochester Institute of Technology (see *Library of Congress Information Bulletin*, January 6, 1986, 5).

Samples of typography, commercial printing, advertising design, and reproductive processes were among the material confiscated from the Arbeitsfont, the Nazi labor organization, at the close of World War II by U.S. Army military intelligence teams. Probably assembled as a study collection by one of the German printing trades unions, the material dates primarily from the years between 1880 and 1930. It is mostly German, although other European countries, the United States, and the Orient are also represented. Among the subject lots are material from the Internationale Ausstellung für Buchgewerbe und Graphik held in Leipzig in 1914, photographs of the headquarters of the Verband der Deutschen Buchdrucker in Berlin, and samples for the Meisterschule für das graphische Gewerbe in Leipzig. There are large groups of the trade ephemera distributed at graphic arts exhibitions, new trade book announcements and advertisements, including many for books by Nazi authors, samples of greeting cards, menus, invitations, and postcards, advertisements for printing machinery and services, and specimens of Japanese and European decorative printing. The collection contains diverse examples of regional and international trends in graphic design and of printing and reproductive techniques.

The production of book and magazine illustrations was transformed by technological developments in the late nineteenth century. From the 1850s through the 1880s wood engraving, a type-compatible process, was used to print very large editions and runs of popular books and periodicals until it was replaced by tonal photomechanical processes. Hundreds of delicate wash drawings in the Prints and Photographs Division of Civil War battles and camps by Alfred R. Waud for *Harper's Weekly* and the *New York Illustrated News* were reproduced as line wood engravings. The division also has drawings by Waud's brother William and by Edwin Forbes, who served as special artist for *Frank Leslie's Illustrated Magazine* from 1862 to 1864. A ten-volume collection of wood engravings by David Nichols compiled by the artist at

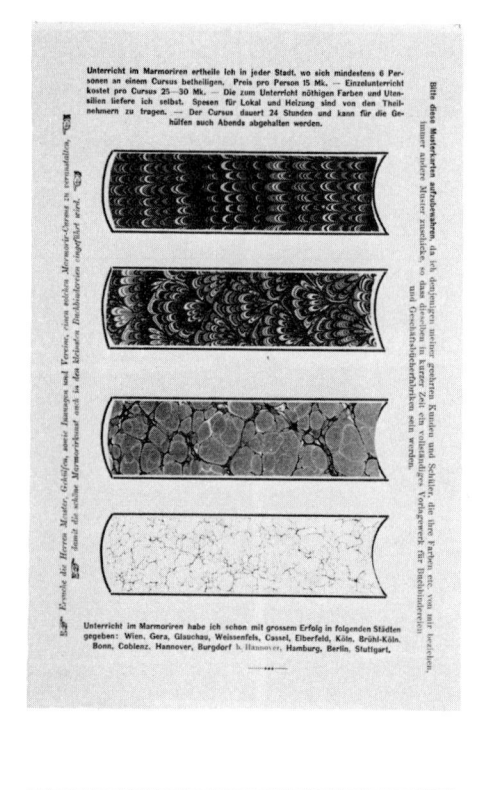

Advertisement for marbling courses offered by Josef Hauptmann of Budapest to individuals and bookbinding guilds in German cities, with samples of styles, ca. 1900. Graphic Design Collection, Prints and Photographs Division.

ABOVE: *Advertisement for the Mittineague Paper Company's display at the Louisiana Purchase Exposition, held in St. Louis in 1904. Graphic Design Collection, Prints and Photographs Division.*

LEFT: *Advertisement for a linotype machine manufacturer, ca. 1900, hailing the greatest invention of the new century, a "two-letter linotype." In this system, two separate characters were carried on each mat, usually the roman and italic of the same letter. Graphic Design Collection, Prints and Photographs Division.*

Pencil drawing by Alfred R. Waud depicting a sutler's cart, which delivered books along with other supplies to Civil War troops. The drawing was reproduced as a wood engraving in the New York Illustrated News, *December 2, 1861. Waud Collection, Prints and Photographs Division. LC-USZ62-7930*

the end of his career documents the turn-of-the-century transition to photomechanical engraving. Nichols worked for *Scribner's Monthly, St. Nicholas,* and *Century.* The volumes, arranged in chronological order, identify the source of the engraving (original drawing or artist), when it was executed, where it was published, and the price received by the artist.

In 1932 William Patten, art editor of *Harper's Magazine* in the late 1880s and the 1890s, initiated correspondence with artists, publishers, and their families for contributions to form the Cabinet of American Illustration at the Library of Congress. Original drawings for works published between 1870 and 1910 predominate, and the collection now numbers slightly less than 5,000 drawings by 200 American illustrators and cartoonists and is being strengthened by acquisitions from before 1870 and after 1910. Book and magazine illustrations, cartoons, decorative drawings, poster designs, and cover illustrations are interfiled by name of artist. Drawings are individually cataloged. Among the illustrators particularly well represented are W. T. Benda, Walter Appleton Clark, Palmer Cox, Arthur Burdett Frost, Charles

Dana Gibson, Oliver Herford, Thomas Nast, Edward Penfield, William Smedley, John Sloan, and Jessie Wilcox Smith. Although the collection is not all-inclusive, the breadth of coverage for this "golden age" of American illustration is impressive.

Several groups of printing blocks and plates are maintained in the division. A collection of 17 blocks and proofs by Alexander Anderson includes biblical illustrations for Thomas Day's *History of Sandford and Merton.* The images on 75 woodblocks engraved by James Richardson of New York range from small vignettes to figures of people and machinery. In the 1940s several book and magazine publishers donated approximately 400 electrotype blocks and woodblocks. The blocks for illustrations by Felix Octavius Darley for James Fenimore Cooper's *The Pilot*, used in several editions published by Appleton's, are in this group, and the original drawings are in the Cabinet of American Illustration. Artists represented in the Harper's boxes include Edwin Austin Abbey, J. W. Alexander, Thomas Nast, and Howard Pyle. The Scribner's boxes contain blocks after illustrations by Pyle and Frederic Remington. Electrotype plates, drawings, and proofs by Edward Gorey to illustrate the poet-psychiatrist Merrill Moore's *Illegitimate Sonnets* were received with the Merrill Moore Papers maintained in the Manuscript Division.

❏   DOCUMENTARY AND ARTISTIC PHOTOGRAPHY

Photography and photomechanical processes revolutionized every one of the graphic arts. For the first time a medium of mass pictorial communication did not require the intermediary hand of a craftsman. Graphic artists had to redefine their role once it became possible to reproduce and multiply an artist's original design and images from the objective world. The photographic collections of the Prints and Photographs Division afford opportunities to study the enormous influence of documentary and artistic photography on the graphic arts and society. The collections contain original prints of all periods from the first days of the medium to the contemporary avant garde and include examples of every photographic technology from daguerreotypes and collodion glass negatives to early color transparencies and contemporary color prints.

Napoleon Sarony, in partnership with Henry B. Major and Joseph F. Knapp, ran one of the largest lithographic plants in the country. In the 1860s

Sarony withdrew entirely from lithography and after a visit to his brother, who ran a photographic gallery in England, returned to become "the swell photographer of his day," with a very successful studio. Sarony accurately gauged the direction in which public taste was moving, for in 1860 Mathew B. Brady had already opened his "National Portrait Gallery" on Broadway and Tenth Street, termed by the press the "Broadway Valhalla." Brady sold gold-framed photographs, photographs "finished in oils," others that resembled watercolors, and paintings after photographs in his elegant gallery, which became an obligatory stop for celebrities.

One year later Brady left fashionable photography to organize a staff of about twenty photographers who recorded people, battles, and battlefields of the Civil War and created the first photographic documentation of a military conflict. In 1871 a proposal to purchase "Mr. Brady's Historical *Gallery of Portraits*" was rejected by Congress, but in 1920, 300 daguerreotype portraits taken in Brady's New York and Washington studios between 1845 and 1853 were transferred to the Library from the U.S. Army War College. The Phelps Publishing Company Collection of Brady Civil War photographs, purchased in 1943, includes 10,000 original and copy glass plate negatives. The Brady-Handy Collection, donated in 1954, contains several thousand plates by Levin C. Handy, who had continued the photographic studio of his uncle and mentor, Mathew B. Brady. Among other developments in Washington, D.C., Handy recorded the construction of the Thomas Jefferson Building of the Library of Congress and photographed the newly organized Library divisions and staff.

The popular stereographic view of the late nineteenth and early twentieth century has left a comprehensive pictorial record of places and industrial processes. Over 150,000 stereographs in the Prints and Photographs Division span the development and decline of this business. A series of 31 photoprints published ca. 1928 by the Keystone View Company, the most successful stereographic publisher, depicts the entire process of book production at the Haddon Press printing plant. The H.C. White Company series on the paper mills at Palmer, New York, in 1909, includes views of machinery, turbines, grinders, beaters, and screens. Other stereographic views record library architecture, interiors, and readers.

Frances Benjamin Johnston, a documentary and portrait photographer, worked primarily in Washington, D.C. Interior and exterior views of the Jefferson Building of the Library of Congress and photoprints taken at El-

bert Hubbard's Roycrofters shop in East Aurora, New York, in 1900 of workers involved in all aspects of hand bookmaking are among the images included in the Frances Benjamin Johnston Collection.

Charles H. Currier maintained a commercial photographic studio in Boston between 1889 and 1909. His views of buildings, interiors, sports, charities, and occupations depict activities and appearances of turn-of-the-century Boston in intricate detail. Prints of public libraries, the Boston Athenaeum, a printing shop, and private libraries in several homes are among over 500 prints in the collection.

Under Roy Stryker, the Farm Security Administration (FSA) gradually expanded the scope of the documentary photographic project begun under

Women bookworkers at Elbert Hubbard's Roycrofters Shop in East Aurora, New York, where village girls were trained in illuminating and bookbinding, photographed by Frances Benjamin Johnston, ca. 1900. Frances Benjamin Johnston Collection, Prints and Photographs Division.

the Resettlement Administration in 1935. Between 1936 and 1942, photographers were sent into the field "to record anything that was significant to American culture." Stryker constructed a very detailed outline that served as a shooting script for his staff photographers, who included Walker Evans, Dorothea Lange, and Ben Shahn. Some of the scenes he suggested were "Home in the evening;" "Group activities of various income levels;" and "American habits," such as "Eating" and "Reading Sunday papers in the park." In 1942 the Office of War Information (OWI) absorbed the files of the Farm Security Administration. The OWI gathered together material from commercial and governmental agencies, industry, and its staff photographers that depicted the war effort from the American point of view and reflected the American way of life in a favorable light. In 1944 these combined files were transferred to the Library of Congress. The photoprints are interfiled, arranged geographically, and subdivided within each region by subject. A microfiche edition of this complete file, published by Chadwyck-Healey, Ltd., includes a cross-referenced index to the subject headings, each of which has an assigned number expanded decimally for subdivisions of topics. Access to the images by specific photographer or location is provided by a microfilm made before the file prints were arranged in the present system.

The regional files are subdivided according to very specific subjects. The Processing and Manufacturing numbers, for example, are further refined to separate paper mills, printing, photography, and reproduction. Files on Intellectual and Creative Activity and Social and Intellectual Activity include specific numbers for research libraries, children reading, people reading at home, and reading for servicemen. Photographs record in great detail activities at the Mississquoi Corporation paper mill in Vermont; a paper mill town, Berlin, New Hampshire; the Champion Paper Mill in Houston; and the Southland Paper Mill in Lufkin, Texas. One of the "popular libraries" is in Greenhills, Ohio, a community planned by the Resettlement Administration. Another is in Yuma, Arizona, a Farm Security Administration library at a migratory farm workers' community. The composing room of the *New York Times,* lithographers in the special skills division of the Resettlement Administration, a Jewish printer on Broome Street, the Cocee Press, which published an Italian-language weekly, *La Parola,* and black printers photographed for a "life of Negroes in New York" are among the printing series in the northeast regional files. For each region photographs reveal a broad range of activities, including producing and reading books and newspapers.

Historians of reading must evaluate the reliability of posed scenes of readers and of books in the home, such as this photograph by Charles H. Currier, showing a private library in Boston, ca. 1895. Charles H. Currier Collection, Prints and Photographs Division. LC-C801-129.

The evolution of photography as a means of aesthetic expression from the 1869 publication of Henry Peach Robinson's *Pictorial Effect in Photography* to the present may be studied in books and master photographs in the division. Among the volumes illustrated by original photographs in the division's Case Collection are Thomas Annan, *Glasgow Corporation Water Works* (1877) and *Memorials of the Old College of Glasgow* (1871); P. H. Emerson, *Idyls of the Norfolk Broads* (1888), *Pictures from Life in Field and Fen* (1867), and *Pictures of East Anglian Life* (1888); John Forbes Watson, *The People of India* (1868–75) in eight volumes; and J. Thomson, *Street Life in London,* issued in twelve parts, 1877–78. Since 1980 the division has transferred approximately 300 volumes from the general collections using an unpublished bibliography compiled by Richard Yanul of pre-1870 publications with original photographs.

The work of F. Holland Day, Arnold Genthe, Gertrude Käsebier, Alfred Stieglitz, Clarence White, and others belongs to the world of fine graphic art. They intended their platinum and gum prints, produced in very small editions for framing, to be treated like original drawings, etchings, or lithographs. Although there was a reaction in the 1920s and 1930s to the painterly, soft-focus style and to their refined processes, the work of documentary photographers for the FSA-OWI units derived power from a combination of precision and emotional expression.

Today photography is put to diverse uses that range from reportage and reproduction to all forms of creative expression. The line between fine and applied graphic art has never been more muted than it is now, when artists can choose from a variety of processes to create or replicate an image for multiplication. Pictorial images appear everywhere—on clothes, packaging, signs, alone or in combination with the printed word—to capture our attention or captivate our imagination. The history and development of graphic arts processes and products illuminate relationships between art and society, culture and technology, information and inspiration, and words and images, which are all an integral part of the history of books.

REFERENCES

A Century of Photographs, 1846–1946. Comp. by Renata V. Shaw. Selected from the collections of the Library of Congress. Washington: Library of Congress, 1980.

English Caricature 1620 to the Present: Caricaturists and Satirists, Their Art, Their Purpose and Influence. London: Victoria and Albert Museum, 1984.

Graphic Sampler. Comp. by Renata V. Shaw. Washington: Library of Congress, 1979.

Popular and Applied Graphic Art in the Library of Congress. 1979. [12-p. brochure]

The Poster Collection of the Library of Congress. 1979. [16-p. brochure]

Prints and Photographs Division. 1984. [22-p. brochure]

United States. Library of Congress. *The American Revolution in Drawings and Prints: A Checklist of 1765–1790 Graphics in the Library of Congress.* Comp. by Donald H. Cresswell; with a foreword by Sinclair H. Hitchings. Washington: Library of Congress, 1975.

United States. Library of Congress. Prints and Photographs Division. *American Prints in the Library of Congress: A Catalog of the Collection.* Comp. by Karen F. Beall et al. Baltimore: Johns Hopkins University Press for the Library of Congress, 1970.

————. *Catalog of the Gardiner Greene Hubbard Collection of Engravings Presented to the Library of Congress by Mrs. Gardiner Greene Hubbard.* Comp. by Arthur Jeffrey Parsons. Washington: Government Printing Office, 1905.

————. *Viewpoints: A Selection from the Pictorial Collections of the Library of Congress.* A picture book by Alan Fern, Milton Kaplan, and the staff of the Prints and Photographs Division. Washington: Library of Congress, 1975.

United States. Library of Congress. Reference Department. *Guide to the Special Collections of Prints & Photographs in the Library of Congress.* Comp. by Paul Vanderbilt. Washington: Library of Congress, 1955.

❑ Index

This book was typeset on the Linotron 202
in a digital adaptation of Granjon,
a typeface designed in the sixteenth century by
Robert Granjon, an engraver of Paris and Lyons
whose type designs include the Greek
characters for Plantin's Polyglot Bible.

Composition by York Graphic Services,
York, Pennsylvania.

Typography, layout, and binding design by
Adrianne Onderdonk Dudden.